The BS of Better

And Other Limiting Language

Brigitte Ranae

www.brigitteranae.com

ISBN: 978-1-7365173-2-1 (Paperback)
ISBN: 978-1-7365173-1-4 (E-book)

Library of Congress Control Number: 2021909314

Copy edits by Karen Tucker of Comma Queen Editing in Byrnes Mill, Missouri.
Front cover image by Andrew Ostrovsky of Port Angeles, Washington.
Book cover design by Peggy Nehmen of Nehmen-Kodner in St. Louis, Missouri.
Back cover photograph by Carly Sullens of Carly Sullens Photography in St. Louis, Missouri.

Printed by Brigitte Ranae, St. Louis, Missouri, in the United States of America.

First print edition 2021.

Contact: For additional information on confidential life coaching services, relationship coaching, team building sessions, or to discuss booking Brigitte Ranae for speaking engagements for your group or organization, feel free to email: info@brigitteranae.com or visit www.brigitteranae.com.

Brigitte Ranae LLC
PO Box 394
Herculaneum, MO 63048

DEDICATION

This book and the ***Reducing Life's Pressure*** series are dedicated to all the special people—all of my family members, friends, colleagues, and clients—who have continually extended love and support over the years in my work and in my own personal development. It is through each of you that I continue to gain strength and courage to fulfill my purpose in life. That is, to love without condition and embrace everyone right where they are through the simplest expressions of acceptance while facilitating growth and healing in the lives of myself and others. To my husband, five children, and our grandchildren, you are my rock, my world, my joy!

A special thank you to the following incredible individuals who have supported me during the continued creation of this series. I am eternally grateful for the countless hours and energy you spent assisting me in molding and placing the final touches on a raw but beautiful concept in order to finish this project. My respect and appreciation for each of you is larger than words. Thank you for all your inspirational, emotional, and tangible support in various forms throughout this project!

Marie Bechard-Layne
Shelly Doty
Loni Eaton
Bear Farley
Carmen Garcia
Julie George
Karen Hoffman
Jennifer Jones Sojka
Dr. Felicity Keough
Terry Lance
Linda McKay
Michelle Keys
Beth Miller
Fran Moore
Kathy Mullins
Madison Norris
Dee Smith
Brittni Thomas
Theresa Thomas
Kala Zurbriggen
John Zurbriggen

CONTENTS

INTRODUCTION

Having coached hundreds of individuals over the years, one overwhelming tendency most of my clients struggle with is negative self-talk and self-sabotage. These tendencies echo a distorted belief system and greatly increase life's pressures unnecessarily. These distorted beliefs often cause immense mental and emotional strain and intensify challenges in my clients' personal and professional relationships while disabling their creative abilities to thrive as individuals and team members. Prior to our coaching sessions, many clients were busy surviving in lieu of thriving and oftentimes felt lost, confused, afraid, drained, and unfulfilled—more like human *doings* than human *beings*. The consensus, the message that always rings louder than any other, is that they almost always feel they are not enough, in one form or another.

Being raised by a mother who was mentally ill, I also struggled with distorted belief systems most of my life that left me questioning myself almost at every turn. This kept me from walking courageously in my own path because I was stuck floundering around trying to find out exactly what I was *supposed* to be doing. Despite the extreme abuse caused by my mother's inabilities to provide a safe environment to rear a child, I emerged into adulthood grasping to one very special gift my mother deposited within me—a secret gift I held onto from childhood and eventually learned to acknowledge and walk within. After embracing and applying this special gift to my life, my world has never been the same.

The most beautiful part of my story is that I have now shared this gift with hundreds of clients, along with many of their friends, family members, colleagues, and organizations. I had the privilege of sitting on the sidelines as they transformed their own lives through personal development, leading to a path of self-acceptance and confidence. While watching their new course ultimately lead them to creating a life of success and significance, a resounding message rang in unison from the heartache they processed during our conversations. In session after session, I began hearing this message loud and clear and decided it was time to do something about it.

So, I began a journey of walking through thousands of pages of client files, which led to the project you now hold in your hands. I traced numerous patterns of thought that projected underlying debilitating beliefs, and, believe it or not, the core symptom of these distortions was expressed in the everyday language they were unmindfully using on a daily basis. Yes, this message was screaming for freedom, and I was forced to stop and pay attention to it through the voices of every single one of my clients. And it didn't stop there; I started looking for the linguistic patterns and found them everywhere I turned, even in the mirror. Almost everyone struggles with some form of debilitating language that adds to daily pressures and represents limiting mindsets. I determined to expose this limiting language and get to the root of the limiting mindsets represented to reduce life's pressures for not only my clients, but for myself, family, and friends.

Hence, ***The BS of Better*** program was born, beginning with this book, more books to come, and training materials included in the ***Reducing Life's Pressures*** series. The objective of this series is for readers to intentionally focus for a few weeks on specific areas to enhance self-awareness and self-acceptance and create personal fulfillment, which in return will strengthen personal and professional relationships. ***The BS of Better*** program and other books in this series are strategically written and structured in a manner that will promote maturation in various aspects of life by focusing on neural pathway development exercises. For sustainable and healthy change to occur, the brain must be reprogrammed, which is exactly what the ***Reducing Life's Pressures*** series is structured to do.

This series is being created in various forms, from paperback journals, e-books, and audio books to support resources, online courses, and live training events. These additional resources are being created to assist readers of varying learning styles with the daily processing materials necessary for mindset and language transformation. This transformation will occur through neural pathway development exercises that will break old habits and trains of thought while establishing new thoughts and habits that serve, rather than limit, participants.

The objective of this specific book in the ***Reducing Life's Pressures*** series is to identify the language we often use that reflects distorted beliefs that create and intensifies internal pressure. This pressure holds us back from feeling at peace, being joyful, or leading a life of fulfilment. And here is the most interesting aspect I found in my years of research: it's not just those with traumatic childhoods or life experiences. Oh no, it's especially prevalent in the lives of those born with a silver spoon, into coddling hands, and in the most loving and healthy environments. This exhaustive language shows no partiality upon which it preys, and from the least to the most fortunate, almost everyone falls victim to its grips.

Don't worry, this resource is not one more book of suggestions telling you what you should be doing to have a better life. On the contrary, the information contained herein will assist you through a process of self-exploration that will lead to one of the most important revelations you will ever encounter. As this revelation unfolds, you will naturally experience clarity as you develop a sense of peace within yourself and courage to step into a place that only your suppressed longings have dared to go. Within this atmosphere of self-exploration, a newfound freedom will unfold as you acknowledge, and are finally released from, the grips of ***The BS of Better*** and other limiting mindsets and language.

This book was not written with the intent of being read. It was written for the purpose of being processed and applied. Contained herein are experiential exercises that I highly urge each reader to take the time to work through. It is not through mine or anyone else's regurgitated information that you will experience healthy change. Healthy change comes only through heartfelt effort in raising self-awareness, identifying limiting patterns of thought and behavior, formulating a plan to overcome those limitations, and taking action to develop new neural pathways in the brain that will serve you instead of limit you.

Therefore, please do not proceed in reading this book until you are ready to commit to processing the information. None of us need more information that tells us all the things we are "doing wrong." That is not what this book is about. It is about lovingly embracing ourselves and committing to growth by accepting ourselves right where we are. So, I am asking you now to first contemplate your readiness and then decide to either proceed in utilizing this book or put it down until you are ready to process and apply. Most importantly, whichever you choose, accept yourself. We are not always ready to embrace change, and that is perfectly okay. Love yourself where you are, and when you are ready, you will create movement and change in your life.

One last thing before we begin; there are a few areas in this program that reference a higher power. This material is written for everyone ready for movement in their lives, regardless of your spiritual beliefs and practices. If you formulate an idea of my beliefs and practices while working through my programs, please do not allow any form of judgment, guilt, condemnation, or pressure to form in your thoughts. I personally have no opinions on the walk of any other individuals and have the privilege of being friends with and work with people of all walks of life. As with any educational or self-help materials you may engage in, absorb and utilize what resonates with you at the time and let the rest go. This program was written for us as individuals to promote autonomy. You are your greatest life coach, and this program will assist all participants in recognizing this truth and walking in it.

You are now invited to engage in the journey of overcoming ***The BS of Better*** to reduce life's pressures by overcoming limiting mindsets and language.

Welcome, Brigitte Ranae

"Our society is brainwashed with self-improvement."
~Fran Moore

1

THE LIMITING LANGUAGE OF BETTER

I knew something had to be done the moment I sat fighting back emotions, behind closed doors working with an executive of one of my corporate clients. He asked with tears in his eyes:

> **"Do you really think I'm doing okay? I feel like such a failure sometimes."**

This beautiful man was working so hard for his company, doing his best to be a healthy mentor for the employees under his management, striving tirelessly to provide for his family, and attempting to create some form of balance with his time to earn, provide, love, and enjoy life and those in it. He followed the instructions, read the manuals, got the degrees, followed the orders given within the proper timeline, stuck closely to all he learned in Sunday School, remained a faithful friend, husband, father, and employee, but it still wasn't enough!

Derek sat across the table from me, and all I could see was the little boy inside who felt like he wasn't doing something right, no matter how hard he tried; he never measured up nor did enough. That little boy who was told what to do and who to be his entire life was now feeling like a failure because he couldn't get past the pressures of the beliefs instilled in him. Those beliefs were killing his joy, robbing him of hope, and pressuring him into a life that wasn't even his own but rather some facade of a man he was supposed to be.

> **Can you relate?**
> **When is it enough?**
> **When are we enough?**

Having coached hundreds of individuals over the years, I have unfortunately seen this mindset Derek was struggling with all too often. One of the biggest challenges we face in the United States is that our society is brainwashed by some need to be better, with a necessity for self-improvement.

First and foremost, remember this simple truth:

> **We are brainwashed with a self-improvement mindset of needing to be better, which reminds us that we are not enough.**

Don't get me wrong; by no means am I suggesting that we stop striving to modify situations and circumstances that may be limiting our personal lives, relationships, and objectives. There is great benefit in personal development; after all, my entire career is facilitating personal development in the lives of individuals, families, and organizations. However, personal development is completely different than wanting to be better and feeling the need to improve. As a matter of fact, personal development has absolutely nothing to do with being better or improving!

BS

Most of the pain or uncomfortableness we experience in life is due to the pressure felt from the need to be better, which stems from the roots of our beliefs. What I am proposing here is that the underlying BS (**B**elief **S**ystem) of our need for better is debilitating many of us emotionally, mentally, physically, and even spiritually—no, especially spiritually. Oh, wait! Did you think I meant something else by BS? Well, yes, that applies too, but in this book, we will simply focus on the distorted **B**elief **S**ystems (BS) that accompany the verbiage and mentality of being better. Before we begin diving into "better," let's explore the BS of our belief systems.

Our **B**elief **S**ystems can be tricky—oftentimes hidden—memories from past experiences that create insecurities, which turn into measurements and judgments. Oh yes, and it gets even uglier because those internal measurements and judgments then turn into internal criticisms we almost always project onto others. When we take a moment to think about that concept, it is apparent how our internal BS can certainly wreak havoc in our personal and professional relationships. Even worse, it sabotages our relationship with ourselves.

BELIEFS

Diving deeper, think about how these sneaky beLIEfs create feelings of not being good enough, feelings that others are not good enough, and/or feelings that certain people or situations are wrong. Oh, did you catch that little word that connivingly sits right in the middle of be**LIE**fs? Yep, the majority of our be**LIE**fs, which form our belief systems (BS), contain distortions of a truth—lies. How can this be?

Here's a tidbit to remember. At the root of all beLIEfs are uncertainties that form the questions that can create an atmosphere of confusion in our thought lives when our BS is faced with contradictions or discrepancies. Our beLIEfs are initially stored as forms of automated solutions to the uncertainties we experienced as our cognitive abilities developed during childhood. It has a lot to do with the brain's hardwiring for survival that likes thoughts and behaviors to be automatic to reduce its workload. The brain doesn't like to work that hard but, by its design, is forced to run constantly; so, it automates things in an orderly fashion by forming beLIEfs that stem from our perceived truths. A collection of beLIEfs makes up our BS, which ultimately form the mindsets from which we function.

One way to maintain order and ease is automation, which basically comprises the thought patterns and habits we live by daily. These thought patterns and habits are the brain's automated way of functioning by having hardwired solutions to the uncertainties we have experienced or may experience. These hardwired solutions are our beLIEfs, which often lead to our anticipations. Those people and circumstances that align with our beLIEfs are experienced as safe and are easy to accept because they seem familiar. On the contrary, those people and things that oppose these beLIEfs are experienced as unsafe, which we often express in judgments or criticisms.

Is this making sense? Those who align with our beLIEfs are typically thought of as right and/or good. The opposite is true, as oppositions are thought of as wrong and/or bad because they are not familiar and were not anticipated. What we anticipate feels safe, even if it's unpleasant and not working, because familiar feels safer. Unfortunately, these hardwired solutions we've established only work in specific instances with specific people under specific circumstances within specific seasons.

Well, those types of duplications only happen in déjà vu. In our ever-changing world, it is difficult to function internally and externally if we put too much stock in our beLIEfs. We will never be able to anticipate everything and are therefore forced into unfamiliar environments that feel unsafe because of our beLIEfs. It's not that things are necessarily unsafe, but rather unfamiliar, which we anticipate will be unsafe because they lead us into the unknown. These anticipations have stolen many moments and opportunities over the years because they turned into uncertainties that we allowed to control us.

Carly Simon wrote it well in her 1971 song "Anticipation." Remember that song? Hop on your phone and listen to it if you'd like to pause for a smile. She explains that we never really know what to expect or what is to come. But she gives some great advice, which is to be in the moment and enjoy the good old days. We're just getting started, but it's never too soon for homework...so, feel free to grab your journal while listening to this song.

What anticipations have you experienced over the last couple weeks? What uncertainties manifested because of those anticipations?

Anticipations keep us stuck and unable to enjoy many moments. They stem from limiting beLIEfs and keep us wallowing in the familiar, left behind, waiting, and disconnected from the moment, beautiful people, and perspectives we deem as unsafe merely because they are unfamiliar. These beLIEfs often stifle our continued growth, slow our maturation, and can also lead to extremely limiting thoughts and actions with harsh impacts on ourselves and others. They keep us from enjoying the present moment, from creating beautiful memories of new adventures, and from experiencing what will ultimately become the good old days we once had with one another.

Strong foundational roots surround beLIEfs, causing many challenges, and they surface as insecurities and uncertainties. Cleaving so tightly to our beLIEfs can be dangerous and cause a lot of damage if we allow them to stay on their own course without supervision and maturation. We will discuss more about this in Chapter 9 when we explore "Altering Our beLIEf Cycle Using a Growth Mindset."

For now, it is important to realize that the dangers and damage in our beLIEfs can oftentimes debilitate us and our objectives. That is why it is important to identify and carefully observe our thoughts and responses to challenges to ensure we are not being suffocated by or suffocating others within the confounds of our own BS. beLIEfs are hardwired and difficult to change, but it is possible through mental exercises that weaken existing neural pathways housing these limiting beLIEfs while establishing new neural pathways that empower and serve us. That is exactly what ***The BS of Better*** program is designed to do.

Too many variables in life exist for our beLIEfs to always serve us. However, sometimes—many times—they *do* serve us. Those are the components we want to preserve, but not by a rigid thought life that keeps us from seeing new information out of fear. Instead, with a sense of vulnerability, openness, and exploration that exposes us to new opportunities that challenge us to reevaluate our insecurities and uncertainties. This will ensure our beliefs are healthy and serving us in the present season and under the current circumstances. If we choose to observe carefully, we can assess our thought lives, the language we use, and our feelings daily to detect if a belief is serving or limiting us. For those ready to go there, this program will take you to a place of careful observation accompanied by peace and acceptance to reach individual and healthy solutions that are beyond the BS we've been taught.

In ***The BS of Better*** program, we will look closely at the language we use daily, which says a lot about our BS. Many of the beLIEFs, and the lies we strive to live by, cause damage in our lives and in the lives of those around us, and it's time to STOP! Stop believing the BS. Stop speaking the BS. Stop living by the BS. And last, stop forcing others to live by the BS. There is so much more to life than the insecurities and uncertainties we allow our BS to keep us wallowing in! One simple and powerful place to begin is by listening to the language in and around us that tells us that we or others need to be better. Our language is an easily recognizable identifier of our beLIEfs that keeps us and others trapped in our BS. We will spend a lot of time in this program identifying limiting language and the underlying limiting mindsets of better.

BETTER

What is better anyway? Let's take a moment to define it. In our society, we typically use the word better as a verb or intransitive verb when describing ourselves in areas where we desire change or improvement. Merriam-Webster defines the verb context of **better** as "to make more tolerable or acceptable; to make more complete or perfect; to surpass in excellence."

We usually use the word better as a comparative word to describe our level of satisfaction with ourselves in certain aspects of our lives, e.g., "I'm trying to get better," or "I used to be better," or "I wish I was better," or "They are better," or "They think they're better." The list goes on.

As an adjective, Merriam-Webster says the word **better** is the comparative word for good, meaning "improved in health or mental attitude; more attractive, favorable, or commendable; more advantageous or effective; and improved in accuracy or performance." By now, you probably get the point, but let's sum it up. If you really read through all these descriptions of "better," what are we really saying when we use that word to describe ourselves, our behaviors, and our circumstances? That we need to be more.

If we think we are not better already, then we are not better currently. This means we are *not* good, attractive, favorable, commendable, advantageous, accurate, etc., but our BS tells us what is better and what is not. If we need to be better, then our minds know we are not enough in our present state. The conclusion our minds come to is: *I am not enough!* or, *My efforts are not enough!*

Listen, stating that we wish to be better automatically implies to our minds that presently *we are not enough*, or our behaviors or circumstances are not enough. Such repetitive thoughts of these limiting beLIEfs build a BS whose foundation confirms daily that we are not enough. Think about this: If we want to be better, then that implies we are not currently better. If we are not currently better, what are we? We are the opposite, or antonym, of better. Our mind knows this subconsciously. The antonym of better is inferior, lower, mediocre, of little or less value or importance, of low degree or rank… Shall we go on? The bottom line is, when we imply we need to be better or do better, we are saying, believing, and living like we are not enough and treating others the same way.

You are NOT inferior! You are not mediocre, of lower degree, or of less value, nor are you of less importance. However, when we allow our minds to tell our brains that we want ourselves to be better, we are identifying ourselves with the very opposite of better. We are telling ourselves that we are not presently good enough, which is why we are striving for better. Let me make one thing clear:

> **You will NEVER be any BETTER than you already are right now!**

I want to emphasize, you are *not* inferior. As a matter of fact, you are the opposite of inferior; you are invaluable, meaningful, and consequential regardless of the changes you would like to make in your life. What you do does not equate to your worth. You are not a human *doing* who needs to do better! No, you are a human *being* who is naturally invaluable, important, and significant simply because you exist. We'll explore more about that in Chapter 2.

Now, if you choose to make changes in behaviors and circumstances that yield the results you wish to see in your life, great! However, no choice you make will increase your worth, nor will it make you any more important, nor will it make you better. No, different choices will yield different results that you may prefer and that others may applaud you for, but no choice will ever make you *better*.

UNDERSTANDING THE BS OF BETTER

Why is it important to understand the BS of better? The language we use says a lot about our hidden beLIEfs, but it also has an enormous effect on our lives. The more we use critical and self-defeating language, the more we believe what we're thinking and saying is true. The more we believe it, the more we live it and create scenarios within our lives that reinforce that beLIEf. We create our own demise, bringing it into existence by the thoughts we allow and the language we speak daily.

In a future publication, I will explain more about the brain and how it stores information, but for now, let me summarize one thing about language and retention. Repeating any words or phrases, whether in thought or speech, day after day, strengthens those specific neural pathways in our brains that house these messages. These strengthened messages within the neural pathways we have built will dictate our automated responses and choices in our daily lives, which ultimately yield our outcomes.

Hence, this is the reason we must be cautious about what thoughts we allow to rumble around in our minds, what words we use that may be limiting us, what moods we allow our state of being to settle into, and what criticisms we allow internally and also extend to others. Our thoughts and spoken words create the foundation upon which our choices will be made. Therefore, it is crucial that each of us observe our thoughts, words, moods, and actions to identify language that may represent a faulty beLIEf system that may limit us. After all, we are enough and deserve words of confidence and encouragement that will breed life and enthusiasm for simply being our own unique self instead of words that lie and tell us daily that we are not enough.

THE BETTER MOVEMENT

Since it's not challenging enough that most of us are taught as children to be good little boys and girls, do our best, and try to be better, we grow into adults surrounded by a pressure-induced culture. Look at the following sample phrases our society inundates us with. The sad part is, we believe it internally, and then we often project it onto others. We see this stuff every day, and it's only getting worse as people and companies attempt to point out our individual pains and discomforts so they can sell us one more thing online or at our local brick-and-mortar stores to "better our lives." News articles, blogs, videos, social media platforms, and other media are loaded with this "better" movement garbage. While they're being sponsored for their captivating headlines that catch our attention, we resonate with the BS that highlights our challenges and struggles, and our confidence and self-worth continue to diminish. Open your eyes and see it—the messages are everywhere!

Be Better!
Do Better!
What it REALLY Takes to be the BEST Version of You!
12 Ways to Have Better Conversations!
You Can Be Better Today than Yesterday!
How Can You Become a Better Person?
8 Habits That Will Make You Better!
Create a Better Body!
How to Be a Better Human!
Be a Better Cook, Wife, Mother, Father, Pastor, etc.
Be Better, Not Bitter!

Be Better Than Just Good!
99 Tips for Being Better in Bed!

Geez! Stop already! All the BS of this better movement—the campaigns, quotes, challenges—enough! Here's the truth one more time: **You will never be better than you already are!** It's true! Nothing you can ever do will make you any more valuable than you already are. You've already arrived; you're already invaluable.

Look...Stop getting sucked into the "be better" self-improvement movement! Your life is so much more treasured than that. A great place to begin is by simply looking in the mirror and seeing your own personal value and self-worth and then making decisions based on that information instead of striving to be some sense of better. Another book in this series will focus more on that because, frankly, some of us have been so busy doing what we think we're supposed to be doing that we don't even know who we are. We're so busy trying to be better that we never realized that forming our own identity was ever an option. Where did that idea of what better looks like in our minds come from anyway? Seriously, think about that for a moment. When using the word, ask yourself, "Where did my definition of better even come from pertaining to this particular matter?"

We'll explore more about this soon, but for now, here's the truth: When we imply *better*, it means that we want something other than what we currently have, and that's not all-in-all negative. However, if "better" is left undefined and unprocessed, it's not helpful. If we feel bad because we have not met an expectation, don't have something, or haven't achieved something we feel we should, then it can be harmful and even debilitating, especially if we live in that mindset of disappointment for an extended period. The only time the BS of Better language is beneficial is when we identify it, define it, and process it to create what we want because it is important to *us* and not because we *should*.

IDENTIFYING THE BS OF BETTER

It's not only the word "better" that insinuates we haven't yet arrived at the place we are supposed to be. We use many terms in our thoughts and vocabulary that imply we are not enough or need to be better. Following are words, definitions, and a few examples of the messages we see in our society. Do any of these apply in your life? Do you find yourself looking to improve or fix yourself, or be your best?

- ☐ Better: facade of needing to be more tolerable or acceptable, more complete or perfect
- ☐ Best: facade of a highest standard or level of achievement
- ☐ Improve: facade of needing to be better or do better

- ☐ Fix: facade that someone or something is broken or in need of repair
- ☐ Feelings of being broken or messed up
- ☐ Feeling disappointed with self

The uncertainty underlying the BS of Better thoughts and words is this:

Is something wrong with me?

Words like better, best, improve, and fix are almost always nothing more than facades—superficial, artificial, or false ideas or suggestions that attempt to resemble the distorted appearances of our faulty beLIEfs. Whatever doesn't resemble these distorted ideas will succumb to not being enough in our minds. See the facades in action? Get the idea of how our society has trained us to internally feel like we're not good enough as we cleave to these facades?

These are not always harmful terms and phrases, but again, undefined, they are not helpful and often lead to negative emotions about ourselves and others. Think about the pressure that accompanies these terms and phrases. There must be some form of communicating that does not consist of terminology that implies we or others are not good enough or need to do something else before we are complete. Holding on to terms such as these and their BS foundation shoves such pressure down our throats, drastically increases anxiety, and creates an underlying tone of hopelessness.

PROCESSING: IF NOT BETTER, THEN WHAT?

Here's the thing...it's not that we never should use the word better or similar terms. The trick here is that we be so completely self-aware that when these BS of better words surface, we immediately define and assess them to see how the words may serve us instead of limit us. How can these words enlighten instead of pressure us, empower in lieu of depress us?

The objective here is to limit the use of these limiting words and to only allow them when we are consciously using them to identify decisions that align with who we are as individuals. ***The BS of Better*** program is full of hundreds of examples on how to consciously use language to promote ourselves in lieu of allowing our subconscious BS to sabotage our lives by trying to be some distorted sense of better.

But how do we do that? We can easily define these better words by changing our language and exploring two other words: **value** and **benefit**. When we acknowledge these terms we use for *better* in our thoughts or spoken words, it is helpful to take a moment to define them by asking what the value or the benefits are in the circumstance we are insinuating are better than the present. For the sake of processing, let's look at some examples.

SARAH'S STORY

Sarah enters into the coaching sessions expressing her concern with how she feels and responds to anger. Sometimes she stuffs her anger so not to have explosive episodes, but then that often manifests internally through surface addictions such as binge eating and channel surfing. Or sometimes the unprocessed anger turns into defense mechanisms such as isolating or giving up if she is trying not to explode. However, on other days, if caught in just the right mood, look out! These behaviors are likely to lead to emotional or verbal abuse of others by yelling, blaming, or name-calling. If those around her are lucky, maybe she will only slam a few drawers and use a little sarcasm instead.

Frankly, the concept of calming and diffusing the situation and verbalizing her feelings and needs is incomprehensible in these moments of pressure. It's simply not something she's practiced, so calming and diffusing feel unfamiliar during this present season and in the current pressures in her life. Sarah states she is ready to make some changes, but very few tools she has used have been effective as they have been difficult to implement. Let's explore some of her thoughts and what may be occurring with Sarah.

Something she thought to herself frequently was, "I'm trying to get *better* at letting go of my anger, but it's hard."

Often throughout our days, what seem to be nonchalant statements like this enter our minds and our conversations. Unless processed internally, our brain stores and reinforces this unprocessed belief that "letting go of anger is hard," which often leaves us with negative emotions and unresolved issues pertaining to the anger. We question our capabilities because we subconsciously tell ourselves we need to be better at this, which means we aren't enough. See how we undermine ourselves with this BS verbiage?

However, we can do something differently and process the situation that is underlying the need for *better* in this situation. Instead of wanting better and feeling bad because she isn't better or enough, Sarah used the following journal topics and exercises for identifying, observing, and processing her anger. Her new solutions all started when she noticed the BS of better language surface in her thoughts and words and then decided to use it.

Sarah Identifies and Observes Her BS of Better Language

"I'm trying to get *better* at letting go of my anger, but it's hard." "I need to *improve* in emotional regulation and anger management so that I can *fix* some of my relationships." "I feel so *messed up* and *disappointed* in myself because I've tried *fixing* this problem for a long time and I just can't do it."

Sarah Observes Her Feelings

"I feel exhausted, crabby, and unattractive because I find myself transferring my anger in other places such as road rage while driving and projecting my anger on my husband, children, and colleagues at work. Then I hate myself later because I keep making people feel uncomfortable and unsafe."

Sarah Processes

Sarah explored the objective of the BS thoughts and words by identifying what she wanted to be better at. "I want to be better at letting go of my anger instead of spewing it on other people to help those around me feel safe and welcome in my life."

She briefly reflected on her patterns when similar experiences surfaced. "When I think of letting go of my anger, it is hard because I deal with the same stuff over and over. I get tired of dealing with it. It makes it worse because I anticipate that it's going to keep happening. This repetitive problem leads me to a feeling of hopelessness when I think of ways to resolve this issue. Then I allow my defense mechanisms and surface addictions to take over most of the time because I'm too exhausted to fight the hopeless feeling and thoughts that things will never change."

Sarah considered the pressure she felt. "When I think of being better or improving in my responses to anger, the pressure I feel is hard because I've been working on controlling my anger for a long time. I feel like such a failure and like I've hurt people to the point some of them may not even feel safe enough to let me back in. I know I should try but again, it feels hopeless."

Sarah pushed beyond the negative energy of the hopeless emotion and contemplated the potential value. "The value I see in letting go of my anger is having peace internally and creating a safe atmosphere where I can stay connected with those I care about, even during challenging times. Wow, imagine the beauty that would bring to my life," she thought as she felt an inkling of hope for a fleeting moment.

She enjoyed the positive energy that moment of hope brought. It heightened her curiosity of the possible benefits that investing more energy into creating change could bring. "Letting go of my anger would bring the following benefits for myself and those around me: 1) Since my anger leads to a lot of resentment and bitterness, letting go of my anger would free a lot of time and space in my mind to focus on other things more important to me. 2) If I did not give so much thought to what makes me angry, it would reduce some of the resentment and bitterness that so often drains my energy. 3) I could be more open to enjoying life more with my family, friends, and even at work without being so uptight. 4) Sometimes I fear people may avoid sharing with me because they fear my reaction, so I could enjoy genuine connection and quality time if I let go of my anger and create a safe space for people to engage with me."

Sarah Establishes Action Plans Based on Her Readiness

I'm ready: "Because I want to reap the value and benefits of letting go of my anger, this week I may try sharing with those closest to me that I am aware that my anger has had a negative impact and that I am working on it. I can ask them to be patient with me and love me through it while I am developing myself and growing so that our relationships can feel safe and enjoyable."

I'm not quite ready: "I'm not confident that I can or am ready to let go of my anger yet, so this week I will work on accepting myself and others right where we are by acknowledging when I feel angry and resorting to some of my destressing techniques, such as going to another room and taking a few deep breaths, diverting my attention by finding something within that relationship or circumstance to be thankful for, or using humor to make light of negative situations in lieu of sarcasm. Humor feels safe, sarcasm doesn't, so I will make sure to consider how others feel before using this defense mechanism."

Establishing my support system: "Someone that I can safely discuss my anger with and ask for support from is my husband, but sometimes he is the one I'm really angry with and I'm not always in the mood to address situations nicely with him. Therefore, if it involves him and it doesn't feel like I can maintain a safe atmosphere, I will lovingly and respectfully table the matter and call my friend Julie to vent because she supports my relationship with my husband and is objective. However, I recognize that venting can sometimes fuel the fire, so I will make sure to express some things that I am grateful for in my relationship with my husband after venting."

Acceptance when not ready: "Even though I am struggling with letting go of my anger right now, I recognize that I am invaluable and so are the other people that may be involved or influenced by my words and actions. Therefore, I will:

A) **Objectively observe the challenge when it surfaces by**...thinking carefully before addressing matters, destressing, not personalizing how others are feeling, and behaving respectfully to myself and others regardless of circumstances and make this my top priority.
B) **Extend grace and respect to myself and others when challenges surface by**...remembering how special they are and how much they mean to me. I will also remember my objective is to create and maintain a safe space for us to engage with one another and stay genuinely connected.
C) **Extend acceptance of self and others when challenges surface by**...reminding myself that I'm okay. They're okay. We're okay. Everything is going to be okay."

After processing, Sarah's life coach asked her a question: "Sarah, that sounds like a plan that will lead to the results you say you desire in your life at this time. When you carry out this plan to let go of your anger, will you be better?"

Sarah replies: "No, Coach; I'm already better! However, when I intentionally identify, observe, and alter some of my choices, my life will be less stressful and my relationships will be more enjoyable. That's what I truly desire."

RONNIE'S STORY

Here's another example. In his twenties and thirties, Ronnie exercised most days. He felt good about the self-discipline he displayed by faithfully working out at his local gym four to six times a week. His body was in great shape, he had so much more energy, and sometimes people even noticed the results of his self-care as they would compliment his physique.

After moving to a new location that was quite a distance from any workout facility and finding himself a soccer dad running his three preteen and teenaged children to and from practices and games most evenings after work, it didn't take long to get out of the swing of hitting the gym. However, Ronnie felt bad about it almost daily, and when the topic would surface, how do you think he would respond?

Ronnie Identifies and Observes His BS of Better Language

"I used to be *better* at exercising, but not anymore. I'm so out of the habit that on a good week, I may exercise one day. But I'm working on *improving* myself, so it will get *better*."

Ronnie Observes His Feelings

"I feel overweight, have less energy, my joints are tight, and I feel restricted because I cannot do some of the things I used to be able to do when I was in shape. I don't like what I see in the mirror, and secretly, I miss having a little time for myself. Sometimes, I feel suffocated, like I'm forced to do everything for everyone else and not allowed time to care for me. The gym is for me!"

Ronnie Processes the BS of Better Language

Ronnie explored the objective of the BS thoughts and words by identifying what he wanted to be better at. "I want to exercise more and have a little personal time for myself at the gym so that I can recharge my mind and body. When I think of being better or improving my exercise routine, the pressure I feel is that I would have to let someone down if I scheduled time for me to visit the gym on a weekly basis. I would probably have to miss one of the kid's games occasionally or not be home for movie night with my wife."

He briefly reflected on his patterns and the pressure he felt when similar experiences surfaced. "When I think of exercising, it is hard because there is literally no time! No time for me ever, just another obligation, followed by another obligation, followed by another obligation... That thinking makes it worse because I anticipate that I will never find time for the gym. I will never find time for me. Then I get frustrated and allow my defense mechanisms to kick in, getting easily irritated with those around me because I'm not doing what I want to do. No matter how disciplined I am, I still sometimes resort to surface addictions like watching TV or hiding out with unproductive work in the garage. At least then I'm home but have a little alone time while disguising it as another important priority so I can at least breathe for a few minutes. But even that leaves me feeling guilty, like I'm lying to everyone else and hiding what's important to myself. It's a vicious cycle."

Ronnie pushed beyond the negative energy of the frustrating emotion and contemplated the potential value. "The value I see in exercising is having a healthy mind and body, increased confidence, and joy from a much-needed sense of autonomy. Exercising would bring benefits for myself and those around me as my self-confidence would increase and I would be less irritable and frustrated. I would also be able to mentor my children in the importance of self-care and show them the benefits of taking care of your body. Not that my wife doesn't find me attractive, but I would certainly like to age in a healthy manner and remain as healthy and vibrant for her as well as myself."

Ronnie Establishes Action Plans Based on His Readiness

I'm ready: "Because I want to reap the value and benefits of exercising, this week I may schedule just one day a week for now so at least I can enjoy the benefits of starting while still giving thought to figuring out my schedule."

I'm not quite ready: "I'm not quite ready to commit to exercising yet, so this week I will work on accepting myself right where I am and by talking with my wife about how much I miss exercise and how important it is to me. Perhaps she and I could explore possibilities together for fitting it in my schedule when I am ready."

Establishing my support system: "Someone that I can safely discuss my exercise goals and challenges with and ask for support from is my wife and my colleague at work who seems to have found a balance with juggling self-care while working and taking care of his family."

Acceptance when not ready: "Even though I am struggling with not exercising much right now, I am invaluable and so are the other people that may be involved or influenced by my words and actions. Therefore, I will, at minimum, remind myself daily of the importance of exercising even if I choose not to do it that day. I will:

A) **Objectively observe the challenge when it surfaces by**...choosing transparency in discussing my desire to exercise more and be open to the ideas others may share on the possibilities of making that happen when I am ready.

B) **Extend grace and respect to myself and others when this challenge surfaces by**...enjoying the moments I have with my family, including all the errands and responsibilities that require a lot of time, because while it's difficult at times, I do enjoy my family and appreciate them.

C) **Extend acceptance of self and others when challenges surface by**...remembering that when I am ready, I will make a way to incorporate exercise into my life, even if it's less time than I prefer. Until then, it's okay. I'm okay, and exercising will not make me better. It will simply add value to my life by giving me some of the benefits that I desire."

After processing, Ronnie's life coach asked him this question: "Ronnie, that sounds like a plan that will lead to the results you say you desire in your life at this time. When you carry out this plan to prioritize exercise in your life, will you be better?"

Ronnie replied, "Not a chance! I'm already better and invaluable; nothing I do will make me any more valuable! However, I will feel somewhat refreshed and my mind will be less weary when I exercise. And, when I intentionally manage my time and lovingly voice my needs to my family for some me-time to exercise, I will feel healthier mentally and physically and ultimately be more pleasant to be around. That's what I truly desire."

IDENTIFY, ASSESS, AND PROCESS

You probably get the point by now: identify, assess, and process any language that surfaces in your thoughts, words, or behaviors that implies the need for improvement in lieu of acceptance. If you want to make alternative choices that yield different outcomes, great. But never strive for better without knowing exactly why it is important to you, and most importantly, accept yourself until you are ready to move a position.

Think about this: whether we are 20, 30, 40, 50, 60, 70, or even 80 years old, we never officially arrive. In our 30s, we know more than we do in our 20s. In our 40s, we know more than we do in our 30s, and so forth. Here's the point: Let's say we took every single aspect in our lives, every challenge that we could possibly *improve* or make *better,* and we *fixed* it all in one single day. What would happen? What then? Nothing, that's what! There would be no room for personal development, no necessity for growing pains to push us into new directions and endeavors. We would still not reach satisfaction after making every single change we think we need to.

That is simply not how we were designed. We will always be striving for something, so stop searching to arrive and simply enjoy being awake, aware, and alive! Enjoy the moment, all the challenges, the quirkiness of being you, the fumbles, the aggravations, the tolerations, the longings for something different or new that doesn't quite seem obtainable in the moment because we're not yet ready to apply the necessary energy to make it happen. These are all beautiful and necessary evils of being human, so stop feeling bad for not being better because you are good enough right where you are!

BE THE COACH

Listen, as a life coach with a ton of experience and education, I have extensive knowledge in the field of psychology, emotional health, communication, and human behavior. But compared to all the knowledge and experiences that are in the world, my knowledge is not even a drop in the ocean! *You* are the most amazing and knowledgeable coach you will ever meet! Yes, hiring a coach is beneficial, but only for the purpose of learning self-coaching.

As a professional life coach, I urge that if you hire a coach, make sure their methodology promotes and trains on self-coaching and includes it as an important part of the end result of the coaching process. Learn self-coaching during any personal development process in lieu of allowing a dependency on a coach to form. This will allow you to practice healthy thoughts and behaviors that will develop healthy neural pathways in the brain, which will eventually generate automated healthy responses in the future.

These healthy neural pathways can quickly lose strength when not exercised, so it is important to learn how to coach yourself in strengthening these healthy pathways for the rest of your life. So, to begin, this book is your opportunity to practice self-coaching and building those healthy neural pathways. Each chapter will come with questions for you to ask yourself, but don't stop there. Trust your *intuition* to guide you to additional questions. Courageously allow *curiosity* and *possibility* to guide you through self-exploration, reflection, and journaling. In each chapter, sample questions are provided to coach yourself, but stretch beyond those and ask yourself the tough questions you've been avoiding answers to, such as:

- What am I pretending not to know?
- What have I been avoiding?
- What am I afraid to acknowledge?

Stretch yourself. Trust yourself. You know what you need and want. Oftentimes, we are afraid to acknowledge what we need and want because awareness brings about feelings that change is necessary or—seemingly worse—essential. This feeling may add pressure to our lives, but don't worry, no action is required, and we will explore ways to regulate those feelings that bring pressure while considering change.

In this book, we are simply deciding to explore those uncomfortable areas and then learning to accept ourselves and others as we mature in life. Human life is a never-ending process of evolution and maturation. We will never "arrive" in this life, but we can increase the peace, joy, and fulfillment we experience on our journey by exploring, accepting, and growing along the way. ***The BS of Better*** program facilitates this process by training in various ways to reduce life's pressures on the road of evolution and maturation.

We do not do what is healthy, but rather what is familiar.

Homework for Overcoming the Language of Better

Ever feel the need to be better? Did the limiting language of better in this chapter resonate with you? If so, you have the ability to break free of these limiting thoughts and debilitating mindset. Do you recognize that our society is brainwashed by the self-improvement movement and that it affects us almost daily?

Ever feel like a failure? Feel like your identity got lost somehow or like you're not good enough? Feeling the need to be better implies to our subconscious that we are inferior and inflicts so much pressure in our minds. When we feel the need to be better, we experience uncertainties and question whether something is wrong with us. Remember, we will never be any better than we already are.

What language are you using that reflects you may be struggling with the BS of Better? We are much more than the expectations that tell us we must be better. Instead of allowing the BS of better language to pressure, exhaust, and increase anxiety in our lives, we can define and assess how to use the better language for our advantage.

We can do this by daily coaching ourselves. You are fully capable of coaching yourself into a life of peace, joy, and fulfillment by capturing limiting language and exposing the debilitating mindsets they represent. Listen to yourself, trust yourself, and courageously connect with yourself through honesty and vulnerability.

TAKE YOUR TIME AND DO THE WORK!

If you have identified that your beLIEf systems have you feeling pressured and stretched thin, trying to be better, to fix or improve yourself, or simply feel like you're not enough, then spend at least the next week processing the following few pages of homework to increase your personal awareness in this area. You deserve to be free from the BS of better.

If you've been struggling with limiting thoughts for a long time, they are ingrained in the neural pathways of your brain and seem familiar. What is familiar seems right, acceptable, or tolerable to some degree in our minds; therefore, we stick with it. A future book in this series will go into the details of the brain and habitual behaviors, but for now, just remember that we do not do what is healthy, but rather what is familiar. Let's drive this home! The reason these habitual thoughts and behaviors are familiar is because those are neural pathways in our brains that exist and are stronger because we've exercised them more than others.

Okay, let's say that again, we do not do what is healthy, but rather what is familiar. Why is this important? Because familiar is only changed through intention. In order to alter our neural pathways, we must intentionally process and apply new information for our brains to establish new neural pathways that serve us instead of limit us. For us to modify these thoughts and tendencies, we must remind ourselves daily to be on the lookout for them and have options readily available to choose from. Simple awareness through processing is the most powerful step in personal development and behavioral modification.

With this homework, the objective is NOT to answer the questions! So, for those of you like me who will want to do all the homework in one day, STOP! The goal here is to be intentional in thinking about this information multiple times a day. Don't worry, it's only a couple of minutes at a time. Just enough to train your brain to think about what you are thinking about throughout the day. During this daily process, we are developing those neural pathways that will keep us thinking about them for the rest of our lives. Otherwise, once we're done with the book, the information will fly right out the window along with most of the other great personal development information you've invested energy and money in but not used. Take the time to journal, ask questions, and process daily so your revelations become your new familiar through repetitious mental workouts. Using *The BS of Better Journal* assists with this process, but working through the homework questions using any journal works as well.

OBSERVATIONS OF THE BS OF BETTER MINDSET

Take a few moments to observe the language, feelings, and uncertainty that often accompany the BS of better mindset. Then observe how others may experience this mindset and how it may limit you. Check those that apply to your experiences and/or fill in the blanks with additional observations you have made pertaining to the BS of better.

The BS of better language:

☐ Better
☐ Best
☐ Improve
☐ Fix
☐ Messed up/broken
☐ Other ________________________

Feelings that often accompany the BS of better language:

☐ Disappointment with self
☐ Dissatisfaction with self
☐ Unfulfilled
☐ Pressure to improve self
☐ Stressed
☐ Other ________________________

Uncertainty: Is something wrong with me?

Others may experience me as:

☐ Unsettled
☐ Hard on myself
☐ Lacking contentment
☐ Sad or unhappy
☐ Unfulfilled
☐ Busy (whether productive or unproductive)
☐ Other ________________________

The BS of better mindset may lead to:

☐ Heightened internal pressure and stress
☐ Projecting internal pressure and stress onto others
☐ Lowered self-confidence; difficulty attempting new things or retrying
☐ Premonitions of repeated failures
☐ Relentless striving but rarely, if ever, arriving
☐ Unrecognized and underappreciated achievements
☐ Judgmental or comparative language (see Chapters 4 and 6)
☐ Other ________________________

Daily Journal Practice

Following are journal topics and exercises for the next seven days, but feel free to continue such exercises until you feel yourself being able to automatically capture and replace the BS of better language within your mind. It will take some time, but the neural pathways will develop as you do these exercises daily, and eventually, you will no longer find it necessary to write things down. The brain will learn to process automatically as you train it through such exercises as those contained within this program. Time varies for each of us, but the more frequent and consistent, the quicker the neural pathways develop.

Every chapter includes processing questions and journal topics that will assist in developing healthy neural pathways in the brain. This includes thought capturing and replacement exercises, a crucial part of bringing you success in this program. Therefore, if you're ready for change, don't skip these processing and journal exercises. Don't stop with those listed either; explore what other questions and journal topics may serve you in the moment. You are your greatest coach! Pay attention and listen to yourself and explore!

Day 1: Journal Your Battle with Better

- Take a few moments to journal about your struggle with wanting to be better or wanting to fix or improve things in your life.
- Write about the pressures of feeling broken or never enough.
- Where might these beLIEfs have come from?
- What does life look like if you are free of these limiting beliefs?

Day 2: Observe Others and Your Surroundings

- Spend the entire day and evening observing your surroundings. In what surroundings do you feel the need to be better, to fix or improve yourself?
- Observe what people around you are saying. What struggles do you hear them having with their own BS of needing to be better?
- What messages do you see or hear on TV, social media, the radio, in advertisements, etc., that could sway you into feeling the need to be better by fixing or improving yourself?

Day 3: Thought Capturing

Write down every single thought you have today that suggests you need to be better or need to fix or improve yourself. It's important to write them all to track their frequency, so make sure to carry a small notepad or your journal with you today.

Day 4: Thought Replacement
Now replace those thoughts from Day 3 with words of encouragement and acceptance that support you with no expectations or pressure.

Day 5: Thought Capturing and Replacement
Now capture and replace those BS thoughts with words of encouragement and acceptance that support you with no expectations or pressure.

Day 6: Thought Capturing and Replacement
Again, capture and replace the BS thoughts with words of encouragement and acceptance that support you with no expectations or pressure.

Day 7: Thought Capturing and Replacement
Again, capture and replace the BS thoughts with words of encouragement and acceptance that support you with no expectations or pressure.

Continue thought capturing and replacement exercises to build neural pathways that support an acceptance mindset.

PRACTICE AND BUILD NEURAL PATHWAYS OF AN ACCEPTANCE MINDSET

Thoughts of the Better Mindset:	Thoughts of the Acceptance Mindset:

Reframe better thoughts with those of an acceptance mindset:

JOURNAL TOPICS TO CONTEMPLATE FOR OVERCOMING THE LANGUAGE OF BETTER

Grab your notebook or *The BS of Better Journal* to contemplate and process overcoming the BS of better. Below are cues and questions to begin assessing the costs and the payoffs of allowing the BS of better to take hold in your brain, but don't stop here. Remember, journal those prompts that stand out to you and ask yourself other difficult questions and concerns that may not be listed but are hiding deep within yourself. You already know these concerns; this is your time to listen! Identify and observe the BS of better so that you can stop what's causing those feelings of disappointment and dissatisfaction when you are ready.

Inquisitive Alternatives:

☐ All the things I love about myself are...
(Keep listing, there's more! Allow yourself to see them.)
☐ What makes me a human BEing instead of a human DOing?
☐ I accept instead of criticize myself by...
☐ Replace expectations and pressure with words of acceptance and support.
☐ What options align with me?
☐ What have I achieved?
☐ What achievements have supported feelings of significance?
☐ How can I recognize and express joy for my achievements?
☐ How can I embrace fulfillment and contentment right where I am?
☐ What things will I eventually explore when I am ready, not to be better, but to yield the results I desire?
☐ Other ________________________

Neural Pathway Development Support

It cannot be reiterated enough that neural pathway development is crucial for sustainable healthy change in thoughts and behaviors. Heightening self-awareness, committing to personal reflection time, and completing acceptance and action plans daily and weekly will develop the neural pathways that serve you. For additional daily processing support, please see **Appendix A – Neural Pathway Development Support**. What would it look like if we asked the difficult yet beneficial questions until the questions were no longer difficult? When you're ready, try it and see.

Who decides when I am enough?

2

THE LIMITING LANGUAGE OF INADEQUACY

One day, I was speaking with a good friend of mine and fellow life coach, Michael (Mike) Elfrank, regarding the topic of self-worth and being enough. I tease Mike because, as a storyteller, he sometimes takes a while to get to the point, but this story he shared, I held onto every single word as he passionately spoke.

Mike recapped the story of the miners as they were trapped for sixty-nine days after the collapse of a mine in Chile. I distinctively remembered that the mining accident occurred in 2010, but once the miners were rescued, I didn't really think much about it. But Mike shed some new light on this incredible story that captivated the world and gave insight to the significance of life.

In Mike's retelling of the Chilean mining accident, he began by shedding some light on many of the details that I hadn't known. I knew thirty-three men were trapped beneath collapsed rock, that their families were distraught with grief on the surface of the mine, and that people and companies from around the world contributed knowledge and resources to free them after sixty-nine long days.

However, Mike continued with important details about this true story that were new to me. The first was the vast efforts from all around the world that were made on behalf of these thirty-three individuals. An estimated $20 million was spent, thousands of necessities were contributed, and hundreds of individuals and many companies from all around the world worked diligently to find any solutions that would lead to the freedom of the miners.

Some contributions may be obvious, such as high-tech equipment, but the effort necessary to engineer, build, and prepare the equipment required a vast pool of willing and innovative team members from different parts of the world. This required time, money, camaraderie, and a level of insurmountable creativity.

But that was only part of the problem. Other factors such as assessing and ensuring their survival while waiting for a successful rescue plan to be put into place were crucial. This included everything from basic survival needs such as food, water, and oxygen preservation to psychological and social needs, along with communication with the outside world while trapped in utter darkness for sixty-nine days.

There were so many details, and so many participants in creating a successful rescue plan and implementing it, that I couldn't possibly describe it in this book. Hundreds of individuals worked and volunteered to cover such details as protective eye coverings to assist as their eyes adjusted when they emerged from the deep. The point is that the enormous pool of contribution from the world to save thirty-three people was incredible.

Mike went on about many more unbelievable details, and then he asked me two questions that shocked me—you know, those eye-opening, aha-moment questions:

1) Why do you think the world pitched in millions of dollars, thousands of resources, and hundreds of volunteers and workers to save just thirty-three people?

This question hit me immediately, lighting a fire under my skin, and I quickly responded because they're people and they matter! Their lives matter! And all the family members who were crying for help because they love them, they matter! Of course, we will do anything and spare no cost, no resource, no amount of time to save them!

Feeling somewhat vindicated in my response, I took a deep breath and waited to hear his. However, it was nothing like what I thought it was going to be as the next question proceeded from his lips:

2) Would they have done it for you? If YOU were the one trapped?

Strangely enough, I was not as quick to respond. I hesitated, being puzzled by the question that had taken a direction I wasn't prepared for. So, I responded with hesitation and reservation, "Just me, or are others trapped with me?"

"No, just you," he quickly replied.

"Well, probably not, Mike," I slowly said as my forceful vengeance to protect human life at all cost quickly turned to sadness, recognizing that my value wasn't enough to simply save me alone.

Whether the world would come together, spending millions of dollars in over two months, to spare my life now became a moot point. The devastation I realized in that split second was that something internally told me I was not enough. All that night, and for the next couple weeks, through many tears, I asked myself, *Brigitte, why do you feel this way? Why do you feel that your life is not valuable enough to invest in your protection and safety?*

I wasn't sure! Was it something I had done? Was it something that I did not do? Was it from past trauma or dysfunction? Why wasn't I enough? I want to know! I have the right to know and the responsibility to figure this out! After all, this is the BS that I am passing along to my children and to my grandchildren and their children unless one of them decides to break it.

I came to a second realization from my conversation with Mike. The value of human life is in the eye of the beholder. Obviously, not everyone values human life in every season of our lives. If we did, abuse, neglect, homicides, and other crimes would never happen. However, most of us would probably agree that most of our world does value human life to the extent of preservation at almost any cost.

That being the case, who decides if and when our individual lives are enough? Who says if and when we are invaluable? I spent weeks and months pondering this question, sorting through thousands of notes from my training in child development and psychology, sorting through hundreds of resources and tools from my coaching classes and certifications. I want to know! Who says?

You are not going to believe this...it's been figured out! So, here it is:

Me! I do! I recognize my own value and protect it!

What happens if I choose *not* to recognize that I am enough and diligently protect my value—my value whose parameters are beyond infinity and completely outside of anything that I could ever do or not do?

What then?

I'll tell you what then! Then we rear generation after generation who devalue themselves, which leads to devaluing one another. That's exactly what we see today. At the heart of most of us, we know the value, but our own distorted beLIEf systems create barriers that prevent us from behaving in a manner that says we and others are infinitely valuable, that I, as an individual, and you, as an individual, regardless of anything, without exception, are enough! When I do not acknowledge that *I* am enough, I will never be able to fully respect that *you* are enough. More about that later, but for now, can we agree that we are enough?

So, my original conclusion was: I am enough! You are enough! We are enough! But that's too easy, not deep enough, and frankly, not applicable. How do we implement those truths and apply them to our lives? Honestly, if we knew how to apply the concept that we are enough, none of us would be walking around thinking that we are not enough nor treating others like they are not enough. We must gain an understanding of what happened to put us into this state, find solutions to emerge out of it, and implement the strategy that will rewire the distorted beLIEf systems that have kept us trapped here, so let's keep digging.

DEFINING ENOUGH, IMPORTANCE, MATTERING, WORTH, AND VALUE

Wait, something isn't sitting well with me. I thought, what does **enough** even mean anyway? So, I pulled out the handy-dandy dictionary. But I didn't pull out just one; I researched every dictionary I could find to help me understand what the word **enough** means because the first definition and everyone thereafter kept falling short of what I thought it would mean.

Are you ready for this? You're not going to believe it. When you look up the word "enough" in the dictionary, you see a couple of definitions. One uses words like satisfactory, sufficient, competent, adequate, tolerable, and suitable. Well, that didn't sound very appealing. Seriously, the world spent millions of dollars, thousands of man-hours and resources because thirty-three individuals were adequate or satisfactory? Stop it! I must be missing something; there had to be more!

So, I continued my search. Another definition is as much as necessary, all that is required or appropriate. My, that sounds special, doesn't it? NO! Being mediocre or average does not sound very valuable. The more I searched the meaning of the word "enough," the more appalled I became. Do you mean I have spent most of my life feeling like I am not enough when all that is required to be enough is simple adequacy? I cannot stand this! Why is this so confusing?

I studied on. **Enough** is also something that you say when you want something to stop, as in, "That's enough!" Well, I've had just about enough of trying to be enough, so that's enough of that!

How disappointing! I thought for sure **enough** meant something relating to my level of importance per se, or possibly that I mattered, if in fact I was enough. So, I explored further. Since "enough" was not sufficient in my mind, perhaps by looking up the words "important" and "matter," I would come to a healthy conclusion that helps us understand our value.

In my research, the new questions then became:

- Am I important?
- Do I matter?

I decided to search the word **matter** first to see where it led me. Well, it could mean anything from the reason for a distress or problem to pus draining from a wound. Well, that doesn't sound very enticing either. However, the good news is that it could also mean important or significant. Well, let's go with that, and see what it means to be important and significant to see how it relates to self-worth and value. Maybe I'm on to something.

Important seems to correlate with value, so let's try a couple more. How about **valuable**? It seems like we might be getting somewhere now because the word **valuable** means of great worth. **Worth** is basically the measurement by which the value is rated. This is a big one for me because, while I am confident and at peace, I have struggled with self-worth all my life.

Recently, someone told me about Brené Brown and her work on vulnerability and courage. I had heard her name in passing a few times but didn't know much about her work. Of course, I did an internet search and watched a couple of her videos and fell in love with the way she so eloquently packages the challenges surrounding "being enough." Brené is definitely on my list of people to follow because I am continually looking to deepen my knowledge around this topic, and she seems to be a great leader in this field of expertise. For now, I'll recap a couple of points I saw on one of her videos.

Brené Brown suggests we live in a mindset of scarcity where it's never enough, we are never enough. It's one of the challenges that surfaced and was addressed with 99 percent of my coaching clients for over fifteen years. I always coach on the awareness of the adaptation level phenomenon that says we never really arrive because every achievement and success we experience eventually becomes the new norm and will no longer be satisfactory. We continue searching even after we arrive at the place we initially desired and strove for. So, yes, I agree with Brené, that we never feel like it's enough.

She mentioned some thought-provoking phrases that are great to journal. Here are a few of her power-packed ticklers on the topic of being enough:

- **The way out of not being enough is enoughness itself.**
- **Our struggle with believing we are enough stems in part by our idea of being perfect instead of engaging with the world from a place of worthiness.**

- **When perfectionism is driving, shame is always riding shotgun and fear is the annoying back-seat driver.**

Listen, I cannot recap Brené's work and words sufficiently; it's too powerful from what I've seen so far. So, when you're looking for your next read or study material on being enough, vulnerability, and courage, I'd recommend her as an excellent resource. A glimpse of freedom seemed so obvious as Brené shared a cornerstone of her theory on enoughness: "Shame cannot survive being spoken."

The tidbit I took away in listening to Brené speak was that in order to experience being enough, exercising courage and vulnerability as weapons against perfection will debunk shame and yield a sense of worthiness. This reminded me of something one of my clients said during a breakthrough session: **"Pooh-pooh perfection!"** Aren't those beautiful words? I found the phrase ingenious. My client was exhausted from her perfectionistic attempts and was exhausting those around her because she never felt like she was enough. However, through many mental exercises, she was able to conquer a lot of that BS in her life. This brought me to realize that:

> **Many are so busy working so hard to be so perfect that the pain of acknowledging they're not is unbearable. Perfection is painful. Break free.**

Perfectionism is impossible and unhealthy. One of my mentors and life coach trainers, Gary Kuzmich, once said to me, "We're all a quart low sometime, someplace, somewhere." Then he shared with me the story behind his comment. A little light comes on in our vehicles that reminds us when our oil may need to be changed or that we're low on oil. This little light doesn't mean our car is messed up; it's simply an indicator that there is something that may need our attention, so we may want to look into it to keep it running smoothly.

The bottom line is that the breach occurs when we allow our value, worthiness, significance, level of importance, or whether we matter in certain situations to be defined by anyone or anything outside of ourselves. This requires listening to, relying on, and paying attention to our own instincts. Unfortunately, our instincts are mostly swayed by external pressures and by the internal BS.

I've found no term that truly defines our significance, for no human language is powerful enough to describe the importance of any human life. In my failed attempts at trying to wrap my head around what it means to be enough, I discovered something beautiful:

> **My value is indescribable. So is yours.**

This is beautiful because that which cannot be described cannot be measured. We live in a world of measuring and comparing in seeking validation. But none of that matters when we simply acknowledge that we cannot be described nor can we be measured. Look at the freedom that comes from the mere acknowledgment of being indescribable and the freedom that comes from being immeasurable.

Human beings are indescribable and immeasurable; human doings are not. Our attempts at arriving by doing create the inadequacy that suppresses us. That's huge and it's scary, seeming next to impossible to overcome in some instances. It may seem impossible to overcome the lies of inadequacy that keep us spinning our wheels by doing...but it's not. Keep going; we're getting somewhere.

WHAT DEFEATS INADEQUACY?

What is the one vital component upon which all healthy characteristics is founded? Many would say love, and I would say perhaps, but there is another characteristic that is a prerequisite even for the ability to love. The greatest gift we can give to ourselves, one another, and our world is acceptance. We cannot love without first accepting.

Acceptance is key. When we accept something or someone, we embrace all the components involved, even the unpleasant or less desirable ones. If simple self-acceptance is the key, then why is that so difficult? Acceptance has a lot to do with how we have been conditioned and what we internally feel is right or wrong. We will explore that more in the next chapter when we talk about our third group of limiting language, guilt-ridden language. But for now, we will visit the foundational component of being enough: acknowledgment that acceptance equates to enoughness.

When we accept ourselves, we are acknowledging that we are more than enough. When we accept others, we are acknowledging that they are more than enough. To love ourselves, others, and the Universe, we must extend acceptance by acknowledging we and they are more than enough—meaning worthy of our love. This is important because we invest in what we deem worthy. Let's take a moment to look at all the healthy human characteristics that stem from acceptance.

Trust, faith, and vulnerability require acceptance, either of ourselves, someone else, or the Universe. Even responsibility requires acceptance. Think about it. So does honesty, optimism, consideration, loyalty, integrity, compassion, creativity, confidence, generosity, enthusiasm, curiosity, ambitiousness, conscientiousness, imagination, kindness, empathy, perseverance, courage, gratitude, patience, forgiveness, fairness, respect, authenticity, self-discipline, reliability... Shall I go on? I asked myself if there was any healthy characteristic that does not require acceptance, and I couldn't think of one. Can you?

Accepting, by embracing all components—even the unpleasant or less desirable ones—is difficult because we are limited by our internal interpretation of what safe acceptance and love actually look like. We are taught through modeled immaturity that acceptance and love are with condition. The only way to pass through the doors of healthy acceptance and love are to lay down our armor of conditions. Man, this is tough! Our conditions solidify what we've been taught is right, good, and safe. Conditions are the gauges by which we measure everything, but these conditions are also the enemy of vulnerability and trust. Conditions sabotage us and those in our lives at every turn by reminding us who and what are inadequate.

Remember I mentioned a special gift my mother imparted to me? This concept is it—beautiful words and actions that stem from a mindset of acceptance and love without condition. My mother had some serious mental health issues that limited her and created a lot of occurrences for pain in the lives of her and her children. However, this one special ability that she modeled for me literally transformed my life once I was ready to embrace it. It didn't happen overnight, obviously. It took quite some time for me to let down my anger and guard in order to be vulnerable and open to receive it. However, with persistence and consistent practice, I literally reprogrammed the neural pathways in my brain to replace conditions and expectations with pure acceptance and uncontaminated love. These are the two gifts I give myself daily, which in return allows me to pass those same gifts along to others.

Unfortunately, most of us have not formed neural pathways in the brain that are strong enough to put down our expectations and conditions. This decreases our ability to make acceptance our primary go-to when we are experiencing challenges with ourselves, others, or our world. Most of us are programmed to take action, and when we do not feel powerful enough to take action, we resort to our defense mechanisms and surface addictions. Think about it: How many times when we face any challenges with self, others, or circumstances do we stop and ask ourselves, "Hey, what am I not accepting at this moment?" or, "What conditions am I imposing at this time?"

Are we trained to do this? No. We are trained to do what is right, to be good boys and girls who grow into good people, and we look around at others and our circumstances as a gauge of whether we are meeting that objective. We are taught that right and good define enoughness, and if we are not behaving in such a manner, we are not enough and then conditions must be enforced. Unfortunately, that's the internal hardwiring for most of us. When we see something that we do not like or feel comfortable about within ourselves or others, our guard goes up because we have not trained ourselves to first accept then respond. Don't worry, this can certainly be reprogrammed, but it will take work. If we're not ready for the work, then at a minimum, let's start by learning to accept ourselves right where we are. Personal acceptance is a great place to begin maturing, and it is the foundation of being equipped to accept others amid challenging circumstances. In upcoming chapters, we will explore healthy critical thinking exercises to increase our awareness of the enoughness of self and others by choosing a mindset of acceptance.

Acceptance is key. When we accept something or someone, we embrace all the components involved, even the unpleasant or less desirable ones.

Homework for Overcoming the Language of Inadequacy

Feel unworthy or not good enough? Do you allow thoughts, words, and actions that devalue yourself? Negating our own value keeps us from protecting ourselves and establishing healthy boundaries for ourselves and others. Being enough is not enough to describe ourselves. We are more than important and significant. We are indescribable and cannot be measured. There is no human measurement because we cannot fully understand our worth and value. When we recognize this, we no longer look to the world to affirm our worth. We are free to live by our own values and priorities.

Acceptance is crucial and is without condition. Acceptance exposes the lies of the inadequate mindset. Rewiring the neural pathways in our brains that tell us we are not enough is crucial. We can live a full life that is beyond obligation and expectation by simply reprogramming our minds with the reality that we are indescribable and worthy.

TAKE YOUR TIME AND DO THE WORK!

The questions and exercises in this program were formed to spark healthy thought and motivate opportunity. We have this same power to reframe our thoughts. The primary purpose of this book is to identify what language we are presently using that is limiting us and then learn to reframe our thoughts that will spark language that promotes us. Let's start practicing acceptance of being enough by using the following questions and journal pages to explore this week.

Remember, the benefits will come not by completing the journal pages in one setting. The true benefits will come as mental muscles are exercised daily, which will develop new neural pathways in the brain by repetitive thought-provoking reflections. The more days we take time to reflect on healthy versus unhealthy language, the stronger those neural pathways will become. As the healthy neural pathways are developed and gain strength in the mind, behaviors will follow suit.

The BS of Better program was designed to assist in developing those neural pathways through consistent and intentional focus on our thoughts, language, and behavior. Grab your journal and begin processing this week; make the time and take your time. You deserve the rewards that come with defeating the limiting language of inadequacy.

OBSERVATIONS OF THE INADEQUATE MINDSET

Take a few moments to observe the language, feelings, and uncertainty that often accompany the inadequate mindset. Then observe how others may experience this mindset and how it may limit you. Check those that apply to your experiences and/or fill in the blanks with additional observations you have made pertaining to inadequacy.

Inadequacy language:

☐ I am never enough.
☐ I am not important.
☐ I do not matter.
☐ I am not worthy.
☐ I am not valuable.
☐ I am not perfect.
☐ I am not smart enough, pretty enough, do not work hard enough, etc.
☐ I prioritize most everyone and everything else over myself.
☐ Other ___________________________

Feelings that often accompany the language of inadequacy:

☐ Worthlessness
☐ Insufficient
☐ Timid
☐ Unhappy with self
☐ Lacking in impact
☐ Other ___________________________

Uncertainty: Do I matter? Am I good enough?

Others may experience me as:

☐ Lacking self-confidence, in need of validation
☐ Unhappy
☐ Frail, fragile, or sensitive
☐ Starved for approval or seeking compliments
☐ Other ___________________________

The inadequate mindset may lead to:

☐ Negative self-image
☐ Seeking validation
☐ Low self-esteem
☐ Needing approval
☐ Fixation on self
☐ Frequent personalization
☐ Being guarded or unreachable
☐ Other ___________________________

JOURNAL ABOUT BEING ENOUGH

Consider Feelings About Being Enough:

- Is "being enough" enough?
- What are my beLIEfs around being enough?
- Do I trust myself?
- Am I vulnerable with myself?
- Whom do I trust?
- Whom am I vulnerable with?
- What would it take for me to trust myself and be vulnerable with myself?
- What would it take for me to acknowledge my enoughness?

Being My Own Enough Coach:

- If I were going to coach myself on being enough, what would I say?
- What questions would I ask?
- What doubts would I challenge?
- What beLIEfs would I reprogram?

How Are Describing and Measuring Feeding Inadequacy?

- How am I describing and measuring myself?
- How am I describing and measuring others?
- How am I describing and measuring my circumstances?
- What does it look like to live an indescribable and immeasurable life?

Where Acceptance Eludes Me:

- What do I have difficulty accepting about myself in this season?
- What do I have difficulty accepting about someone else in this season?
- What do I have difficulty accepting about my circumstances in this season?
- My thoughts of how acceptance eludes me are...

Now, Let's Add a Little Touch of Acceptance:

- What can I accept (embrace) about myself in this season?
- What can I accept (embrace) about someone else in this season?
- What can I accept (embrace) about our world or my circumstances in this season?

How might my beLIEf(s) and expectations around enoughness be affecting my ability to accept myself, others, and circumstances?

Daily Journal Practice

Following are journal topics and exercises for the next seven days, but feel free to continue such exercises until you feel yourself being able to automatically capture and replace the limiting language of inadequacy within your mind. It will take some time, but the neural pathways will develop as you do these exercises daily, and eventually, you will no longer find it necessary to write things down. The brain will learn to process automatically as you train it through such exercises as those contained within this program.

Day 1: Journal Your Battle with Being Enough

- Take a few moments to journal about your struggle with not being enough. If prompts would be helpful to you, refer to the questions in the previous homework, "Journal About Being Enough."
- Write about acceptance; where is it easy and where is it difficult?
- Where might your beLIEfs of being enough have come from?
- Where might your beliefs of what is necessary to be accepted have come from?

Day 2: Journal About Importance

- When do I feel important, and what are the surrounding circumstances?
- When do I feel unimportant, and what are the surrounding circumstances?
- How might this affect my ability to accept myself?

Day 3: If You Were the Miner

- Remember the story in this chapter of the Chilean miners? If it were you in the mine, would the world have invested so many resources to ensure your safety and well-being?
- What might your response indicate? Will it limit or promote you? How?

Day 4: What Did I Accept/Not Accept Today?

- Who and what did I accept in myself, others, and circumstances today?
- Who and what did I not accept in myself, others, and circumstances today?

Day 5: Find the Value

What value would come by adding acceptance in some of the areas noted during Day 4?

Day 6: Thought Capturing and Replacement
Capture and replace the inadequate thoughts with words of encouragement and acceptance that support you with no expectations or pressure.

Day 7: Thought Capturing and Replacement
Again, capture and replace the inadequate thoughts with words of encouragement and acceptance that support you with no expectations or pressure.

Continue thought capturing and replacement exercises to build neural pathways that support an indescribable mindset.

PRACTICE AND BUILD NEURAL PATHWAYS OF AN INDESCRIBABLE MINDSET

Thoughts of the Inadequate Mindset:	Thoughts of the Indescribable Mindset:

Reframe inadequacy with thoughts of an indescribable mindset:

JOURNAL TOPICS TO CONTEMPLATE FOR OVERCOMING THE LIES OF INADEQUACY

Grab your notebook or *The BS of Better Journal* to contemplate and process overcoming the inadequate mindset. Below are cues and questions to begin assessing the costs and the payoffs of allowing the lies of inadequacy, but don't stop here. Remember, journal those prompts that stand out to you and ask yourself other difficult questions and concerns that may not be listed but are hiding deep within yourself. You already know these concerns; this is your time to listen! Identify and observe the inadequate mindset so that you can stop what's causing those feelings of worthlessness and beLIEfs of not being enough when you are ready.

Inquisitive Alternatives:

- ☐ What I have difficulty accepting about myself and my circumstances is...
- ☐ I accept (embrace) myself right now by...
- ☐ I am enough, so I...
- ☐ I am important, so I...
- ☐ I matter, so I...
- ☐ I am worthy, so I...
- ☐ I am valuable, so I...
- ☐ I am ready and choose to change my circumstances right now by...
- ☐ For now, I will accept the following until I am ready to make some changes...
- ☐ Other ______________________

Neural Pathway Development Support

It cannot be reiterated enough that neural pathway development is crucial for sustainable healthy change in thoughts and behaviors. Heightening self-awareness, committing to personal reflection time, and completing acceptance and action plans daily and weekly will develop the neural pathways that serve you. For additional daily processing support, please see **Appendix A – Neural Pathway Development Support**. What would it look like if we asked the difficult yet beneficial questions until the questions were no longer difficult? When you're ready, try it and see.

Lost congruency leads to distorted belief systems that form our expectations in the roles we assume. This BS ultimately defines the rules we feel obligated to live by.

3

GUILT-RIDDEN LIMITING LANGUAGE

LeAnn is a beautiful mother in a blended household with a loving husband and four precious children, with a rich heritage of strong moral and family values. From the outside looking in, one can obviously see she has her life together and is doing an incredible job in giving care to her family and meeting her responsibilities. Why is it, then, that mom guilt sabotages her thoughts, torments her mind, and robs her of peaceful rest as she lays her head on the pillow many nights? Why is it she feels like she's suffocating by the noose of exactness reminding her day-by-day that she is not doing enough? She certainly could do more to support her husband, but let's face it, he could do more also. Her perfectionistic tendencies drive the internal overachiever to the brink of exhaustion. It sounds something like this:

"I *should* play more with the kids."
"I *should* be more patient."
"I *should* be more joyful."
"I *should* be spontaneous and more fun."
"I *need to* set a schedule so I can fit in everything I want to do with them every day."
"I *need to* spend more one-on-one time with each child."
"I *ought to* start tomorrow with a fresh restart."
"I was *supposed to* play a game with my child, but I didn't."
"I was *supposed to* fit in self-care today so I could be a more positive role model for my kids."

The list goes on and on... It's the never-ending story of mom guilt. And, of course, it doesn't stop at the borders of momhood. Oh no, LeAnn could also be a better wife, daughter, friend, sister, Christian...you name it. Basically, she feels like a failure in most of her roles to some degree; it's never enough. She's never enough.

One week, when working with her coach to get to the bottom of these thoughts, she remembered something and proceeded to say:

"I read this week an article [Christian-based] on how to be a better mom. At the end of the day, I realized how this, and other pressure-induced resources, can have an enormous effect on me. When I was trying to fall asleep, constant thoughts of what I didn't do well enough as a mom kept haunting me. Thinking about that article, I felt like, 'I didn't play enough, wasn't joyful enough, I didn't do this' and more ran through my mind."

What is going on here? Look at the ridiculous way we mentally torture ourselves with thoughts and words of disapproval. Most of these thoughts do not even belong to us. Many times, these thoughts are not pointing out our weaknesses, but rather the weaknesses of societal conditioning and ideas. Oftentimes these internal pressures are ideas that form imaginary role expectations according to the molds of society. Unfortunately, many of us live buried in condemnation, living in a constant state of disapproval of ourselves, especially Christians or those of strong religious affiliations. I am personally a woman of faith, by the way, but just look at ways the world pressures us. This next paragraph was taken from one of my favorite study Bibles:

"**Conscientious** consumers shop for value, the **best** products for the money. **Wise** parents desire only the **best** for their children, nourishing their growing bodies, minds, and spirits. **Individuals with integrity** seek the **best** investment of time, talents, and treasures. In every area **to settle for less would be wasteful, foolish, and irresponsible**. Yet it is a natural pull to move toward what is convenient and comfortable." (This quote is from the *Life Application Study Bible*, Tyndale New Living Translation, Commentary of the Book of Hebrews, Tyndale House Publishers, Inc., 1996.)

LOOK AT THE PRESSURE!

LOOK AT THE EXPECTATIONS!

LOOK AT THE BS OF BETTER LANGUAGE!

This pressure is everywhere. Listen, it's not that I don't like this resource anymore; I still love it. However, my thoughts are way beyond the limitations of better, and I refuse to be pressured by a society that interjects such ridiculous and undefined words to pressure me into action. The healthy actions we take will not stem from pressure-induced words and mindsets. No, it will stem from a place of peace and acceptance that is in alignment with our sense of autonomy and commingled with grace and mercy. And you know what? Sometimes, convenience and comfortability are more important to certain individuals in certain seasons, and it doesn't mean we are settling for less. It just means how I define best, conscientious, wise, and integrity in this season may not be how you define it, and that is perfectly acceptable.

Beautiful LeAnn, other moms, and many other precious individuals live with this type of pressure and guilt daily. However, like chains broken from the prisoners' feet and caged birds set free, we can enter into a state of peace by breaking the bonds of guilt-ridden language. Let's start by identifying what some of that language looks like.

GUILT-RIDDEN LANGUAGE EXPOSED

First and foremost, let's define **guilt**: having committed a specific or implied **offense, crime, violation** of law or principles, which are deserving of or lead to feelings of blame. Whether real or imagined, these offenses or violations often lead to self-reproach and a sense of inadequacy. Okay, now would be a great time to reread those last two sentences. Please, before proceeding, make sure you understand exactly what that underlying guilt is doing to your subconscious mind.

Seriously, think about it: What offenses, crimes, or violations are we actually doing that lead to these feelings of self-reproach? This may seem harsh to some, but this truly is what is happening as we internally condemn ourselves. Ready to see if this applies to you? Following are some examples of guilt-ridden language. Which ones do you find yourself using?

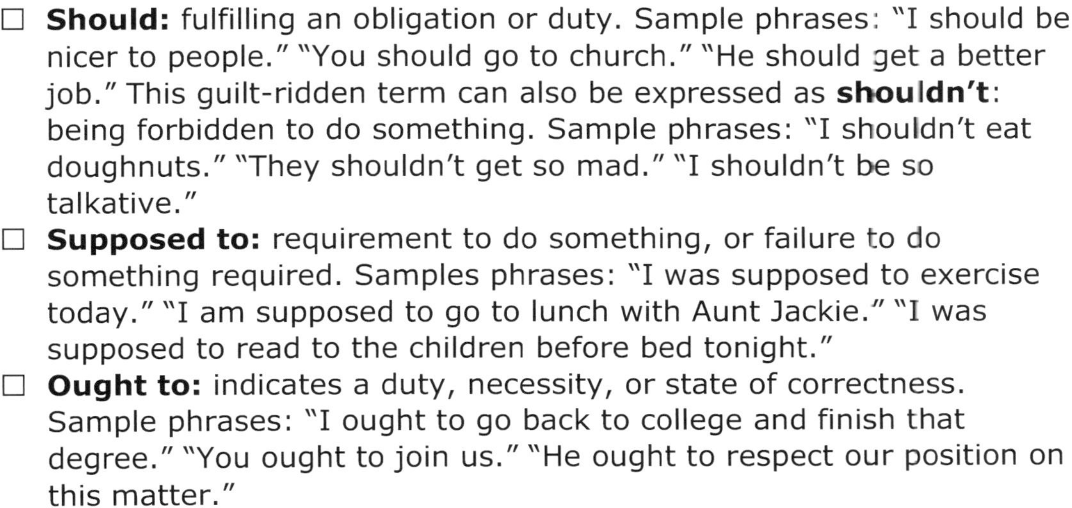

- ☐ **Should:** fulfilling an obligation or duty. Sample phrases: "I should be nicer to people." "You should go to church." "He should get a better job." This guilt-ridden term can also be expressed as **shouldn't**: being forbidden to do something. Sample phrases: "I shouldn't eat doughnuts." "They shouldn't get so mad." "I shouldn't be so talkative."
- ☐ **Supposed to:** requirement to do something, or failure to do something required. Samples phrases: "I was supposed to exercise today." "I am supposed to go to lunch with Aunt Jackie." "I was supposed to read to the children before bed tonight."
- ☐ **Ought to:** indicates a duty, necessity, or state of correctness. Sample phrases: "I ought to go back to college and finish that degree." "You ought to join us." "He ought to respect our position on this matter."

- ☐ **Need to:** a required obligation or essential. Sample phrases: "I need to stop smoking." "You need to mind your own business." "They need to be held accountable."
- ☐ **Shaming:** humiliation for wrongdoing, loss of respect or honor. Sample phrases: "Shame on you for..." "Shame on me for..." "You should feel ashamed for not being more humble." "Don't think so highly of yourself." "Nobody likes a show-off."

What other thoughts, words, body language, or behaviors surface among guilt-ridden emotions?

WHAT HAPPENED TO US?

Okay, yes, we know cognitively that it sounds ridiculous that we do this to ourselves, yet we continue to allow this underlying guilt to sabotage so many of our days. Why do we do this? Where did this come from? What happened to us? Well, I'm so glad you asked. We are going to explore one theory now.

Let's take a look at Susie. Beautiful Susie is five years old, born into a healthy and thriving family unit, the only child of two loving parents who work hard to give Susie the best life possible. They nurture her, provide for her, lovingly correct her to guide her along her journey of learning, encourage her, respect her, and do everything to the best of their human abilities. As a matter of fact, Susie is one of the few born into a healthy family unit with minimal dysfunction.

Around Susie's fifth birthday, she is playing in her room and smells something yummy coming from the kitchen. She gaily skips to the kitchen and sees Mommy putting brownies in the oven. On top of the stove, Susie's favorite, vegetable and chicken soup, is being made by her Mommy for dinner. As sunbeams pour through the window on Susie as she dances around the breakfast nook, she excitedly awaits daddy to get home from work. You see, they plan to play with her new baseball bat and glove before dinner. As Susie is happily prancing around, she feels a little chilled as her sundress exposes her shoulders.

She hops into the kitchen, twirling about, and says, "Mommy, I'm cold."

Mommy lovingly looks down at Susie and gently says, "Oh Susie, it's not cold in here," as she smiles into Susie's vulnerable little eyes.

Here's a question for you: What just happened to Susie?

It's really important that we get this, so take a moment to think about it. How did Susie feel when Mommy told her it was *not* cold?

What thoughts were going on in Susie's mind?

What message was she receiving?

How might these well-intentioned words of her loving mother have impacted Susie's development?

Let's explore a little further. At a minimum, Susie's feelings were certainly invalidated. There is no fault with her loving mother, who was standing over a hot stove in the kitchen as she prepared dinner for her family for the last hour. When you look at the big picture, it was nearly impossible for Susie's mom to recognize the needs and feelings of her 45-pound, five-year-old precious daughter being chilled as she's dancing around in her sundress. However, the impact is bigger than you may think.

As children, in most cases, we are taught that the grown-ups are "right" and that we should listen to them. If a grown-up says something that contradicts our thoughts or feelings, or that we disagree with, obviously, we think we are "wrong."

Diving deeper, to explore the true impact, what happens to Susie when she starts kindergarten in the fall? She is sitting at her desk in a new classroom, with a new teacher, with a bunch of children she's never met before, and with a whole new set of rules and expectations.

As she is sitting at her desk trying to be a "good girl," listening to the teacher, she feels chilled. Her jacket is hanging in her cubby along with the jackets of the other children. She looks around to see if anyone else is wearing their jacket, which they are not. What does Susie do?

Does she politely raise her hand, express her feelings to her teacher, and ask permission respectfully to go get her jacket? Probably not! More than likely what happens is that she begins questioning herself, her feelings, and her thoughts get derailed from the present lesson she is supposed to be learning as the teacher is speaking.

For the next 20 minutes, she is plotting and planning how to properly get her jacket. "Recess should be coming up soon, maybe I can grab my jacket then if everyone is grabbing theirs to go outside." She's trying hard to pay attention and be a good girl, but she's distracted once again by the goose bumps appearing on her splotchy pale arms and light quivering of her bottom lip.

As she's looking around to see if the girls around her have pale skin and goose bumps, the teacher calls on her to give the answer. Startled, she sits in silent embarrassment as the teacher and all her peers stare at her while she doesn't know the answer. Anxiety and confusion rush through her young mind; fear takes over as she realizes yet again that she didn't do something right. She only knows that she is cold and afraid to say anything because, once again, she may be wrong and doesn't want to feel bad for being wrong again.

The teacher kindly corrects her, reminding her to pay attention so that she can get a good grade on her assignment so that everyone will be proud of her. This cycle continues throughout her childhood. Susie's peers make fun of her because she wears glasses, lost a tooth, tripped over her shoelaces that she didn't know how to tie, cried a couple of times in class because she missed her Mommy, and for some reason, kids call her Toothless Susie-Q. "That's not my name. Why do people call me that? Why is everyone so mad at me and mean? What am I supposed to be doing? I must be really bad."

She's trying to do everything right, but she can't. Her parents; homeroom teacher; music, art, and PE teachers; bus driver; Sunday school teacher; grandmother; aunt; and elderly neighbor all remind her constantly of what she is not doing right.

What once was a perfect little girl full of hope and freedom is slowly being dwindled to the behaviors and habits of cultural norms in order to fit in. By the early years in elementary school, Susie is likely to be on a path of lost congruency where her identity is now dependent on modifying her behaviors and habits to be accepted.

Her identity is no longer free-spirited and aligned with how she thinks and feels because that would require vulnerability and expose her to more criticisms and corrections. It is terribly confusing, and Susie feels like she can never say or do anything right and like she is always letting someone down, including herself. Unfortunately, Susie grows into a teenager, college student, and eventually an adult who feels the exact same way. She is continually being taught what is acceptable, which is ever-changing. These experiences are ultimately the conditioning that will later become Susie's conditions by which she gauges and measures herself and those around her. This is where she learns to measure whether she and others are good enough.

WHAT HAPPENED TO SUSIE?

While I prefer psychiatrist Carl Jung's inner child work and psychologist Carl Rogers' person-centered approach for healing, John Bradshaw was an incredible American educator and counselor who developed some remarkable material on congruency and healing the inner child. For those of us who can identify with Susie's struggle as a child, I highly recommend researching some of Bradshaw's work. *Homecoming: Reclaiming and Championing Your Inner Child* has been a helpful resource for many.

In studying Bradshaw's work, how this incongruency began and developed over time was a powerful revelation, so I will do my best to touch on that here. I highly encourage those who identify with the following struggle to consider researching his work on inner child healing, but here I provide a quick summary of one aspect regarding the lost congruency Susie and most of us experience. Following is a simple display of the process that occurred in Susie's development as she goes from congruent to incongruent.

Congruency: Congruency is when our words and behaviors reflect our internal wants, needs, thoughts, and feelings. It means our internal dialogue is in alignment with our external behaviors, which are in agreement with our personal identity and individual priorities. Some call this state inner harmony. When we are not in this self-aligned state of mind, some professionals may suggest we are experiencing cognitive dissonance, which is lost congruency.

In Susie's beginning years, her behaviors aligned with who she was, a free-spirited, innocent, invaluable child. When she was born and needed a diaper change or to be fed, she voiced her needs without any thought of how others may have perceived her, and she was cherished and invaluable. She didn't consider that it may be 3:00 a.m. before crying for food; no, she had a need and she vocalized it. In her terrible twos and the *three*nager stages, she vocalized a lot more; yet she was still seen as adorable and accepted for the most part. It was cute when she had mishaps; sometimes people laughed at her many shortcomings, which she didn't even realize she had.

Incongruency Starts: However, this quickly changes as life expectations and experiences occur while her cognitive abilities are developing. At some point, Susie starts recognizing what *good girl* and *bad girl* mean. She notices the surrounding body language of the adults in the room with a display of disapproval when she makes a *wrong* move. Susie quickly realizes that she will disappoint those around her if she does or doesn't do certain things. Suddenly, it's not funny anymore. Where did the smiles and acceptance go? Then, she experiences guilt and shame, which leads to attempts at earning approval to be accepted instead of freely expressing herself; hence, incongruency starts and the juggling act begins. Now, this isn't necessarily a bad thing; after all, we have a responsibility to protect our children and teach them healthy from unhealthy, loving from unloving behaviors. But it's an art that not one single parent has mastered and never will because there are too many variables at play. More about that later, but let's go on.

At a young age, Susie reads these social cues and begins separating from the truth of who she is into what she thinks she is *supposed to* be. She's trying to figure it out, but that's impossible as well. The separation creates distance between her private thoughts, fears, and desires and her public self, which attempts to display everything she thinks she is supposed to be to be accepted. Sometimes it feels like she's two different people: the big public self on display for everyone and then her small, still voice hiding her truth inside so she doesn't experience more shame and humiliation.

She grows into school-aged and experiences trying times in elementary school, disappointing everyone at every turn with little hope in sight of figuring all this confusing stuff out. She watches carefully when she is praised and finds comfort and migrates there as often as possible, learning how to protect herself along the way with defense mechanisms, which we will talk more about in the next book of this series. She tries so hard, listens intently, watches, and absorbs everything like a sponge, hoping she can figure it all out and get it right. While she's still enjoying some freedom and has moments where she naturally expresses herself, she's still secretly exploring what she can do to be a good little girl.

Lost Congruency: As Susie continues to develop, the distance becomes more prominent between her true self and her public self, and scars begin forming on her heart as it begins to harden. As she continues to develop, the scarring becomes deeper and her true self shrinks even more, ultimately leaving little more than a shell of a public person manifesting the behaviors she thinks she is supposed to manifest to be accepted. Middle school and her teenage years are tough on her, and she almost loses herself completely. Her mind seems to be in a constant state of confusing thoughts that clash and where cognitive dissonance reigns.

While she still wants to be that good girl and to be accepted, sometimes she doesn't even try because, secretly, she knows she's never going to measure up. Her hidden voice whispers repeated lies to her by now as she has almost completely lost congruency. She hears things like, "Why even try if I'm never going to be good enough anyway," or "Why do I even care? No one else cares about me or what I have to say." Other lies run wild during this phase and form beLIEfs that ultimately become her BS.

Susie eventually loses touch with who she really is and has morphed into the enigma of someone she doesn't understand and doesn't really care for. This little girl, scarring into a young lady, turns into a hardened shell of a woman who may not ever fully find herself again. As an adult, what she has left is this ever-so-small inner voice crying silently inside without words to describe the pain. She knows she's lost and out of connection with herself but doesn't know where to look to find herself.

Everyone around adult Susan is going through almost the same feelings with different circumstances, but most people don't talk about it and wouldn't know what to say if they did. The biggest challenge is that she is no longer sitting in a kindergarten classroom assessing whether it's safe to go get her jacket because she is cold. Now she has adult responsibilities and is trying everything possible to be the best mommy, wife, daughter, employee, Christian...but at the end of the day, it's never-ending and she's never enough. The voices that tell her all the things she *should* be doing, were *supposed to* have taken care of, *ought to* focus on, and *need to* be completely drown out that precious voice crying for someone to accept her and help her to feel safe and worthy of love.

Does anyone hear her?

Does anyone see her?

Will anyone love her?

Will Susie ever be enough?

Susan isn't the only one who struggles with this. We all have varying degrees of this exact reality. Sounds terrible, doesn't it? Like we're lost and alone to some degree? Well, we're not lost, and we are certainly not alone! Susan is thriving today, and there is plenty of hope and opportunity for us to thrive as well. The key for her and for us is breaking the debilitating cycles of the BS of better mindset that stems from lost congruency. Healing begins as we start hearing ourselves, seeing ourselves, and accepting by lovingly embracing ourselves. It starts in the mirror. Keep reading.

HOW ROLES NOW DEFINE US

As if losing congruency isn't bad enough, Susie grows into adult Susan and assumes additional roles and responsibilities during her teenage years and into adulthood, where she experiences further disconnection. She attempts to survive by assuming life roles. As a teenager, perhaps it's star student, head cheerleader, volleyball star, cross-country state champion; as an adult, it's beauty queen wife, mommy of the year, supportive friend, employee of the year, and community service star. Unfortunately, Susie eventually realizes, she can't be everything for everyone, and to comfort herself, she relies on her defense mechanisms to keep her safe and functioning. There has to be more beyond roles, right?

Let's take a few moments to explore roles and the impact they have on our individual lives. In general terms, **roles** are defined as parts played, as in a character; a function or position; or the characteristics or expected social behaviors of a member of society. In psychology, roles are defined as parts played in specific social settings and are highly influenced by the individual's ideas of what is appropriate.

This means that the individual has a fairly fixed idea of the appropriate rights, obligations, and expected behaviors that are usually associated with their particular roles within their social status. However, what happens when these ideas are challenged, when we behave outside of these expectations, or when we do not play the part according to our internal expectations? Even worse, what happens when our behaviors do not measure up to the ideas and expectations others may have pertaining to our roles?

Let's dive into some of these roles to get a clearer idea of what this may mean for us as individuals. Take being a mother, for instance; what does being a "good mother" look like? With a few minor variations, most of us have a fairly fixed idea of what healthy parenting looks like. What happens when we deviate from these fixed ideas in our role as mothers? Whether intentional, unintentional, or due to extremely challenging circumstances, if we do not behave according to the clearly defined and rigid ideas of the role of motherhood, it will likely have a negative impact on our internal self-worth and personal value. No one wants to be associated with the label of "bad mom."

As we develop in childhood and into young adulthood, we lose our sense of congruency, alignment, and harmony with our inner selves while trying to find the right way to properly fill our roles. This leads to forming distorted beLIEfs that create our expectations in life for the roles we assume, which is extremely difficult because of all the various expectations.

And if devaluing ourselves according to the failures in our roles and responsibilities isn't enough, we set ourselves up and others for more disappointment through many failed expectations. Do you realize that disappointment would be nonexistent without expectations? If we could get rid of expectations, we could relieve ourselves of disappointment. This obviously is not reasonable, possible, or even beneficial, but it is certainly something to keep in mind because, frankly, most expectations simply are not necessary. All expectations are is a strong belief that someone will or should achieve something or do something. Here we go again—more BS. When does this stop? There are ways to experience progress without rigid expectations. However, lost congruency is filled with expectations and leads us searching for more expectations so we can identify what we should do next.

Ultimately, our development often leaves us looking for what we should be doing, while being hypersensitive to our needs and the needs of others and taking action where we feel we are supposed to be instead of following our own hearts, interests, and passions. Lost congruency leads to distorted beLIEfs that define the roles we assume, which will ultimately determine how we should, need to, and are supposed to be behaving. There we go: human *DOings* instead of human *BEings*, like puppets on strings controlled by imaginary BS, which leaves us feeling confused and unfulfilled.

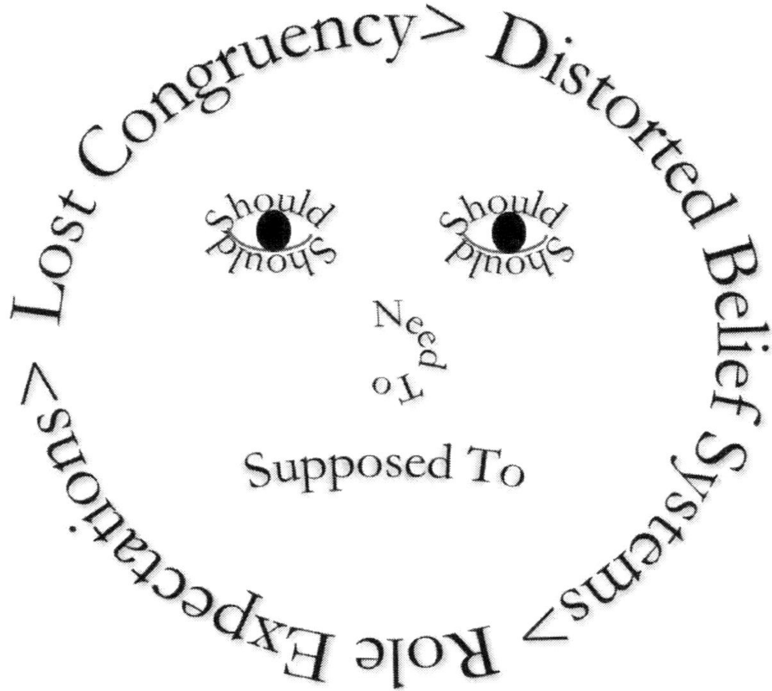

Often empty and void of passion, we are not doing what we *want* to do, but rather what we feel *obligated* to do. This sense of obligation not only directs our lives in many instances, but it also increases our stress levels as we attempt to fill our obligations "correctly" without really identifying if these obligations are things that really interest us as an individual.

How many times a week do we stop and ask, "Does this obligation or expectation work for me?" or, "Is this really *my* personal preference and priority?" Probably not very often. The pressure we feel from internal and external expectations leads to many challenges. For instance, at the end of the day, we often feel shamed or guilty for not meeting certain expectations and obligations. Or we may feel frustrated that these ridiculous expectations and obligations are present in the first place.

Expectations: The Four Tendencies Framework by Gretchen Rubin

One huge challenge with expectations is that we are not all wired the same. Because of that, we guilt and shame ourselves and others for the way we handle meeting or not meeting expectations. Gretchen Rubin is an author, speaker, and blogger who worked for years in the legal system, and she has a wonderful theory on expectations that I summarize below. However, she also has done a lot of the same type of work I do and has other great work on habits and human tendency, so feel free to check out her information if you find yourself struggling with expectations.

Warning: Gretchen, along with almost every other professional in the self-help and psychology fields, uses some "better" language; she even has a book called *Better Than Before: What I Learned about Making and Breaking Habits*. So, when you see that language, define it and replace it to serve you instead of pressure you, but seriously, Gretchen has some great work out there.

Okay, so here is a quick summary on her Four Tendencies Framework regarding how people respond to expectations. Gretchen suggests that there are four basic types of categories that people fall into, which will most frequently decide how they will respond to expectations: Upholders, Questioners, Obligers, and Rebels.

Upholders respond the same to the expectations of others and themselves most of the time and do what's expected of them. They might even stick to expectations that are not serving them or others anymore because they are so committed to meeting all expectations.

Questioners will only meet expectations if it makes sense to them. They will meet inner expectations but will completely disregard expectations of others if it doesn't make sense to them. Questioners need a lot of information and justification before they will ever meet an external expectation.

Obligers will do their best to meet the expectations of others because they don't want to let anyone down, but they will frequently let themselves down by not meeting their own expectations. Obligers can really find value in external accountability because it's much more difficult to keep commitments with themselves alone.

Rebels will most frequently resist all expectations, whether their own or someone else's. They usually do not like habits because they don't like to be held to any expectation unless it's something they choose in the moment. Choice, freedom, and flexibility are crucial for rebels, and they may have difficulty when feeling obligated.

Regardless of which type resonates with you, all expectations add pressure that leads to stress. This is not a bad thing if it's a stress that is serving your own purpose and objectives. Stress can be healthy if it is acute stress that motivates us to complete tasks, hit deadlines, and meet goals that are important to our long-term individual objectives and successes.

Other types of expectations are not so helpful. Sometimes we may feel like a failure who can rarely win, and other times we may feel like a rebel kicking against the grain. Which do you experience more frequently? Think about the way you view life's expectations and obligations. Take a moment to record your thoughts here:

1) What roles have I assumed?

2) What internal and external expectations accompany those roles?

3) How do I feel about my internal and external expectations and my responses to them?

4) What obligations am I allowing that are not representing nor serving me?

> **"Reexamine all you have been told..., dismiss whatever insults your own soul."**
> **~Walt Whitman**

Homework for Overcoming Guilt-Ridden Language

Guilt-ridden language can "should" us to exhaustion and be the near death of ourselves sometimes, killing our joy and robbing our peace. We often feel like we are never enough no matter how much effort we give. Societal conditioning creates our ideas for the many roles we assume, and we allow these ridiculous beLIEfs to mentally torture ourselves with thoughts and words of disapproval while remaining buried in condemnation. Healthy actions do not stem from the pressures of condemnation, but rather from a place of acceptance that is commingled with grace and mercy. We all define acceptable behaviors differently; therefore, we must understand and accept ourselves from within first in order to define what acceptable looks like for us as individuals.

TAKE YOUR TIME AND DO THE WORK!

Instead of focusing on what you should, supposed to, ought to, or need to be doing, ask yourself if these things align with your authentic self and personal values. Where did this guilt-ridden language come from? Perhaps a childhood expectation or belief carried over from your micro- or macro-cultures? Ask yourself what the benefits are of doing the things you are considering.

Remember, little Susie grew into a woman who carries around the internal pressures of the expectations she learned during crucial years of development. You are doing the same. The shoulds, need tos, ought tos, and supposed tos represent some of those pressures. So, here is your homework for this week. Let's identify when those words and phrases are being used, where they stem from, what they mean, and what you may be ready to do about them.

Grab your journal and begin processing using the following pages, but don't stop there. If you realize that guilt-ridden language is embedded with deep roots, keep coming back and reassessing by using the following identifiers and journal topics. Make sure to pay special attention to your own heart; what new neural pathways would be beneficial for you to begin developing through repetitive exercises? And if you can't seem to work your way through this, hire a professional to assist you in kicking this guilt-ridden BS to the curb! You are worth investing in, taking time for, and paying special attention to.

OBSERVATIONS OF THE GUILT-RIDDEN MINDSET

Take a few moments to observe the language, feelings, and uncertainty that often accompany the guilt-ridden mindset. Then observe how others may experience this mindset and how it may limit you. Check those that apply to your experiences and/or fill in the blanks with additional observations you have made pertaining to this limiting mindset.

Guilt-ridden language:
- ☐ Should/Should have
- ☐ Supposed to
- ☐ Ought to
- ☐ Need to
- ☐ Must
- ☐ Have to
- ☐ Other ______________________

Feelings that often accompany guilt-ridden language:
- ☐ Shame
- ☐ Guilt
- ☐ Condemnation
- ☐ Humiliation
- ☐ Remorse
- ☐ Regret
- ☐ Disgrace
- ☐ Overwhelmed
- ☐ Other ______________________

Uncertainty: Am I wrong or on the wrong track?

Others may experience me as:
- ☐ Carrying unnecessary burdens
- ☐ Hard on myself or others
- ☐ Apologetic
- ☐ Intense
- ☐ Unforgiving of self or others
- ☐ Other ______________________

The guilt-ridden mindset may lead to:
- ☐ Responsibility overload
- ☐ Self-condemning
- ☐ Taking on too much
- ☐ Difficulty setting healthy boundaries
- ☐ Needing forgiveness or validation
- ☐ Other ______________________

Daily Journal Practice

Following are journal topics and exercises for the next seven days, but feel free to continue such exercises until you feel yourself being able to automatically capture and replace the guilt-ridden limiting language within your mind. It will take some time, but the neural pathways will develop as you do these exercises daily, and eventually, you will no longer find it necessary to write things down. The brain will learn to process automatically as you train it through such exercises as those contained within this program.

Day 1: Journal Your Battle with Guilt-Ridden Language

- When do you find yourself using words like should, need to, ought to, or supposed to on yourself? When do you shame yourself?
- When do you find yourself using words like should, need to, ought to, or supposed to on others? When do you shame others?
- Where might the BS of these expectations have come from?
- What does life look like for you and others if you are free of these limiting beliefs?

Day 2: Journal Your Relationship with Expectations

- Spend the entire day and evening observing your expectations.
- What expectations do you have of yourself and of others?
- Is it easier to meet expectations of yourself or others? What are your tendencies in meeting expectations?
- How has your relationship with expectations served you and where has it limited you?

Day 3: Journal How Your Obligations Are Serving or Not Serving You

- What obligations or expectations do you have that are serving you?
- What obligations or expectations do you have that are not serving you?
- How may you consider changing those obligations and expectations of self or others to serve in lieu of limit?

Day 4: What Would It Take? What May Stop Me?

- Think outside the box and write down any options that may be possible for you to change those expectations of self or others that are not working.
- List anything that might keep you from making changes in areas where your expectations of self or others are not working.

Day 5: What Am I Ready For?
Write down what you are ready to explore and what action you are ready to take in changing those expectations of yourself or others that are not working.

Day 6: Acceptance Plan
In the areas you are not ready to explore or alter at this time, journal words of encouragement and acceptance that will support you with no expectations or pressure.

Day 7: Thought Capturing and Replacement
Capture and replace guilt-ridden language with thoughts, words, and behaviors of a self-aligned mindset without expectations or pressure.

Continue thought capturing and replacement exercises to build neural pathways that support a self-aligned mindset.

PRACTICE AND BUILD THE NEURAL PATHWAYS OF A SELF-ALIGNED MINDSET

Thoughts of the Guilt-Ridden Mindset:	**Thoughts of the Self-Aligned Mindset:**

Reframe guilt-ridden thoughts with those of a self-aligned mindset:

JOURNAL TOPICS TO CONTEMPLATE FOR OVERCOMING THE LIES OF THE GUILT-RIDDEN MINDSET

Grab your notebook or *The BS of Better Journal* to contemplate and process overcoming the guilt-ridden mindset. Below are cues and questions to begin assessing the costs and the payoffs of allowing guilt-ridden thoughts, but don't stop here. Remember, journal those prompts that stand out to you and ask yourself other difficult questions and concerns that may not be listed but are hiding deep within yourself. You already know these concerns; this is your time to listen! Identify and observe the guilt-ridden mindset so that you can stop what's causing those feelings of shame and condemnation when you are ready.

Inquisitive Alternatives:

- ☐ Where did the BS that says I should, ought to, need to, or am supposed to come from?
- ☐ Who says?
- ☐ What aligns with me and my values in this instance?
- ☐ Are the options I am considering healthy and safe for me and others?
- ☐ What BS or responsibilities might I consider letting go of?
- ☐ What responsibilities might I consider delegating?
- ☐ Regardless of choice, I will accept, in lieu of shame, myself by...
- ☐ Other ________________________

Neural Pathway Development Support

It cannot be reiterated enough that neural pathway development is crucial for sustainable healthy change in thoughts and behaviors. Heightening self-awareness, committing to personal reflection time, and completing acceptance and action plans daily and weekly will develop the neural pathways that serve you. For additional daily processing support, please see **Appendix A – Neural Pathway Development Support**. What would it look like if we asked the difficult yet beneficial questions until the questions were no longer difficult? When you're ready, try it and see.

Limiting Language

Are you seeing a pattern yet to the limiting language we use? Let me give you a huge hint. The key component to all limiting language has to do with mere questioning. These patterns of language are disguised uncertainties. We question any uncertainty, which we will cover more in Chapter 9. In this chapter and the next few chapters, the key question will be:

What am I questioning?

Answering this question will pinpoint the uncertainty(ies). In this chapter pertaining to guilt-ridden language, the uncertainty is:

- Am I wrong?
- Am I on the wrong track?

The questions that keep our tails spinning are:

- What is right?
- Who is right?

Internally, we feel we must know what is right so that we can know who is right because the uncertain possibility of being wrong is too painful. But then the problem becomes determining who and what is right, which is subjective more times than not. Therefore, if we are going to live in a mindset of peace and joy, we must become comfortable with the fact that many times, we will not be able to definitively determine who and what are right, and it's often futile to put effort into that quest and frame of mind.

Then how do we decide and move forward when difficult questions surface? Look around us. Our society is inundated with debates pertaining to almost everything: legalities, politics, religion, race, health, and safety. In truth, these debates will never stop, society as a whole will never be satisfied; it's too diverse and beautiful for a single solution to any one concern.

Does that mean we give up, shut up, and sit down? No! It means that every day, I, as an individual, stand up firmly in the eyes of injustices and exercise my voice—not based on some BS definition of what my childhood taught me was right or what someone tells me is right today, but rather, based on my individual and evolving values in the moment while recognizing the infinite value of all life.

However, this is only possible and effective when I allow you to do the same. It's a joint effort, and we have much more in common than not. The challenge is that many times we aren't looking for the commonalities and opportunities to promote one another because we are too busy attempting to be right within the BS of our own minds.

While it may be difficult to find common ground in some of these areas, it is always possible to respect, listen to, and accept ourselves and others. If at any time it is not, the immediate call to action is to step back for a moment and set healthy boundaries. When proving a point or being right is more important than respecting, listening, and accepting, then we have serious internal problems superseding any potential solutions. When we put the need to be right above the responsibility to be human, we have failed! We will find peace and joy when we stop requiring ourselves and others to live by the guilt-ridden language of rightness and correctness because, many times, it is impossible to define.

Instead of "Am I wrong? Who is right? What is right?", let's change the line of questioning during times of uncertainty. Let's try this instead:

- Is this safe?
- Am I safe?
- Are they safe?
- What will create a safe space for all involved?

This not only pertains to physical safety, but safe in every area about which we are personally concerned for ourselves and others. After all, this is ultimately the underlying uncertainty of it all. If I feel unsafe, I will not be vulnerable because I am not comfortable with the possibility that I may be wrong. If I am not comfortable with the possibility that I may be wrong, I must prove you wrong to make myself feel right in lieu of being open and vulnerable to explore ways to connect.

This mindset creates power struggles that divide families, organizations, and even countries. Does anyone win here? No! Unfortunately, these scenarios fester into broader problems as we engage in even more limiting language in the form of judging, worrying, comparing, living victimized, and uncertain with little acceptance of one another.

Until we get comfortable with uncertainty and respecting and honoring ourselves and others among the varying definitions of right and wrong, we will be little more than preschool children in adult bodies attempting to solve world problems. I deserve the freedom that comes beyond limiting language. You deserve the freedom that comes beyond limiting language. Our world deserves the freedom that comes beyond limiting language.

Truth without grace and mercy is not truth. Illusions of facts that are void of grace and mercy are nothing more than arrogance disguising itself as correct.

4

JUDGMENTAL LIMITING LANGUAGE

"She is so stupid. Every time I talk to her, she digs a deeper hole for herself. I told her to stop doing that, but of course, she won't listen. I've talked until I'm blue in the face, and I'm just sick of it. It makes no sense at all. She's as dumb as a box of rocks sometimes, and she won't listen to anything anybody says. I'm sick of it, and when she calls next time, I'm not even going to answer the phone. If she wants to act like that, she can go ahead, but I'm not going to be a part of it. All she's doing is lying to herself and everyone else anyway, walking around like she's got it all figured out. She doesn't have a clue! She'll fall on her face again and come crawling back, and then we'll see; we'll see. Then all those people who are following her on social media will also see what she's really all about..." On and on the critic goes!

EXPOSING THE JUDGMENTAL MINDSET (JM)

Does this mindset sound familiar? Maybe you or someone you know? Come on, be honest, we've all seen this mindset in action, and we've all acted upon it to some degree. It's the judgmental mindset, and boy, is it smart. It knows almost everything except how not to be judgmental and how to exercise grace. Let's take a few moments to expose the judgmental mindset.

The judgmental mindset (JM) is so sad and is often lonely, although it believes this to be true by its own choice. It is sometimes quite difficult to spend time engaging with someone who has an active JM. Unfortunately, the JM will likely become a lifestyle of isolation if it remains active for too long. This is because it has difficulty loving itself; it secretly loathes its perceived self-inadequacy. The JM, or critic, spends most of its time attempting to prove it is lovable by making sure it, and everyone else, knows it is correct.

We are referencing the critic as "it" because IT is not YOU! It is a learned behavior that was established as a coping mechanism to preserve itself. The critic keeps us in line so that we will not be rejected for wrongdoing or be ridiculed by looking unwise.

This self-loathing is expressed in various forms such as criticisms and blaming of self and others. Following are some common characteristics of the JM. Gently observe by checking those that may apply below, but be cautioned: the JM will most likely have difficulty acknowledging many of these characteristics. If the JM even allows us to acknowledge that we may be battling with it, it will begin justifying why some of these tendencies exist.

Most importantly, be gentle with yourself! There's no need to justify anything—that's actually part of the JM. The JM tendencies protected us at one time, and while they may not be serving us now, at one time they did. It is important that we allow ourselves to acknowledge them and simply begin observing when they surface in the upcoming weeks. This alone will promote maturing beyond the limitations of the JM. Simple and gentle observations are all that's asked for right now. If you're struggling, it may be helpful to ask a trusted friend or family member with whom you feel safe to read through these tendencies with you to assist in seeing beyond your current blind spots. This is a great time to grab a journal and begin logging thoughts as you scroll through the following checklists.

Cognitive distortions (irrational thought patterns) of the JM:

- ☐ Personalizing: relating things to itself whether it is directly involved or not
- ☐ Magnification or minimization: inflating or deflating the importance of achievements or failures
- ☐ Negative predictions: assumptions stemming from negative impressions
- ☐ Catastrophizing: seeing the worst possible scenario
- ☐ Setting extremely high standards
- ☐ Critical of self and others
- ☐ Guilt-ridden or judgmental language
- ☐ Fixed beliefs: inability to remain open when challenged
- ☐ Cognitive labeling: labeling someone by describing an individual by a characteristic rather than seeing others outside of the JM's faulty label
- ☐ Overgeneralizing: using words such as *always, all, every, never, everyone*, and *nobody*
- ☐ Blaming others and frequently finding fault

- ☐ Disqualifying positives: acknowledging the negative aspects of certain instances while having difficulty seeing the positives
- ☐ Overvaluing its own things above that of others
- ☐ Self-serving biases: viewing things in a manner that makes the self look and feel good, even if circumstances may suggest otherwise
- ☐ Jumping to conclusions
- ☐ Mind reading: interpreting the thoughts of others without inquiring of their actual thoughts and beliefs
- ☐ Fortune-telling: making predictions of negative outcomes
- ☐ Emotional reasoning: relying on emotions to determine reality

Some behaviors manifested by the JM:

- ☐ Unforgiving
- ☐ Bottling up anger
- ☐ Vengeful
- ☐ Spiteful
- ☐ Ungrateful
- ☐ Egotistical
- ☐ Intolerant
- ☐ Critiquing
- ☐ Griping
- ☐ Complaining
- ☐ Criticizing
- ☐ Bashing others
- ☐ Gossiping
- ☐ Rigid
- ☐ Prideful
- ☐ Arrogant
- ☐ Knowing it all
- ☐ Condemning others
- ☐ Often lacking in empathy
- ☐ Giving unsolicited advice
- ☐ Mocking or ridiculing people
- ☐ Labeling or categorizing people
- ☐ Expressing unrequested opinions
- ☐ Rejecting those the JM disagrees with
- ☐ Untrusting of others' motives or intentions
- ☐ Haughty, thinking it is correct most of the time
- ☐ Easily agitated by the actions and sayings of others, whether or not it has a direct impact on the one criticizing
- ☐ The decider of morality—will certainly let people know when someone has stepped out of line
- ☐ The perfection police, noticing everyone's imperfections
- ☐ Negative outlook more days than not

- ☐ Difficulty outwardly acknowledging one's own challenges and modifying them but easily picking others apart
- ☐ The master of jumping to conclusions and difficulty waiting to hear all the information outside of itself because it thinks it already knows all the facts
- ☐ Often perfectionistic, self-critical, and hard on self, which is then projected onto others because of low self-worth
- ☐ Sometimes paranoid, like others are secretly lurking to make it look bad or stupid
- ☐ Downplaying the achievements of others or assuming luck was obviously on the victor's side
- ☐ Inflating perceived mistakes of self and others; blowing things out of proportion
- ☐ Difficulty negotiating—would rather poke needles in both eyes because the JM is obviously right and others are certainly wasting its time
- ☐ Loves its own perspective above anything else
- ☐ Easily triggered by social media (because others are usually fake and stupid, of course)
- ☐ Difficulty listening and fully engaging to perspectives outside of itself
- ☐ Justifying own behavior
- ☐ Disrespecting others verbally or with body language
- ☐ Having and sharing lots of opinions about lots of people with minimal relevance
- ☐ Can be lacking in genuine empathy, love, and respect for others
- ☐ Minimal responsibility for personal change because it's usually others who are the problem
- ☐ Inability to dissociate circumstances and characteristics from individuals
- ☐ Harboring perceived grievances
- ☐ Feeling vindicated after the JM feels it's proven its point to be truth
- ☐ Sometimes envious or jealous
- ☐ Inability to appreciate the differences in others
- ☐ Putting its own perspective above protecting others and relationships
- ☐ Difficulty staying in long-term relationships or difficulty forming healthy relationships, which often creates a series of shallow, distant, and/or temporary relationships
- ☐ Often feels anxious in social settings or like it must do or say something
- ☐ Usually prefers to keep its circle pretty small because of its inability to tolerate the ignorance of others and because it doesn't want anyone to discover its own perceived inadequacy

Some things the JM may say:

- ☐ Might as well do it myself; nobody else will do it right anyway!
- ☐ I don't care, let them be mad—that's their problem!
- ☐ They think they're better than everybody, but they're nothing special!
- ☐ Fake! I know them, they're fake.
- ☐ I'm sick of it! They do this all the time, you'd think they'd figure it out already.
- ☐ That is so stupid! They are acting ridiculous.
- ☐ Here we go again! I can tell you exactly what's going to happen now.
- ☐ I told you so or I told them not to do that, but they never listen.
- ☐ I can't stand...
- ☐ Well, that's what they get, they should've known better.
- ☐ I don't like being around people.
- ☐ It's not that big of a deal; anyone could do that.
- ☐ That person makes me sick!
- ☐ I can't stand so-and-so, they always...

If you checked off quite a few of these identifiers, it is likely you may struggle with the JM. Remember, be gentle with yourself as you proceed through this chapter. Chances are, if you don't struggle much with the JM, while reading through the list above, you were probably shaking your head while thinking of someone you know who does struggle with it. The following information on judgmental mindsets and language in this chapter are important to consider regardless of who is struggling. This chapter will reveal the most important component to overcoming judgments, so let's get started.

THE JUDGE

The JM stems from the internal judge, but where does this judge get its information from anyway? As parents and caregivers, we naturally model our values. Therefore, our children interpret our thoughts and behaviors that reflect and protect these values as the correct thoughts and behaviors. As you can imagine, when a child is faced with an opposing value from that taught by their parents or caregivers, they will naturally feel like it is incorrect. Instinctively, they may resonate more so with the opposing value and that can certainly create conflict externally or lead to cognitive dissonance. We take this into adulthood and internally feel torn between what we learned is important and what is right versus what we feel is instinctively our preference as more information floods our developing minds.

This really kicks in as preteens and teenagers when we start considering everything from menial to actual lifestyle choices. We instinctively assume everyone is wrong or bad if they are not behaving in a manner that aligns with what we've been taught is important and correct. Honestly, this practice can be rather helpful when it pertains to safety and humane concerns such as harming, intimidating, disrespecting, or damaging others, their property, or our world, for instance. Some of these unspoken and spoken rules keep our world safe and functioning. However, if we really take some time to think about it, for the most part, these big-ticket items are not really the ones that keep us up at night. Most of the time, the divisions stem from where we individually place importance in aspects like values and personal desires or preferences.

These variations are innumerable, and we frequently have conflicting values and priorities within ourselves and with others that cause criticisms and judgments. This is so confusing at any age, so we can appreciate why we sometimes feel torn internally and why we feel divided in many of our relationships. The key here is not to debate or decide which value or priority is right, but to respect that regardless of the values and priorities themselves, those who possess them are important and valid. The people who are placing emphasis on certain values and priorities, even when they oppose ours, are invaluable and deserve our respect. When our approach is built on respect for self and others while acknowledging the value and validity of all parties, it is much more likely that we will engage in healthy and considerate communication efforts.

The judge is selfish and robs us and others of this freedom through criticisms, forcing a specific emphasis be placed only on what the judge deems important at that time. The judge makes us feel angry (including irritation or frustration), resentment, disrespect, or disapproval of self or others. Feelings like this are indicators that our judge doesn't feel safe. When we acknowledge these feelings and identify our judge, it is a wonderful opportunity to gently calm the judge by creating a safe place to begin observing instead of criticizing. We always have the opportunity to identify and calm our judge, but it isn't done easily if we are not used to it. Calming and quieting the judge requires us to develop new, or strengthen healthy, neural pathways in our brain that house responses other than those that are automatic, familiar, and more than likely reactive.

This is one of the biggest challenges we all have because, to gain the benefits, we must do the work necessary to facilitate growth and healing in our neural pathways. Within the confines of personal development, mental muscle exercises to develop and strengthen new neural pathways are a must. If we want the benefits, we must exercise our physical muscles to develop strong muscle fibers that support our bodies, and we must exercise our mental muscles to develop strong neural pathways in our brains to support our minds and emotional responses. If we do not want our judge running rampant, it is crucial to identify, choose, and practice safe and healthy responses in lieu of criticism.

It is possible to prioritize safe connections and strengthen bonds with others instead of criticizing during opposition. Another book in the ***Reducing Life's Pressures*** series will focus solely on communication and relationship development. But for now, let's start with the first step, which is what this entire chapter is ultimately about. The judge doesn't feel safe with itself and its current uncertainties. Remember this valuable concept:

When I am judging others, I do not feel safe.
When others are judging me, they do not feel safe.
When I feel judged, I do not feel safe.
When others feel judged, they do not feel safe.

Judging is all about self-preservation, and it never feels safe no matter how we look at it. If we remember this and keep it at the forefront of our minds while working diligently to overcome any undertone of criticism, our lives and relationships are likely to eventually experience a healthy transformation that feels safe for us and those around us.

The Judge Gone Wild

It is important to acknowledge that we all have a judge that has a negative impact on our lives and relationships. The severity of that impact varies for each. Some of us are more aware of it than others and are more likely to catch our thoughts and modify our behaviors using empathy, self-awareness, and healthy coping skills to minimize the damage. However, others have literally allowed the judge to take over, at some point criticizing nearly everyone and everything in its path. This mindset is the judge gone wild and will be obvious to anyone who spends time with a judge on a regular basis. Let's explore how we may submit to this mindset and what it looks like when we do.

Why do we critique and judge and then justify our actions in our minds by validating those behaviors? Much of the time, these behaviors stem from the internal critic that developed in an environment not rich in grace and mercy for self and others. For those of us who engage in judgmental limiting language frequently, an inner critic runs wild that developed over time as a sense of protection.

During some phase of development, we probably felt criticized, or heard others being criticized, and developed an internal critic to escape the probability of external criticisms. Judging and critiquing are immature defense mechanisms. By identifying what is right or correct, and aligning our behaviors with such, the judge expects to avoid the uncomfortableness of external criticisms.

Unfortunately, since we do not live in a black-and-white world, this is an impossible feat. The harder the internal critic fights to keep itself in line so that it does not subject itself to external criticisms, the more it becomes the external critic. It is the convoluted golden rule in action. Instead of doing unto others what I would like done unto me, I now do unto myself and unto others what was previously done unto me.

Often, the critic exhausts itself and anyone enduring enough to get close and stay close to the critic. For those of us who are the critic, we've pushed most others away with our harsh expectations. For those holding on tightly by trying to love the critic, at some point, we often succumb to the exhaustion. The environment of the critic is a lonely and sad world, which everyone, except the critic, can plainly see. As the battle rages internally to keep criticisms at bay by projecting external criticisms, the judge often makes it near impossible for those around to simply be themselves, which ultimately forces our loved ones to fake, modify, or exit the relationship.

The strange thing is, we often see those exact behaviors manifesting in the critic. Because it is too painful to look in the mirror and modify itself, the critic often fakes *nice* temporarily when necessary and exits most relationships because, frankly, people are too ridiculous to deal with in the mind of the critic. In reality, the critic doesn't want anyone to get close enough to see all the imperfections they fear within themselves.

The critic doesn't participate well in reciprocal relationships because it is too perfect to change itself. Usually the only modification that occurs, since the critic doesn't want to modify itself, will be by those desiring to stay close to us; however, those precious people will be forced to modify by aligning with the critic's faulty beLIEfs; that, too, will usually be temporary. At the end of a painful season, with little reciprocity given to a relationship, the perfect critic remains unchanged and alone, justifying itself by sulking in external blaming until it finds a new temporary victim to project its false sense of perfection onto.

GRACE IS A MUST

Grace is crucial for the critic. The critic must first experience grace to learn that grace even exists. It is not until the critic experiences continued grace that it can even acknowledge that healing is a safe option. The critic is forced to judge or be judged, and it is much more likely to bite first to prevent being bitten.

The judge is a frightened little child too afraid to consider leaving the abusive home that torments itself and others. It often gripes, complains, critiques, gives unrequested and unwanted suggestions, and eventually pushes itself into a lonely corner. The critic is often one of the last to be invited to the party, if invited at all. Why? Because the critic exhausts itself and all those around it; it's too opinionated to even have a safe conversation that may lead to its development. The critic demands control, which ultimately leads to one of two places: alone or engaged in unsafe relationships that rely on a false sense of correctness dictated only by the critic's faulty beLIEfs.

This does not work for long-term relationships because none of us are performers needing to be told what to do. While we are adapting through life's many seasons and changes of personal development and enhanced awareness, we all attempt to maneuver life safely. Three overwhelming pressures are present during this process: our beLIEfs (the past), our expectations of self and others (the present), and our fears (the future). It all boils down to control. Our beLIEfs, expectations, and fears are juggling the past, present, and future, all while trying to control the outcomes. We have no business attempting to control another individual's outcomes, but the ring-leading critic sure tries. Does it feel like a circus sometimes? Now you know why. However, we are not performers in the circus of life! We are individuals who are beautiful, autonomous, free spirits with a need for self-expression and creation. We are more valuable and powerful than the controlling critic and the lying judge! However, only grace will allow us to see and live this truth.

OVERCOMING LIMITING IMPRESSIONS

For some time, the idea of individual impression has been on my radar. Impressions are like images that get burned into our memory, and they have an enormous effect on our personal and professional lives and relationships. Many of our beLIEfs have a direct relationship with these impressions. The negative impression that the world has created during our development has left such a negative impression of ourselves, others, and Creator.

Think about it. How many debilitating impressions do we succumb to daily? We subconsciously know it's often, but we are so used to being led by these damaged impressions that we walk blindly by them without question much of the time. You know, that quiet voice that whispers, "Something feels awkward here," only to be followed quickly by a louder voice who refuses to take a closer look in fear of personal realization.

It is time for our minds to reset! During our development, we were so impressionable, and our environment introduced us to many lies now stored in our beLIEfs. These beLIEfs form the foundation that defines our interpretation of truths. This is why it is often difficult to decipher truth because we all have distortions of it based on our own impressions, which often makes it difficult to fully trust anyone or anything. These impressions keep us uncertain and in fear instead of open and curious.

These negative first impressions are stored in our minds during development and stem in large part from our individual micro- and macro-cultures, which ultimately form our judgments. Take a moment to think about the continual evolution of our personal judgments:

1) Judgments come from our ideas of right and wrong.
2) Ideas of right and wrong stem from what we believe to be acceptable and unacceptable.
3) Acceptable and unacceptable beLIEfs stem from our impressions that were framed during development.
4) Those impressions change over time as we grow and experience more of life.
5) Continued growth is always available through experiencing new information that will reset those impressions that may be limiting us and others.

What keeps us from being comfortable with recognizing we do not know everything and being open to continued growth? Often, it's fear that is likely to stand firm on our expected norms and moral beLIEfs, defending them to the grave. "It's black or white, and that's the way it is no matter what you believe." We hear it all the time. Ummm...no, it isn't, so I suppose we may disagree, but I'll love and support you anyway. Life is not black and white. Listen, no one is questioning if murder is okay, for instance. In this example, the questions stem from whether murder is the course of action during certain circumstances, even though murder itself violates most moral codes. Doesn't the context change things? Of course it does.

No one can really debate context because it varies for every single person in every single situation. We beat one another up over varying contexts that we cannot possibly fully understand from our individual and limited impressions. The reason we do that is because we beat ourselves up while trying to define this moral code in every context and then we project that onto others. STOP! It's impossible because it would require concrete interpretations of truth. Varying context does not allow for such, which is exactly why grace and mercy must be at the core of every single thought, mood, attitude, intention, objective, word, and action. If any of these aspects of our being are not fully saturated in grace and mercy in every context, then our responses and actions will not be based on truth and love.

Truth itself is based on individual standards and authenticity, which, when mature, will include grace and mercy. Our attempts to cleave to an immature truth are futile. *Truth without grace and mercy is not truth!* Illusions of facts that are void of grace and mercy are nothing more than arrogance disguising itself as correctness. Criticisms and judgments always stem from distortions of an immature truth. Personal truths mature as we develop.

Fully matured, truth will include mercy and grace. When we fear our idea of truth may require growth (change), we may attempt to debate truth. Truth matured does not debate; it acknowledges, accepts, and continues to look for opportunities to mature. Unfortunately, it is difficult for us to grasp that it is not the actual truth that is changing, but rather the implication of that truth that always varies by interpretation and context.

This is where only our Creator can, and does for those who are open to it, beautifully reveal today what we were not mature enough to experience yesterday amid some challenging life experiences. Creator does this through grace and mercy as we grow, and if we are ever going to heal internally and in our relationships, we must extend the same to ourselves and others in this ever-changing, ever-evolving world. And for those of us who mentally demand concrete truth, here it is, from the Greek philosopher Heraclitus: "Change is the only constant in life." So, loosen up and get ready for development if you truly wish to rely on something concrete, as it will require change. And I hate to break it to some of us, but this does not mean change of others; this means patiently embracing change of ourselves internally as individuals. The JM has a real struggle with this reality.

God created the framework of growth and development and fully understands our human design that requires patience during this process. God patiently extends grace to us daily in part because our human nature requires time and experience to grow. It's not God that is lording over us with a giant gavel, but rather our interpretation of Him that was formed in part by our impressions and the beLIEfs, expectations, and judgments of the humans around us during our development. How unfortunate that our views of such a loving Father are often tainted by the human immaturity around us as we develop.

Our views of Creator, self, and others were distorted in large part by the inability of those around us to appreciate the differences in those they didn't understand who simply had different impressions and contexts. When our ideas of acceptable and unacceptable differ from others, it is often difficult to disassociate the other person's ideas from their actual *being*. This frequently causes us to judge the person instead of identifying that the other person has beLIEfs that simply formed in a different environment than our own beLIEfs. The difficulty here is that when we do this to one another, we position others in a place that forces them to be a human *doing* versus a human *being*. In this mindset, we and others must do certain things in certain ways to be worthy and accepted, and those beLIEfs are expressed as judgments and criticisms.

As we are developing, our ideas of acceptable and unacceptable are observed and tweaked as we experience what others are doing and how others are reacting. This certainly feeds the problem, and hence the judgmental mindset starts forming within each of us. In early childhood, we quickly learn the "right way" is to conform and do what we are supposed to be doing. When we can identify ourselves as human beings instead of human doings and realize our behaviors and outcomes do not define our value and worth, then, and only then, can we extend those same opportunities for grace to others. Until we master this beautiful little concept, we will remain human doings and expect everyone else to do so as well.

Every single one of us have distortions in our beLIEfs, and every single one of us can alter those distortions through continual development. It's called learning, which is the never-ending plot in life. Learning is exposing ourselves to new impressions and altering our beLIEfs through plasticity in our brains. This happens by exposing ourselves to concepts outside of our current beLIEfs and actions while developing and reinforcing new neural pathways in our brains that become opportunities of viewing and choosing for the future. It is literally rewiring the brain with new options through an openness to new impressions. Learning by remaining open is by no means about steering us away from our healthy values, behaviors, and foundations that are serving us. Rather, it's about assessing those that may be limiting us and learning how to create healthy environments to safely connect with ourselves and others when these important aspects of life may clash.

OPENNESS OR INSECURITIES?

Such rewiring requires openness. **Open** is defined as without obstruction or confinement; not closed, not barred. At the root of **judgments** are **expectations**, which are ideas of complete *confinement to a particular beLIEf*. Would you mind rereading that sentence please? Does this state of mind make anyone else sad? It sure does me because, looking back, I often lived confined by my insecurities while demanding others do the same. While feeding that mindset, we create an atmosphere of insecurity where no one really feels safe. One of the most powerful commitments I made to myself after unearthing this crucial truth years ago is this:

> **I will not live confined by beLIEfs, not mine nor anyone else's. NO! I am free to explore, express, and learn as I go! That's that!**

Listen, I didn't ask for approval to walk in this personal freedom. No permission was requested nor necessary. I simply accepted my right to openly explore and choose how I wish to express myself as new knowledge and opportunities unfold from day to day, from season to season. The decisions made today may not be the decisions made tomorrow; but today is available, and I will choose healthy decisions based on my limited understanding of the context within today. I am okay with that. The JM is not okay with that because the judge has difficulty seeing outside of itself.

Are you? Are you okay with making decisions knowing they may not be the "best" or "right" decisions, and they may change tomorrow as we gain more knowledge and our impressions change within the future? Coming to an agreement with ourselves that we will remain open requires that we feel secure even while learning life's lessons and gaining additional knowledge that we later realize we were void of. This mindset allows us to be secure in the fact that we will never fully understand anything in our limited human capacity but will walk through the fear of uncertainty anyway. The beauty: when we remain secure and continue moving among uncertainty, we allow others grace as they experience this same freedom.

Many of us struggle with being open to the idea that we are all making decisions based on limited and ever-evolving impressions that require constant resets. That's why we interject and often project our limited impressions onto ourselves and others under the guise of helping. Let's not be mistaken—the judge is never helpful to us or anyone else. The judge is the great closer! This lying thief shuts down every opportunity to move beyond the present state in a healthy manner. It is so easy to identify; the hard part is *being willing to identify* the lying thief because it requires self-reflection and possible change. The JM is not comfortable with this. For those who are ready to see it, simply look to see if the **Mindset of Judgment** or the **Mindset of Acceptance** is present. Here's more on how to identify if the great closer is active in our thoughts and behaviors.

Mindset of Judgment vs. Mindset of Acceptance

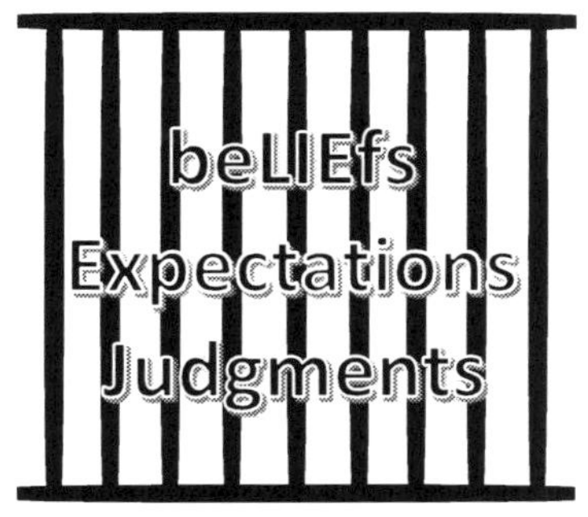

Leads to Insecurity vs. Leads to Freedom

A mindset of judgment stems from distorted beLIEfs, projects expectations on self and others, and yields judgments that lead to insecurity for one or more engaged parties. These insecurities keep our thoughts and actions confined to rigid expectations. However, a mindset of acceptance stems from a place of openness, extends grace to self and others, and yields peace, which leads to freedom for all engaged parties. Think about this for a moment: Would you rather be right or encourage a sense of autonomy for all parties involved?

Think about the impressions that we possess and are instilling in others. Are we living and instilling impressions from a closed mindset of criticism that breeds insecurities, or are we living and instilling impressions from an open mindset of acceptance that breeds autonomy and freedom?

We raised five beautiful children in a Christian home with healthy principles stemming from our interpretation of the Bible. Most of the time (not all, unfortunately) when they were younger, and certainly as adults, we chose to not tell our children what they *should do*. Rather, we encouraged our children not to do what we, or others, tell them is right, but rather to search their hearts, exercise their personal freedoms of choice, while remembering to weigh the potential outcomes of consequences and rewards. Most of our words and actions as parents empowered critical thinking and personal autonomy over correctness.

Obviously, with children, this is a very fine line, and we cannot say that we always got it "right" as we were not, and still are not, always modeling healthy behaviors. It's tough to do, but at the end of the day, our children ultimately know that their choices will define their outcomes, *not* their worth. They are always invaluable, accepted, and loved without condition regardless of the choices that led to their outcomes.

Free will is an important teacher. While not always easy to watch and allow, it grants children of all ages the ability to mature through experience. Promoting critical thinking and allowing rewards and consequences prepare children and those we love for what's to come. Experience is a powerful teacher because it is usually accompanied by deeper emotion, which is what drives memories into our memory banks. Boundaries will be included in another program within the ***Reducing Life's Pressures*** series. But for now, realize that boundaries are essential when we're struggling to find a balance between promoting critical thinking and free will while deciding how to participate in the lives of those we care about.

What we can say is that the environment of promoting critical thinking and personal autonomy over an authoritative style demanding obedience led to every one of our children being strong and independent freethinkers. They all work hard, take care of the responsibilities they deem important, exercise their voice firmly, and set boundaries often when necessary. Every one of them are open to the beauty of the diversity around them, and they usually second-guess themselves when they feel themselves criticizing or judging others. When they do, you can usually hear grace and mercy pushing its way through the confusing time they are in to acknowledge some form of human beauty in those with whom they share opposing views. This is in large part due to their abilities to push through their own insecurities.

Oh, our children do have insecurities occasionally, and so do we. However, as a family unit, our sense of respect and loyalty to promote autonomy and freedom encased in unconditional acceptance and love gives each of us strength to fight and push beyond those limiting impressions manifesting as insecurities. Through practice, this mindset becomes the beautiful gifts we can choose to give to the world around us. While we may not always choose it, those healthy impressions are there whispering:

> **"There's another way; see the human and love beyond the context, insecurities, and criticisms of this moment."**

In all honesty, our children taught us more than anyone how to love without condition, how to forgive, how to embrace, and how to extend grace. Through them, we were forced to look in the mirror more times than we'd prefer to reset our mindsets and grow. We didn't know it all then, we don't know it all now; rather, we are open to continually growing and developing with our children as we all learn together—no criticisms necessary. Isn't that great? Yes! Is it easy? No! Does it always happen? No, but we are aware of limiting human tendencies and have all agreed to always work together to find our way through them.

Chances are, we'll never master these efforts, but the more we keep our commitments with one another and work together through awkward humanistic times, the more comfortable it becomes. What's the alternative, anyway? I'll tell you, without agreements to accept and love despite human behaviors, we allow our criticisms and judgments to create unsafe environments. This leads to divisive defense mechanisms, surface addictions, and unhealthy behaviors that run rampant and escalate the original challenge we chose not to face head-on together in the first place. What we choose to avoid today will present itself in the future in one form or another.

MAKING ALLOWANCES

A powerful example of the difference between a mindset of criticism and one of acceptance was written by one of my favorite authors. His name is Paul, and he wrote about it in Ephesians, one of the books of the Bible. In chapter 4, Paul writes that love displays humility, gentleness, and patience, while making allowances for one another's faults, which unites us together in peace. Paul also suggests the idea is for us to understand that we all have different gifts and that we have the opportunity to use those gifts to do works that build one another up as we mature within ourselves and in our unity with one another and Creator.

This maturity is an ever-evolving process as individuals and in our relationships with one another and God. By mere reasoning that maturation is a continual process that never stops in this lifetime, we can certainly understand that at any given time, we will experience areas for growth, which usually requires grace. The fork in the road requiring the choice that will lead to broadening confined insecurities or freedom is found when we experience ourselves or others as being somewhat immature in certain areas. We experience immaturity as faults, and Paul's suggestion is so powerful: make allowances for one another's faults because of your love. That is exactly what love is: making allowances for one another! The JM has difficulty making allowances.

By now, you probably recognize that I am cautious with words and the phrases they form because every single one symbolizes and communicates something that will give formation to that which is to come. My words are literally forming some aspect of the future. Words are a powerful responsibility and opportunity that are not taken lightly. One of the reasons Paul's words are so important and are included in this chapter is because of where he came from. Paul was not some made-up character. Historical evidence has traced his existence, his evolution as a human, and a major paradigm shift he experienced that completely changed his mindset and life course.

What everyone can agree on in the life of Paul is the undeniable transformation he experienced in his mindset, thoughts, and behaviors. What is admirable is that he went from being a persecutor of a certain group of people to devoting his entire life to serving that same group. This paradigm shift brought him powerful revelations and great wisdom that he passionately and lovingly shared with a group of people he had previously maltreated. The interesting aspect is that it all started with how he identified himself. When Paul recognized through a painful process that his beLIEfs and standards were harming others, he chose to look in the mirror and reposition his internal compass. After exploring himself and his own beLIEfs, he made some serious internal changes, reprioritized some things, and chose to be open to maturing. The JM has the opportunity to experience a paradigm shift as well.

Like Paul, when we are immature in certain areas, especially our own sense of personal identity, we are easily confused and influenced by hurtful untruths. Then we painfully project those untruths onto others. As we mature and connect with ourselves internally, we can begin seeing and speaking truth in love. This is the most wonderful opportunity of life and relationships: to speak the truth as we know it, always in love. What a heavy choice. The likelihood of making that choice is solely dependent on our level of maturity, which is nothing more than developed and healthy neural pathways in the brain. So, what is the actual choice? We choose every day in the mirror, with one another, and with Creator whether:

Truth is masked by beLIEfs, expectations, and judgments.
OR
Truth unfolds as the byproduct of openness, grace, and acceptance.

Paul goes on to provide another form of hope in Ephesians chapter 4 that, as we grow in God, we speak the truth in love. God makes us fit together perfectly, and as each of us grow, we promote growth in others so that we are all healthy, growing, and full of love. Together in unity, we are all growing, learning, and making allowances for one another when things look and feel uncomfortable because we individually recognize that none of us are fully matured in every area. He suggests for people to let everything we say be helpful so our words are an encouragement to those who hear them. Paul sums up this chapter by telling his readers to get rid of all bitterness, rage, anger, harsh words, slander, and all types of malice, which acted upon are signs of immaturity and signs of an active JM. Instead, he reminds us to choose to be kind, tenderhearted, and forgiving of one another, which acted upon are signs of maturing.

All judgment and criticism come from a preeminence mindset, a place of superiority in our thoughts that we project onto others. Oftentimes, this mindset is masked with the facade of being helpful, and we may find ourselves extending advice or various types of support even when not requested. It is difficult to understand the difference between helping and judging. This chapter contains a few tips that will help us understand where limiting judgmental thoughts and words may be stemming from and how we may contemplate moving beyond them.

One of the first things to consider before extending our ideas of what is correct for someone else's life is whether this information is being solicited. If someone is not specifically asking for information from us relative to their life, then we can assume that they are not soliciting advice. Anytime we are thinking judgmental thoughts, verbalizing criticisms, or even extending advice—even when it comes from the purest of hearts and motives—it's important to catch, stop, and assess what's going on. Unless someone first asks for or invites a response from us, any internal or outward responses of expectation and correctness may likely be an indicator that we are lacking empathy.

Even when someone asks for advice, have we ever really considered how arrogant it may be of us that we feel we have the answers for another unique individual's life? This is not being written with a harsh tone, but it is important that we get this: Most adults and even young people are capable of devising their own solutions. When we attempt to provide advice or solutions for another's challenges, even if it is not haughty, it most certainly is not usually as helpful as them working through and finding their own solutions. So, we give someone a fish; when do they learn how to fish for themselves? Oh, trust me here when I tell you that I've given *plenty* of advice, solicited and unsolicited, but am extremely aware and cautious of that practice now.

MATURATION

There are two goals of this chapter. One is to learn the value of not judging ourselves and start being the healthy, loving, and patient teacher of ourselves instead. One sign of maturity is when we proudly embrace being a lifelong student who engages in self-acceptance during all phases of continual learning and growth. The guilt-ridden language we explored in the last chapter is one way we judge ourselves, so if you struggle with self-judgment, feel free to copy the exercise pages in Chapter 3 and practice those exercises for as long as it takes until you conquer the torture of guilt.

The other goal is to learn how to stop judging others and start being respectful and accepting of free will and differences. Critiquing and judging self and others are immature tricks the mind plays as it attempts to assure us that we are in control and are correct. On the contrary, when we are critiquing and judging ourselves and others, we are anything BUT in control and correct. Critiquing and judging often looks like guilt-ridden language on steroids, and when that internal battle is raging, we will certainly project it onto others. Another sign of maturity is being able to put down the gavel instead of forcing ourselves and others into a courtroom, demanding actuality, justice, and fairness.

Even when rearing children, the goal is not about teaching them the "right" way. The objective is to help them develop critical thinking and promote a healthy sense of autonomy in our children. How do we do that? Here's one way to know if we are criticizing and judging. We can ask ourselves:

> **Is my objective here to show someone the right way, or is it to promote choices based on the other party's own healthy free will?**

If we would rather another individual's behaviors align with our idea of right than to align with their own idea of healthy, then we are the one with the concerning issue in that moment. Exceptions to this concept certainly exist, such as giving care to a child or stepping in when there is a threat of danger to yourself or someone else. However, those moments are in the minority when it comes to the many times we feel justified in usurping someone else's free will by critiquing and judging. How many times do we give unrequested and unwarranted criticisms? If it is frequently, beware; those around us will become exhausted pretty quickly and may envision ways to gag our immature critic, or at least escape it.

WHEN WE FEEL JUDGED

The judge surfaces in life in so many scenarios, so use your imagination, but I will give you one scenario that occurred in my life many years ago. Warning: This is going to sound a little rough, but it's raw and real and millions of people experience it, so I'm throwing it out there fully anticipating that our pain and healing will resonate with someone and bring hope for healing.

I was part of a religious organization for many years, teaching at multiple levels within the local church and in other churches and events. I was involved, fully vested, and considered the people there my family. With no warning, a devastation occurred in our personal family, and my children and I were blindsided by traumatic events. It was inconceivable, and no one knew how to handle the situation we had been forced into—not me, my friends, family, church, leaders nor even the community authorities. In one day, my three young children and I went from a middle-class neighborhood with all the amenities we could want to finding ourselves homeless with barely enough clothes in our bags to get through the week.

While I was drowning in circumstances and gasping for air, I was doing my best to cling to anything familiar and stable. The few people I spoke with and asked for help within the first few days did their best to accommodate. That was short-lived, and no one in the church initiated any support. Emotional support was what was needed, but the circumstances were so bizarre that, frankly, people were afraid to get their hands dirty by even asking if we were okay. So, it was silence. Complete silence. Crickets.

One friend initiated being there for me through it all, though. She called, drove me a couple places, held me and told me no matter what, it would be okay, and then she took me and my three children into her home. She literally gave us her bedroom while she slept on the couch for a few weeks while I repositioned myself to make other employment and living arrangements. There were eight of us living in a small single-story home with one small bathroom. It was not easy, but it was safe. It was not pleasant, but there was love.

Within a few weeks, we were able to pick up the pieces. I got a new job paying enough money to support my children and myself well with some overtime, eventually sold my home, and we got another place to live. Month after month went by, and while many people at the church I was so involved in knew of our circumstances, no one approached me to see how we were doing—ever. Out of all those hundreds of people whom I served, worked with, trusted in, hugged week after week, exchanged "I love yous" with, no one, not even once, reached out.

It was utter devastation, our world turned upside down, and then crickets. It was crickets because it was terribly awkward circumstances that no one felt safe with. Eventually, I quit the church and got to the place where I never wanted to attend another church as long as I lived because all those years felt like a fallacy. "That's not love," I told myself. "They never really loved me." "It was all a big lie." Oh...do you see the judge? The lying thief? The critic?

I wasn't the only one judging. The lying thief was whispering everywhere around me in the minds of hundreds of people who were never strong enough to break through those lies and support our family that was devastated. Not even a simple phone call? Really? Yes, that's how powerful the judge is. It makes us think we have to know it all before we can take proper action. Well, that's a lie too because all it does is keep us stuck in the unknown with no hope of embracing or supporting anyone outside of its limited idea of the facts. We do not need facts to love and support. All we need is the strength to push beyond the lying thief, the judge, the critic.

The point of sharing this story is to explore what it can look like when parties do not feel safe amid the judgments. We criticize and question what we do not understand or do not know how to deal with. If we do not have answers to those questions and concerns internally, then our defense mechanisms will kick in. That usually looks like avoiding, confrontation, bad-mouthing, or gossiping. But man, we see this all the time in businesses, various organizations, and even families.

This was a beautiful learning experience for me. But trust me, it was not beautiful while I was going through it, and I still occasionally fight the critic when I look back at that time in my life and when I think about "church." A few of my experiences hurt then; the memories of them hurt even now sometimes. The breach is simply in my expectation of what a church is "supposed to do" when some of their members are hurting. It's not the people, it's my expectations. We're all just doing what we know, where we are in this moment, which will never measure up to expectation.

Obviously, this is commonplace in many churches, but it is also prevalent in many families, businesses, and other community organizations. But here's the reality: well-meaning, beautiful individuals oftentimes feel unsafe and concerned by our circumstances or our actions and they simply do not know how to cope with it. They don't know how to respond, don't know what to say, and don't know what we need. Instead of us rising above the uncomfortableness of their uncomfortableness, we often allow their defense mechanisms to trigger our own defense mechanisms, which often manifests as us validating our position, bashing the other party, making insinuations, avoidance, and much of the time, writing people off.

With that being said, when we feel we are being judged, or others are exercising their defense mechanisms against us, it is important that we understand the positions of the parties we feel condemned by. Assuredly, most of the time, they are not actually condemning us. They are walking in their defense mechanisms because they feel unsafe by our circumstances or behaviors or insecure within their own lives. Choosing empathy and grace over personalization during times like this is much more likely to yield healthy outcomes for everyone involved.

As far as my defense mechanisms during that time, I've learned from them because I certainly didn't make the healthiest of decisions during that time either. I'm telling you right now, with absolute certainty, that almost any single one of those hundreds of people that I walked away from in that church would have been there for me if I would've pushed even a little bit to explain my feelings and share my needs. I was responsible for getting my needs met during that season, not the church. I was part of the crickets!

As a matter of fact, at the beginning of the traumatic events, our pastors, youth ministers, and a couple of my closest friends were there the few times I stepped up and voiced a need. While I didn't ask for much, when I did ask, someone was there! Every single time I voiced a need, even though they didn't fully understand it, and even though it made them feel uncomfortable, they were there. Looking back at one particular day, it was very ugly and extremely exhausting for myself and everyone present, so I can totally see why people were afraid to engage. Sometimes life is ugly, and boy was that an ugly season in my life.

As things escalated, and news of our family's pain started spreading in the church, I felt the whispers in the air instead of direct communications and support, which led me to my defense mechanisms of shutting down and isolating. Looking back, I realize that these whispers were mainly out of concern—not always, but most of the time. But I was so distraught in my pain that I experienced all of them as condemnations and rejection.

I became a part of that body of believers when I was 17 years old, and it completely changed my life—in most ways, in a healthy manner. I thought we were a family, but in my mind, a family doesn't just love you when you look and act like them and ignore you when you don't. That's not a family, and that was painful for me to realize. The church was not my actual family; they were a body of believers doing their best to live a healthy life and love and support others. But at the end of the day, they went home to their families, their jobs, their responsibilities. Were they wrong? No!

The church body is a beautiful unit, but I realized that my expectations were misdirected, and they had been for a long time. My expectations were too harsh, and it was my immature expectations of the church to be my family (because much of my family was so dysfunctional) that fed into many of my challenges. I had the responsibility of me and my children at that time, not anyone else. During times of discord, we have an opportunity to proceed cautiously and look in the mirror. We always have a level of individual responsibility and an opportunity to take some sort of healthy action ourselves regardless of what anyone else does.

The church as a whole and its members are often stereotyped as judgmental. I hate to break the news, but that, along with many other biases about "church," are an absolute fallacy. The problem lies within each of us as individuals when we have difficulty communicating and working through our own feelings of inadequacy and fear. As a matter of fact, it doesn't matter what organization you are a part of, you will experience the same type of feelings and challenges, just under different circumstances.

Regardless of what roof we choose to participate in and engage under, if people are involved, we will experience uncomfortable times. It could be our local church, our place of employment, the gym, the VFW, or our own family—especially our own family. The only difference is that in a healthy family unit, we push through it and hang on anyway. That's the difference. These other groups are often disposable, but for most of us—not all—family is not disposable, so we fight!

We push through the uncomfortable moments and have the difficult conversations because there is a bond that we will not allow to be broken. The JM is less powerful than some units, we decide. While family structure is different than all these other groups, it is possible to commit to forming unbreakable bonds, and that absolutely exists within some churches and organizations, albeit not most, unfortunately. These bonds, at their core, rely heavily on listening, seeking to understand instead of being understood, having those difficult conversations, being willing to be held accountable, and having an open mindset with a commitment to individual and corporate growth.

Sometimes, that takes a lot of work, and for most, it's not worth the effort, so the idea of packing a suitcase and moving on to the next job, church, or even family seems much more appealing. The JM has a heyday here. The challenge is that we take the same problem with us, which will eventually resurface in the new environment unless we have identified and learned from it as an individual. That huge part, the problem that will resurface because we cannot escape it without facing it, is the judge.

IS THERE ALWAYS A SOLUTION?

In most scenarios, solutions can be found when we work together. I say most times because in some situations such as abuse or pain where trust is violated, termination may be the healthiest option. In the situation when I felt betrayed by my church, I did voice a need to a leader within the church at the time and was unquestionably accused and condemned. It was the youth minister, and I called him voicing my pain as a mother because the church as a whole knew what my children were suffering through and not one individual reached out to my children over the course of many months. I called to ask him to reach out to my children because they needed support outside of the four walls of the church building.

I voiced my pain and frustration that we were alone in the most difficult battle of our lives, and I simply wanted someone besides myself to step out of the church zone into the real lives of my children to extend some form of compassion and comfort to them. Instead of hearing our needs, the youth minister interpreted my expression of our needs as criticism and returned assumed fire by extending criticism. He reminded me of my own personal responsibilities and mistakes and told me to stop projecting our pain and expectations on their leadership. Our JM often sparks the JM of others; see how that works?

Now let's stop for a moment before this sounds like I am criticizing the youth minister. To put it into perspective, this is the same man who opened his home to me and my children for a couple days while we were in a crazy place of transition. Did he care? OF COURSE HE CARED! I'm about as far from a needy person as you can get, but at that time, the needs of my family were overwhelming to the few I did speak with, and frankly, I was in so much pain, I certainly didn't voice my needs in the safest form of communication. I was also in so much pain that I violated my own morals and values, the guilt of which drove me to the point of not wanting to live anymore. Holy cow! Looking back, this was a terribly rough season, to put it mildly!

Okay, yes, this seems somewhat harsh on both ends, and frankly a little absurd even to me, and I'm highly objective. However, I still chose to look in the mirror (later, of course) after I stopped blaming and accusing the youth minister and others who I felt deserted us at that time. Oftentimes, pain demands action in the moment. When we as individuals feel powerless to take that action, we sometimes search to relieve the responsibility and often wind up blaming or accusing others when we cannot find a healthy outlet ourselves. The JM is really good at that. See the back-and-forth cycle that gets us nowhere as a society? I'm pretty sure this is what the youth minister was ultimately saying, in unhelpful and unfortunately hurtful words. But there was some relevance to his point that I later found value in after much self-reflection. At some point, if I ever see him again, I hope to hug his neck and embrace the humanness we share. So, was the youth minister wrong? Was I wrong? No, we were in two different places in life.

So, my story was that no one reached out to my children in the midst of our pain, so I judged the church and left it. Then I judged the church because I left and no one cared enough to reach out to me—seriously, like I really wanted to talk to anyone at that point anyway. My JM certainly kept me bound to an ugly attitude then. It was much easier to blame them for not reaching out. See the cycle. If I blame someone else for being wrong, then I'm pushing my responsibility to take action off on them. And if they never take action, we remain broken and it's their fault, right? No! Who was responsible at that time in my life? Me! I was responsible all along! But I allowed the pain to remain through blame while cleaving tightly to my criticisms and judgments.

In lieu of accepting responsibility for my own pain, I didn't only blame the church, but a bias formed against all churches, and I pretty much wrote organized religion off for quite a few years. Look at how the JM can alter your entire lifestyle! I became antireligion, antichurch, and wanted so badly to even write off God. After all, if a loving God allowed such pain and devastation to a family, why would I believe in Him? And if all the people who claim to serve God don't give a rip about me unless I live by their rules and regulations and fit their mold, then I don't want any part of it anyway. This is not the reality, though. It's just an indicator that churches, like every other organization, are full of hurting people who do not feel safe enough to work with one another to overcome some obstacles sometimes. Church is not a terrible place, regardless of the lies our JM tries to keep us stuck in.

Literally millions of people have similar experiences, so I challenge all of us, in church or out of church, to pay attention and start putting forth some effort to heal because division is never healthy. Boundaries, yes; division, no. The JM is an expert in criticisms and judgments, which lead to division unless processed together in a healthy manner and worked through. Our family attends a beautiful church once again, and we are so glad that we put ourselves out there. It was scary and required us to muzzle the JM, but wow, the rewards are so worth it. We've been part of a small loving group of believers for a few years now and have not had any challenges. However, at some point, we may; after all, it is a group of imperfect people. This time, we are prepared to catch the beLIEfs of the JM and stop it quickly so that we can engage in healthy communications and find solutions within our organization instead of making matters more difficult for everyone.

We have the ability to look at these experiences as growing opportunities to strengthen bonds and to point us in a different direction when beneficial, which is certainly not what the youth minister and I did. No, we pointed fingers at one another and walked away. That was the last genuine conversation we ever had. How sad because I love him and his family, and he would probably say the same of us. And both of us have had genuine experiences with Creator that cannot be denied, so while we may have walked away from one another and our church, we will never walk away from humanity, so we are still connected.

This youth minister and I both terminated our relationship with one another and with the church for quite some time because of our individual inabilities to work through challenges and internal and external judgments and criticisms. There is always a healthy solution, but it is sometimes difficult to define and even more difficult to put into practice as it will require us working together. This process is often uncomfortable because it is unfamiliar. As we mature and healthy responses overpower unbridled reactions, it gets much easier. Conflict resolution takes practice—a lot of practice when the JM is leading the way!

How many times has something similar happened in your life—people terminating one another amid differences? Unfortunately, for most of us, it's more times than we would want to admit. Take a few moments now to reflect on a couple of times where judgments and criticism wound up in finger-pointing and defense mechanisms instead of strengthening healthy bonds and growth. Did you allow the relationship(s) to terminate? What did you learn from these events? What can you do differently during times of conflict in the future? Use your journal to reflect on these questions.

Control vs. Freedom

One of the biggest limitations that often runs parallel with the language of better, self-improvement, and judgment is the need to control. The need to control stems from internal pressure, which is likely to be projected onto those around us. This pressure often stems from us feeling out of control in areas we are not choosing movement, which may lead to an underlying sense of guilt, shame, or feelings of not being good enough. We, then, are more likely to be sensitive to the words and actions of others, raising the probability that we will project that internal pressure onto them when they are going against something we feel is best or the correct way of conducting matters. When we feel the need to be better, the need to control often heightens; hence, we attempt to control others when we feel out of control ourselves.

Control and freedom can be viewed as opposites relative to our thoughts and behaviors. We can strive for something through demanding or manipulating thoughts, words, and actions or through a mindset of freedom, which reflects acceptance and vulnerability in our thoughts, words, and actions. Now, we may likely achieve what we were aiming for through control and through freedom alike, but rest assured, the journey of control will be much more painful for you and everyone involved. The JM is always attempting to control.

Let's break this down more. According to the Oxford and Merriam-Webster dictionaries, **control** can have many definitions such as influencing behaviors or the course of events; managing, restraining, or restricting tendencies or activities; to limit or regulate; or to have power or authority over. **Freedom**, however, is the absence of coercion, constraint, and restriction; liberation from hinderance, restraint; being free of the power of another. In short, control involves having power, and freedom involves being released from power.

The word **power** stems from the Latin word *posse,* meaning "be able." Power is our independent ability to be, to do, or to take action. Freedom is obtained when we independently exist and take actions under our own will and authority. Control is often exercised by us attempting to use our own authority to seize the authentic expressions and abilities of another. So, here's the question: When and why would we ever want to do that to another person? Aside from raising children and giving care to those who cannot care for themselves—and even then, that approach is questionable—why would we want to usurp anyone's power?

When we critique, express our uninvited opinions, and internally or verbally judge others; when we think someone should or could be doing better, needs to improve, or fix situations...guess what? We're attempting to control them. Freedom is free of opinions and judgments and goes well beyond our limiting thoughts and expressions. The JM does not understand or have respect for freedom. And let's take this one step further before moving forward; if we are critiquing someone else, it's simply a mere reflection of our own internal critic.

Following are some exercises to process for those who acknowledge controlling language internally or projected. Be careful here to acknowledge this information while bestowing grace upon yourself. We all do this in some form, and we all have it done to ourselves. Simply process this information and attempt to be more aware of it. Your intentional awareness will lead to the modifications that will yield the results you desire and create a healthy environment for you and a safe environment for others. In the meantime, keep in mind, we're all doing the best we can, where we are, with the information we presently have. As you bestow grace and mercy upon yourself first, you will then be able to extend it to others. Do not be hard on yourself, thinking you'll be a better person if you stop the controlling thoughts and language; remember, you're already better! You're already more than enough! So are those around us!

The judge is an internal critic attempting to escape external criticisms by making sure self and others align with its limited idea of correctness.

Homework for Overcoming Judgmental Language

Do you recognize the internal judge that formed during your development? What does it look like? What does it sound like? What lies does it tell you? The JM can be a harsh little booger, so watch for it carefully. Identifying the JM within self and others assists us in calming the triggers. There are alternatives to the JM during times of opposition. Triggers do open doors for the JM to criticize and condemn, but they also open doors to explore and extend grace; both are choices, and we decide what we choose.

When we are judging, it is a sure sign that we do not feel safe in some regard. The JM often lashes out or shuts down when it doesn't feel safe. Its criticisms and condemnations are projected as reminders to itself of its superiority. After all, the JM is too right to be wrong or waste its precious time in objective collaborations that focus on connection if not in alignment with its own perspectives.

The JM makes everyone uncomfortable because it is terrified of being wrong. So terrified, in fact, that it often isolates us and pushes others away so no one sees its imperfections. The JM's uncertainty must focus on the wrongness of others because it is not courageous enough to look in the mirror and explore its own reality. The antidote for the frightened JM is making allowances for one another through grace, and that takes a lot of practice and rewiring through neural pathway development.

TAKE YOUR TIME AND DO THE WORK!

If you recognize that your beLIEf systems have you projecting your personal pressures onto others where you may be attempting to "assist" them in being better, fixing, or improving them, wouldn't now be a great time to modify those tendencies? After all, having a clear understanding of the damage these tendencies can cause now, do you really want any part of any opinion or behavior that may suggest someone else is not good enough by implying they need to be or do better? Great, me neither! Here is an opportunity to spend the next few days processing the following exercises to decrease your personal power and manipulations over others. Once again, awareness is the key, and those we engage with certainly deserve to be free from the BS of our judgmental mindset; so do we!

For the next week, pay special attention to attitudes. They will be obvious when watching body language, facial expressions, and defensive behaviors, and listening to words and feelings expressed.

- ☐ Feeling attacked
- ☐ Attacking someone else
- ☐ Feeling triggered
- ☐ Defense mechanisms
- ☐ Raised voice
- ☐ Judgmental mindset kicking in
- ☐ Attitude reflecting negative emotions
- ☐ Rolling eyes
- ☐ Squinting eyes
- ☐ I-don't-care attitude
- ☐ Crossed arms or legs
- ☐ Keeping physical distance
- ☐ Raising hands
- ☐ Raising eyebrows
- ☐ Shrinking shoulders
- ☐ Placing self behind objects (chair, desk, etc.)
- ☐ Frowning
- ☐ Snarling lip
- ☐ Wrinkling forehead
- ☐ Making fists

Be hypervigilant this week and notice what you hear in your thoughts, words, body language, and behaviors. Where is the JM attempting to control? Notice others as well and what judgmental limiting language they may be manifesting—not to critique, but rather to understand the pressures they may be experiencing. Journal any thoughts, words, or behaviors where you have the urge to criticize or judge or where you take action in the form of criticisms or judgments. Ask yourself questions like the following to gain a clearer understanding of where the JM may be lurking and hiding in your thoughts and words.

- Who did you think was wrong?
- What could someone have done better?
- Who acted inappropriately?
- Who could improve?
- Who was acting ridiculous?
- Who did you attempt to give advice to?
- Who did you project your opinions on?
- What conversations felt unsafe, and where was the JM active?

When you find yourself engaged in an unsafe environment where the JM of yourself and/or others may be running wild, take some time to diffuse the situation by calming the JM. Begin developing a new mindset by building new neural pathways in the brain to replace the JM by making safe statements such as:

- This feels unsafe or awkward right now. I respect and appreciate you and would like to work with you to create a safe space where we can work through this challenge. How can I assist in creating a safe space for you at this time?
- I appreciate you sharing, and I hear you. What I believe you said would be helpful for you is...
- Thank you so much for clarifying your needs to feel safe at this time. If you don't mind, I would like to share my needs with you as well. For me to feel safe, it would help if...

OBSERVATIONS OF THE JUDGMENTAL MINDSET

Take a few moments to observe the language, feelings, and uncertainty that often accompany the judgmental mindset. Then observe how others may experience this mindset and how it may limit you. Check those that apply to your experiences or fill in the blanks with additional observations you have made pertaining to this limiting mindset.

Judgmental language:

- ☐ Right/wrong
- ☐ Correct/incorrect
- ☐ They should...
- ☐ They are supposed to...
- ☐ They ought to...
- ☐ They need to...
- ☐ Shaming, guilting, or critiquing others
- ☐ Attempting to control others
- ☐ Giving unsolicited advice
- ☐ Other ______________________

Feelings that often accompany judgmental language:

- ☐ Angry, irritated, or easily aggravated
- ☐ Impatient
- ☐ Disapproval
- ☐ Arrogancy
- ☐ Superiority
- ☐ Like others are wrong, stupid, or don't know what they're talking about
- ☐ Other ______________________

Uncertainty: What is wrong with someone else or their circumstances?

Others may experience me as:

- ☐ Arrogant, haughty, pompous, or pretentious
- ☐ Presumptuous or high-and-mighty
- ☐ Demanding
- ☐ Unappeasable
- ☐ Rigid, strict, or inflexible
- ☐ Opinionated or uncompromising
- ☐ Skeptical
- ☐ Abrasive
- ☐ Authoritative
- ☐ Unsafe or untrustworthy
- ☐ Other ______________________

The judgmental mindset may lead to:

- ☐ Perfectionism
- ☐ Fault-finding
- ☐ Accusations
- ☐ Isolation because of irritation due to being superior to others
- ☐ Avoidance of others due to an inability to create a safe environment
- ☐ Obsessive thinking, ruminating about the behaviors of others
- ☐ Shallow, superficial, or minimal relationships
- ☐ Other ________________________

Daily Journal Practice

Following are journal topics and exercises for the next seven days, but feel free to continue such exercises until you feel yourself being able to automatically capture and replace the judgmental limiting language within your mind. It will take some time, but the neural pathways will develop as you do these exercises daily, and eventually, you will no longer find it necessary to write things down. The brain will learn to process automatically as you train it through such exercises as those contained within this program.

Day 1: Journal Your Battle with Judgmental Language

- Take a few moments to journal about your struggle with wanting certain people in your life to be better or wanting to fix or improve them.
- Write about the pressures or feelings of brokenness that others may experience by you projecting your beLIEfs on them.
- Where might these beliefs and requirements you have about the lives of others come from?
- What does it look like if you allow others to be free of your limiting beLIEfs?

Day 2: Observe Others and Your Thoughts About Them

- Spend the entire day and evening observing others and your thoughts about them. In what surroundings do you feel the need to control by requiring others be better, fix, or improve themselves?
- Observe what people around you are saying and doing that trigger you into opinions, demands, manipulations, and coercion, or attempting to limit, regulate, restrict, or usurp the authenticity or authority of another.

Day 3: Thought Capturing

- Write down any words you think or say or actions you exhibit that portray your need to control by requiring someone to be better, to fix or improve themselves or circumstances, or where you feel the need to prove incorrect.
- Define the word **grace** in your journal and describe what it looks like when you extend it to yourself and others.

Day 4: Thought Replacement

Take the thoughts, words, and actions from Day 3 and replace them with thoughts, words, and actions of acceptance and grace in lieu of expectation and pressure. How can you let go of the circumstances and cleave tightly to the person behind them? How can you extend grace?

Day 5: What May Stop Me?
List anything that might keep you from extending grace during an active JM.

Day 6: What Am I Ready For?

- Write down what you are ready to explore and what action you are ready to take in overcoming the limitations of the JM.
- What value comes when you extend grace to yourself and others?

Day 7: Acceptance Plan

- In the areas you are not ready to explore or alter at this time, journal words of acceptance and grace that will support you with no expectations or pressure as you work to develop neural pathways not driven by the JM.
- How will you extend grace to yourself and others regardless of your readiness to change?

Continue thought capturing and replacement exercises to build neural pathways that support a gracious mindset.

PRACTICE AND BUILD THE NEURAL PATHWAYS OF A GRACIOUS MINDSET

Thoughts of the Judgmental Mindset:	**Thoughts of the Gracious Mindset:**

Reframe judgmental thoughts with those of a gracious mindset:

JOURNAL TOPICS TO CONTEMPLATE FOR OVERCOMING THE LIES OF THE JUDGMENTAL MINDSET

Grab your notebook or *The BS of Better Journal* to contemplate and process overcoming the judgmental mindset. Below are cues and questions to begin assessing the costs and the payoffs of allowing the judgments and criticisms, but don't stop here. Remember, journal those prompts that stand out to you and ask yourself other difficult questions and concerns that may not be listed but are hiding deep within yourself. You already know these concerns; this is your time to listen! Identify and observe the judgmental mindset so that you can stop what's causing those feelings of arrogancy and disapproval when you are ready.

Inquisitive Alternatives:

- ☐ What or who am I attempting to control?
- ☐ What struggles do I have with guilt-ridden language (see Chapter 3)?
- ☐ What options promote freedom and safety for myself and others?
- ☐ What can I accept instead of criticize?
- ☐ Where can I make allowances for another?
- ☐ Where might I mature at this time to promote the freedom of myself and others?
- ☐ Where might I extend grace to another?
- ☐ Where might I extend grace to myself?
- ☐ Other ________________________

Neural Pathway Development Support

It cannot be reiterated enough that neural pathway development is crucial for sustainable healthy change in thoughts and behaviors. Heightening self-awareness, committing to personal reflection time, and completing acceptance and action plans daily and weekly will develop the neural pathways that serve you. For additional daily processing support, please see **Appendix A – Neural Pathway Development Support**. What would it look like if we asked the difficult yet beneficial questions until the questions were no longer difficult? When you're ready, try it and see.

When we worry, we are allowing perceived difficulties to harass our minds, seize our thoughts, and strangle our peace, joy, and potential.

5

WORRY-INFESTED LIMITING LANGUAGE

"*What if* I don't like it? *What if* they don't like me? *What if* I don't do a good job?" Mary asked her husband as she considered switching careers. "I *could* get hired, or it *could* be something completely different than what I thought it was going to be. *Maybe* some things about this job will be too difficult for me. I *might* get in there and realize it's the biggest mistake I've ever made in my career," she continued.

"Seriously, John, think of all the *possible* challenges I *could* be facing. This is a completely different industry, and it is *possible* that it won't be a good fit for me. After all, I've spent over twenty years in my current position, and the *possibility* of me finding security like this is pretty low." Mary continued ruminating for the next few days and felt like she was stuck on a giant seesaw. She was teetering back and forth between the what-ifs, maybes, mights, could-bes, and all the unpleasant possibilities of her potential career move.

She spent time reflecting on another opportunity she had passed on a few years ago. To this day, she still *regrets* not taking that chance, and this scenario felt like déjà vu. The closer she came to making the decision to move, the louder the thoughts of *uncertainty* became.

"Come on, Mary, you question and overthink everything to death!" John said. "I'm not trying to be mean, but look at the opportunities that you have squelched because you're so worried about making the *right decision*."

"Yes, John, I agree with you, but my decisions have also paid off in a lot of ways and kept us from suffering a lot of potential consequences of wrong decisions."

"That is one of the things I really respect about you," he replied, "but can't you do something in life without trying to make it perfect or control every single outcome? It's impossible! There is life beyond perfection and fear, Mary. We deserve what is on the other side of some risks that you are too concerned to take simply because you may not be able to cover every base beforehand. I will always love you and support you no matter what decisions you make. And right now, I really hope you will calm your mind and push through your fears because you deserve this new opportunity. We deserve the possibilities on the other side of your worry."

THE FOUNDATION OF WORRY-INFESTED LANGUAGE

Sound familiar? Can you identify with Mary's uncertainties? These worrisome thoughts are treacherous for us to live with and often exhaustive when decisions are necessary. They deflate us and all those around us who are put on hold while we attempt to control the outcome by weighing every negative possibility.

While in the thick of it, do you ever take some time to stop and think about what worry is? Or about what's going on when you worry? Unfortunately, most of the time we don't. For those of us who spend a lot of time worrying, it has become a way of life. Many of us have modified our behaviors and surroundings toward the path of least resistance and with the least amount of risk as possible. The biggest challenge here is that, without resistance, there is no growth; without risk, there is little to no reward. All too often, worry robs us of our reward. It can also rob our family, friends, and business.

Dictionaries define **worry** as allowing thoughts to dwell on difficulties, uncertainties, and actual or potential problems. Worry is an old English word stemming from German origin that means to strangle. Right now, I'm going to ask you to rethink that last sentence and visualize it. *Worry* is derived from the word *strangle*. Get the picture? Let's keep diving deeper.

As the meaning of worry evolved, the middle English term came to mean seize by the throat, tear, or harass. Sound familiar? Do you recognize that when we worry, we are allowing perceived difficulties to harass our minds? To seize our thoughts and strangle our peace, joy, and potential?

If you identify with this chapter, and worry-infested language is a challenge for you, I want you to reread this chapter however many times it takes for you to fully understand what is going on in your mind when you worry. This is serious!

We often laugh and embrace labels such as worrywart or overly cautious to justify this devastating mindset. It's not a joke! When we give way to this form of language in our thoughts and verbiage, we open our minds and bodies to mental, emotional, and physical exhaustion and illnesses, along with spiritual unrest.

THE ANXIETY OF WORRY

Worry is a symptom of anxiety. All of us experience anxiousness at certain times, and that can help keep us from unpleasant circumstances or out of harm's way. Anxiety is a natural emotional response to protect us from perceived danger, so it can be valuable. Anxiety can be experienced at varying levels, from mild to extreme, from beneficial to debilitating. One way to understand the seriousness of the level of anxiety we may be experiencing at any given time can be observed by how much of our lives are being affected by our anxiety. When our anxiety is debilitating, it may require specific types of therapy.

When we avoid anxiety or do things to escape certain triggers of anxiety, the next time we encounter a similar scenario, it is likely going to be more difficult to cope without attempting to escape again. Anxiety is not the problem itself; it is a helpful emotion. Learning to use it is the challenge. Many times, we experience anxiety simply because something is unfamiliar and not because there are legitimate unhealthy concerns.

Are there things in your life you alter due to anxiousness? Are you able to function with your current level of anxiety? Is anxiety affecting your relationships, jobs, abilities to complete tasks, make decisions, or thrive in life? If anxiety has affected your ability to function in a healthy manner, then professional assistance is highly recommended. Specific types of treatment can assist in breaking through to enjoy the benefits of living and taking healthy action despite anxiety.

Being a symptom of anxiety, worry is another component of life that we must learn to cope with and push beyond to fully experience many of the joys life has to offer. However, many of us have allowed worry and festering thoughts and language to control so much of our lives that it becomes a mindset that we live in daily. A worrisome mindset can cultivate illnesses and unrest and become a permanent state. Healing is necessary to reprogram our minds, which takes time and requires us to build mental muscles to protect us from the havoc worry can wreak in our lives, relationships, and desires.

It is possible to combat worry and overcome anxiety. I know this to be true not only from my training in psychology, but because I worked for quite a few years to push through worry and anxiety in my own life. Let me tell you, the mind that refuses to be controlled by worry and anxiety is beautiful and—my personal favorite—is FREE! Freedom is my favorite part of breaking through the muck we are discussing in this chapter. The struggle here is that worry and anxiety sneak up on us, disguised as our protective friend, and eventually take over. This ugly proactive reaction has one objective, which we will look into now.

Worry ultimately stems from the need to control, and the need to control comes from fear. Unfortunately, most of what goes on around us is out of our control. We know that worrying does not help matters, yet we allow it anyway. Many times, we worry because we are delaying making a decision or taking action. We fear making the wrong decision or taking an action that could possibly lead to results that we don't want or others would disapprove of. In this next section, we will put things into perspective when it comes to decision-making, taking action, and yielding an outcome despite worry.

CONTROL – THE BIG FALLACY

Seriously, what percentage of the time do you worry about something, weigh out your options, do the pros and cons, explore potential outcomes, choose a decision along the course you feel is safest and most favorable for you, and then yield the exact results in the exact way that you originally planned for? Yeah, me neither.

Rarely, if ever, are things the way we think they are going to be. This may seem like a curse, but it is actually a blessing. It is no secret that things do not usually work out the way we planned, but they always work out. How do we know that it will always work out? Well, how much proof do we need? We have survived everything to this point and are still here, so I would say the odds are in our favor. Think about that for a minute. We're still here, right? Perhaps even death itself or serious health or injury has affected our lives? Does worry help? No, worry never helps; it strangles us and others. Yes, many of us are dinged up, and we've gotten some scars along the way, but we are here and we are still living. Yes, it's scary sometimes, but worry debilitates instead of strengthens us, so, what value is there in worry?

Control is somewhat of a fallacy, is it not? We can control our mindset and our actions, but we will never be able to control all our challenges and outcomes. This bears repeating:

> **The only things we can control is our mindset and our actions. We will *never* be able to fully control our challenges and our outcomes.**

Now, I know this is hard to hear for some of us, but we must understand this principle before we can even begin to let go of worry. Worry is a failed attempt at controlling.

CONTEMPLATING VS. WORRYING

Most of us realize that we cannot control much of our circumstances, but many of us attempt to control the outcome through worry. Oh yeah, I forgot—we're not worrying, we're contemplating our options to make a calculated decision, right? It is important that we not fool ourselves, so let's be honest about the difference between contemplating and worrying.

Contemplation stems from a Latin word meaning *place of observation* and *to survey*. When we contemplate, we observe, gather factual and measurable data, collect information, and ask that small, still voice in our gut what resonates with us and our personal values. Doesn't this sound like a peaceful process? Imagine yourself contemplating for a moment. Put the book down for one minute and experience yourself observing, gathering data and information, listening to and trusting that small, still voice inside, and hearing the voices of others from a place of observation without judgment. Doesn't this feel safe? Even though contemplation may be accompanied by a sense of motivating stress, it has a calm about it.

Is that what happens when we worry? No, it isn't. Worry is anxiety in action; there's nothing calm about it. We've already defined worry, remember? As a recap, it's seizing, harassing, or strangling our peace and joy. There's a huge difference in the mindset that contemplates and the mindset that worries. Worry is all about control, and most information that is gathered is done so with the intent to control the outcome. Any surveying or observations conducted are distorted because they are done so through the lenses of finding and controlling the "best" outcome. There it is—the BS of better again.

Worry keeps us hyperfocused on the past and reminds us of all the reasons we cannot trust the people and circumstances currently involved. Worry makes us the great martyr and validates itself by reminding us that we have to worry because no one else probably will. Worry strangles us to the place of inaction and/or heightened stress. Does this feel safe?

Take a couple minutes to journal the difference between contemplating and worrying in your own life. What does it look like when you **worry**? What does it feel like? How does it affect you and those around you? How does it affect your decisions? Does it feel safe?

What does it look like when you **contemplate**? What does it feel like? How does it affect you and those around you? How does it affect your decisions? Does it feel safe?

How can we break the cycle of worry? We've already touched on it: stop the need for controlling the outcome. But, how realistic is that? For those who identify with having a true worrywart mindset, the worry neural pathways in the brain are so strong that it doesn't seem that another option is readily available. We must begin weakening those neural pathways by developing new neural pathways in the brain that give us another option. This will come through repetitive mental muscle exercises, some of which follow.

MENTAL MUSCLE EXERCISES

Let's do a realization exercise now. Say we are worrying about something and have two options to choose from: Option A and Option B. Think about something now that concerns you and consider two choices you could make. Often there are many more options, but for the sake of this exercise, we will say there are only two. The realistic outcome of any option you will ever have is going to fall within one of these five categories:

1) Absolutely nothing like what I thought it was going to be and less pleasant
2) Something like what I thought it was going to be but less pleasant
3) Absolutely nothing like what I thought it was going to be but more pleasant
4) Something like what I thought it was going to be but more pleasant
5) Pretty close to what I thought it was going to be, not quite, but pretty close

Where is option A likely to fall in your scenario? What about option B? Regardless of how hard we fight it or do our best to control it, we're going to wind up with one of these outcomes, and most of the time, we cannot predict which one it will be. The only difference is the actual option itself and the mindset we choose (but we'll get to that soon). The outcome is not always predictable other than to fully know and accept that at any given time, one of these five outcomes will assuredly occur.

Unfortunately, we spend so much time worrying about the option itself, which one is **best**, which one is **right**, that we have a hard time getting to the other side of it for fear of the outcome. That is where control comes in. **Control** is fear in action. Now that we understand that nearly all outcomes are ultimately uncontrollable, let's explore how we consider the options themselves.

Here's the truth of the matter: At any given time, you have multiple options in front of you. Any one of the paths that you could choose will most likely come with bumps in the road. Typically, what happens is that we make a decision, hit that bump in the road, and then question why we took that path, possibly regretting that we did and wishing that we would've taken a different path. This is exactly what we are attempting to avoid when we worry.

If we have someone along that path with us, it is even worse. We then suffer embarrassment and shame because we were responsible for choosing the wrong path that possibly affected someone else. However, it is crucial that you and the other individuals on the path with you recognize that the other paths that you could've chosen also have bumps in the road; those paths also have hardships. They may look different and yield different outcomes, but there will be challenges and victories on every single path.

Challenges in general are impossible to avoid as these obstacles are a natural and necessary part of human life. While through calculated choice we may avoid some challenges, ultimately, we will run into another. Every path leads to another challenge, and our mindset will be the primary factor between a healthy versus unhealthy outcome, a striving versus thriving life, and a life of freedom or one strangled by worrisome entrapments. Every choice will ultimately lead to a challenge, so let's stop fighting it!

The Choice and Challenge Cycle

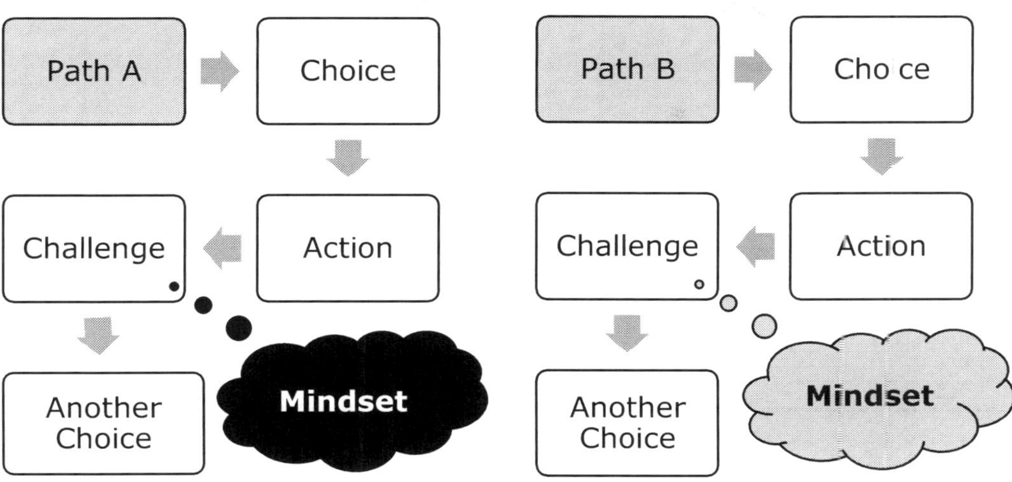

Do you get the point? Every **path** leads to a **choice** that requires an **action** that will ultimately lead to a new **challenge** that will require another **choice**. Our **mindset** along the paths we choose determines our ability to overcome the challenge(s) in a healthy manner or to pick ourselves back up when we fall on our faces after making the choice.

Every day of our lives are filled with this process. Choice leads to action, which leads to challenge(s), which leads to more choices. It doesn't stop. It will never stop as long as we have breath. The only thing that we can control is the mindset we choose along any given path at any given time. Our mindsets promote or limit us; therefore, the mindset itself is the choice to contemplate and invest energy in.

Those days when we feel exhausted and overwhelmed, we've probably been exposed to this cycle more often than we'd prefer with more challenges than we are comfortable with in that season. That is why self-care, unplugging, and recharging are crucial components of a healthy life. We can only handle this rodeo for so long before we need to stop and take care of ourselves.

Everyone alive has a 100 percent failure-and-survival rate, but worry attempts to keep us from the inevitable rodeo by choosing the safest and most secure path that will yield the results we think we want at the time. The path we choose is much less important than the mindset we choose when we come face-to-face with the challenge along the path we've chosen. That's a mouthful, so please, take a minute to digest this diagram and previous three paragraphs because we must surrender to these truths to move ahead in breaking the chains of worry.

WHAT ABOUT BEING "RIGHT" SPIRITUALLY

We all have the responsibility to decide on the standards upon which our moral compass rests and work toward aligning with what we feel makes sense. For my family, we rely on a certain divine scripture and faith in Creator. We do not rely on religion, although we attend a place of worship. Why? Because everything is affected by our limited understanding of its truths. However, as all parents know, our children are also growing and learning, and we extend grace along the way as we love them without condition (when we are healthy). The Divine also knows His children are learning and growing. Grace is real, and we can rely on it when we are working to understand and develop ourselves throughout our lifetimes.

To the believer, Creator is perfect and all-knowing, and His ways are infallible. Those ways are ever present along the course of our journey. However, our understanding of His ways is often distorted, which is why we frequently feel confused and bump into one another with our criticisms. His ways are *not* the paths we are traveling that we spoke of earlier in this chapter; those are *choices* we make. His ways are the grace, mercy, protection, and love without condition that accompany us along those paths. So many of us get it confused. We're always searching to make the "right" decision so that we can take or stay on the "right" path, as if that path is His way. **No, the support along the path is His way: grace, mercy, protection, and love without condition. This is His way!**

Many of us, especially those of faith, are constantly searching for *the* path—the one right path that we are supposed to be on—yet rarely feel like we've found it. On the rare occasion when we do feel like we've arrived on the path, it is fleeting. That's because we are trusting in our ability to choose the "right path," but it doesn't exist. The faith we exercise and healthy characteristics, such as respect, humility, forgiveness, and so many more, are His ways and will accompany us on every single path we choose if we are receptive and trust in Him.

Visualize this with me: There could be 100 paths lain before our front door every single morning. Our subconscious is secretly searching for *the* path. That subconscious is directed by our beliefs. Our fear of the future will use our expectations of the present to try and direct us in choosing *that* path. And of course, amid our personal pain or confusion, when we intentionally or unintentionally choose *the* path, we feel guilt and condemnation for having chosen one that ultimately led to pain. That same guilt and condemnation that we feel is the creature that is projected as we criticize and judge those around us as they step out of their front doors that day attempting to find their own path as well. That projection is not His way, and the constant questioning and rehashing of failures for having chosen certain paths are not His ways. Our paths are bumpy and sometimes run into others', creating challenges. Our response will be, or will not be, His way; it's not the path, it's the response.

Listen, if you are someone who does not believe in Creator, please don't take this information as judgmental or imposing. In all sincerity, I respect your position, value you as an individual, and completely support your expressions, however they may differ from mine. I don't think you're wrong and will never engage in debating religious beliefs. You and your thoughts are just as valuable as mine and everyone else's, and I mean that sincerely without a patronizing spirit. If you knew me as an individual, you would know how true that statement is.

My view here is that if you are not connected to Creator, you simply have chosen to disconnect yourself from the possible benefits that come with that connection. The majority of people in this world have some sense of relation to Creator. That connection brings with it immense benefits to the participant. If that is not something that you are interested in or long for, you are just as loved, accepted, and valued as "believers," without question and without expectation.

As an individual, and as a coach, I promote individuals in defining their own healthy path through personal acceptance and exploration. I never have an expectation of what that's going to look like. One aspect of the coaching process does give clients an opportunity to explore their spirituality. That is because it is important to identify what you feel spiritually, outside of your environment and upbringing, so that you can align your behaviors to match what your heart tells you is spiritually healthy. Not doing so creates internal pressure in the subconscious mind, making it difficult to reach contentment and thrive as an individual.

Therefore, spiritual and behavioral alignment is a goal in many coaching processes, but the client chooses what that looks like. I dare not ever be haughty enough to dictate anyone's spiritual walk. In this realm, I personally accept myself, others, and Creator along my journey as I attempt to align my own thoughts and actions with choices that will yield healthy outcomes in this life and that life to come when my energy changes form. Of course, hindsight is 20/20, so I am constantly tweaking my ideas of what this alignment looks like, but I am assured in my gut that grace, acceptance, and love without condition will go with me wherever I go in any life, here or in that to come.

We all decide what is important to us. From my limited understanding, God Himself promotes free will as recorded in the Bible, so who am I to question it? I'm a science person and tend to be pragmatic in thought, so I needed more factual prodding when I spent years questioning spirituality itself. One thing that has always stood out to me, especially understanding how the mind functions, is that there is an energy present within each one of us that is separate from our bodies. The law of conservation of energy states that energy can neither be created nor destroyed; rather, it can only be transformed or transferred from one form to another. Having taken a lot of science courses over the years, this resonates with me, so I began looking for spiritual validation of this law.

I focused this search during one season, and I found something that has never left me. Ecclesiastes 12:7 says when we die that our (earthly) bodies return to the ground where it came from and that our spirit (energy) returns to God where it came from. So, if science is accurate, our energy came from somewhere, and it will go somewhere when our old bodies give out. This is the main reason I make decisions based on this life and that to come. However, many of us—including me over the years—feel like there is some big God in the sky with a gavel waiting to pounce on us every time we make a mistake. We don't say it, but subconsciously, many of us have had similar beLIEfs drilled in our minds. These misconceptions often make us feel angry and increase our uncertainties, driving our worrywarts insane, always secretly searching for the "right" spiritual path. That's a fallacy in our BS; we'll never choose the "right" path.

Listen, relax! Regardless of what you believe, live in a manner that allows your decisions to align with it and remain open to exploring possibilities as life unfolds for you. And when you don't live accordingly, receive the grace and mercy of yourself, others, and Creator (if you desire this connection) as you learn along your path. And if you're unsure, then I encourage you to simply be open to growing in your spiritual life; that's all any of us are doing anyway. It's simple: humble yourself and ask Creator to guide you in what is true. That's it. Just acknowledge Creator and allow Him to whisper to your soul (your energy). And then receive His grace, mercy, protection, and love without condition, which will, from my personal experience, support you along your journey. Our uncertainties associated with a higher power absolutely cause worry, especially when we fear karma or the law of sowing and reaping. Know this...God loves! So, be on the lookout for worrisome thoughts associated with spirituality and gently communicate with yourself, others, and Creator to find your own sense of spiritual peace as we continue maturing together.

DOES IT REALLY MATTER THEN?

I am not suggesting that it doesn't matter what path you choose; of course it does, as every choice will lead to a reward or consequence of some sort. I'm not suggesting you stop being cautious or stop weighing the possibilities. These are important parts of calculated choice, which I work with people through the coaching process on a weekly basis. What I am saying is that the mindset we choose along any path is the most important aspect of our journey, not the actual path itself. Worry in lieu of contemplation will strangle us, stifle our growth, and rob us of opportunities every single time.

Am I saying it is "bad" to worry? No! I am saying it is not helpful and will not yield the outcomes we desire. We try to avoid internal regret and external criticisms or blaming by choosing the "right" path, and it's simply not going to happen most of the time. And while this strategy of choosing the "right path" may on occasion be successful, there are many, many times when it is not. We cannot see into the future and will never be able to control most outcomes, so we must learn how to cope within this reality to keep worry from strangling our peace and joy and stealing our opportunities.

I am not suggesting that our choices do not matter. They certainly do as they will yield outcomes. The measurement by which we gauge what is healthy versus unhealthy or right versus wrong is absolutely different for everyone. The closest gauge we have is a moral compass, which is certainly skewed by our limited human capacity for understanding; however, it is important as it will yield outcomes.

THE UNCERTAINTY BEHIND WORRY-INFESTED LANGUAGE

Anxiety will attempt to avoid uncertainty at great lengths. As with any of the language mentioned in this book, it is important to identify the uncertainty behind the worry-infested language. What are some of the common uncertainties when you worry? The ultimate uncertainty with worry is "How can I control an outcome?" Think about that for a moment. Put a few thoughts below or take some time to grab your journal and reflect calmly.

What decisions can you make or actions can you take to eliminate some worries? What can you delegate or let go of? What can you accept?

Time is torture when worry is involved. Indecisiveness is what prevents this torture from ending.

Homework for Overcoming Worry-Infested Language

Do you find yourself worrying, what-ifing, maybe-ing? Did this chapter hit home for you? Worry is about controlling outcomes and often chooses paths of least resistance. It can strangle and debilitate us, stealing our opportunities and questioning our choices to death. Worry lies, acting like our protective friend while robbing us of healthy options and freedom. Worry gets us nowhere fast and keeps us there as long as it possibly can. It ineffectively delays, waits, collects as much information as possible and prolongs healthy decisions to abate its uncertainties in an attempt to control outcomes.

There are alternatives to worry. While worry controls, contemplating explores. We live in an unpredictable world that is full of choices. Every choice is associated with a level of uncertainty. Calmly contemplating options and outcomes can be helpful, but the reality is that almost every choice will ultimately be followed by some sort of challenge. Our fretting over various choices while attempting to find the path of least resistance is futile. However, it is the mindset and characteristics we choose along the path chosen that is important, not the various choices themselves.

TAKE YOUR TIME AND DO THE WORK!

Listen, I know, I know. We've all heard, "Don't sweat the small stuff." And, yes, no matter how optimistic we are, some things are *not* small things. The point here is not to gauge our struggles as we simply cannot measure challenges. Frankly, no measure of fear or pain is pleasant; we simply hope to minimize it instead of amplifying it through choosing a healthy mindset to decide and then cope with the outcomes. You and I currently have a 100 percent track record of making it. Perhaps with a few scars and maybe even maimed, but we've made it and will continue to do so.

Most important this week, do not be hard on yourself if you find yourself battling a worrier mindset. At some point in life, worry served you well. It kept you safe from something. It became a secure defense mechanism to protect you and those you care about. Simply acknowledge that there is an alternative to worry, and that we will transition to that healthier mindset by paying close attention to our thoughts and through mental exercises that build new neural pathways.

Time is torture when worry is involved. It's important to understand the difference between contemplating and worrying, and how to make a decision as quickly as possible—not necessarily a decision for action; it could be a decision to accept for now until action becomes the decision we choose. Indecisiveness is what prevents this torture from ending. Indecision and worry are oftentimes partners. When we are ready to escape the havoc that the dynamic worry-and-indecision duo wreaks in our lives, we follow this course: 1) Decide and choose a course; 2) take action; 3) accept; 4) learn and make alterations by repeating this course.

Our goal in these next few days is to begin shifting our mindset from a worrier to a warrior mindset. We will do this by learning to contemplate in lieu of worry. Training our brains to decide, take action, accept, learn, and then alter by making new decisions within the present moment will free our minds and build our confidence. When catching the worry mindset in action, remember to stop and take care of yourself. Take some time for self-care by unplugging and recharging, which will assist in calming the worrywart.

OBSERVATIONS OF THE WORRY-INFESTED MINDSET

Take a few moments to observe the language, feelings, and uncertainty that often accompany the worry-infested mindset. Then observe how others may experience this mindset and how it may limit you. Check those that apply to your experiences or fill in the blanks with additional observations you have made pertaining to this limiting mindset.

Worry-infested language:

- ☐ What if this or that...
- ☐ Maybe this or that
- ☐ This or that might happen
- ☐ This or that could...
- ☐ Ruminating on all the negative possibilities
- ☐ Other ______________________

Feelings that often accompany worry-infested language:

- ☐ Anxiety of various degrees
- ☐ Distress
- ☐ Anguish
- ☐ Agitation
- ☐ Apprehension
- ☐ Nervous or on edge
- ☐ Uneasy
- ☐ Other ______________________

Uncertainty: How can I control an outcome?

Others may experience me as:

- ☐ Tense or high-strung
- ☐ Delicate or sensitive
- ☐ Perfectionistic
- ☐ Nagging or controlling
- ☐ Excessive
- ☐ Other ______________________

The worry-infested mindset may lead to:

- ☐ Ruminating on negative possibilities
- ☐ Limited opportunities due to blind spots that keep me fearing risks
- ☐ Being preoccupied with distracting thoughts
- ☐ Inability to relax or enjoy the present moment or season
- ☐ Debilitating thoughts
- ☐ Strained relationships due to micromanaging or hovering
- ☐ Anal-retentive behaviors such as excessive orderliness, obsessiveness, or perfectionism
- ☐ Other ______________________

Daily Journal Practice

Following are journal topics and exercises for the next seven days, but feel free to continue such exercises until you feel yourself being able to automatically capture and replace the worry-infested limiting language within your mind. It will take some time, but the neural pathways will develop as you do these exercises daily, and eventually, you will no longer find it necessary to write things down. The brain will learn to process automatically as you train it through such exercises as those contained within this program.

Day 1: Journal Your Battle with Uncertainty, Worry, and Anxiety

- Take a few moments to journal about your struggle with uncertainty, worry, and anxiety.
- Write about the effects this trio has on your life.
- Where might this fear of uncertainty have come from?
- What does life look like if you are free of worry and anxiety?

Day 2: Journal the Following What-ifs

- What if uncertainty was not dangerous and you could actually tolerate it?
- What if worrying were pointless because it cannot stop "bad things"?
- What if worrying caused more suffering now without saving you from any suffering in the future?
- What if worrying did not require attention at all?

(Taken from Michael Stein, Psy.D., "Avoidance of Uncertainty: Generalized Anxiety Explained," *Psychology Today*, February 28, 2020, https://www.psychologytoday.com/intl/blog/understanding-the-anxious-mind/202002/avoidance-uncertainty-generalized-anxiety-explained.)

Day 3: Thought Capturing

Write down any worrisome thoughts you have today, what-ifs, maybes, coulds, and all the negative possibilities. Pay special attention and log *all* of the worries and negative what-ifs.

Day 4: Thought Replacement

Now replace the worrisome thoughts from Day 3 with words of contemplation, without the fear of uncertainty: observing, gathering data and information, and listening to and trusting that small, still voice inside. What is possible with this mindset?

Day 5: Thought Capturing and Replacement

Write down any worrisome thoughts you have today, what-ifs, maybes, coulds, and all the negative possibilities and immediately replace them with positive possibilities through calm contemplation.

Day 6: Where Am I on My Current Course?

☐ Deciding and choosing a course
☐ Taking action
☐ Accepting
☐ Learning and making alterations along my course

How might my current course and decisions limit or promote me?

Day 7: Transition from a Worrier Mindset to a Warrior Mindset

Categorize and list all your concerns of the day into a worrier column or a warrior column. Once listed, use calm contemplation and gentle observations to reframe all the items in the worrier column to make them into warrior statements.

Continue thought capturing and replacement exercises to build neural pathways that support a warrior mindset.

PRACTICE AND BUILD THE NEURAL PATHWAYS OF A WARRIOR MINDSET

Worry-Infested Thoughts of the Worrier Mindset:	Possibility-Infested Thoughts of the Warrior Mindset:

Reframe worrisome thoughts with thoughts of positive possibilities:

JOURNAL TOPICS TO CONTEMPLATE FOR OVERCOMING THE LIES OF THE WORRY-INFESTED MINDSET

Grab your notebook or *The BS of Better Journal* to contemplate and process overcoming the worry-infested mindset. Below are cues and questions to begin assessing the costs and the payoffs of allowing the worry-infested mind, but don't stop here. Remember, journal those prompts that stand out to you and ask yourself other difficult questions and concerns that may not be listed but are hiding deep within yourself. You already know these concerns; this is your time to listen! Identify and observe the worrisome mindset so that you can stop what's causing those anxious feelings of distress and anguish when you are ready.

Inquisitive Alternatives:

- ☐ When challenges have previously occurred, I overcame them by...
- ☐ If this or that happens, I am capable of handling it because...
- ☐ Consider all the positive possibilities.
- ☐ What can I let go of?
- ☐ Is this my responsibility, or does it belong to someone else?
- ☐ What are the optimistic opportunities?
- ☐ What personal growth may I explore?
- ☐ What reward may come from the risk?
- ☐ What boundaries will assist in me feeling safe with decision-making?
- ☐ How does it look when I replace anxious worry with calm contemplation?
- ☐ The warrior vs. worrier mindset will change what?
- ☐ Other ________________________

Neural Pathway Development Support

It cannot be reiterated enough that neural pathway development is crucial for sustainable healthy change in thoughts and behaviors. Heightening self-awareness, committing to personal reflection time, and completing acceptance and action plans daily and weekly will develop the neural pathways that serve you. For additional daily processing support, please see **Appendix A – Neural Pathway Development Support**. What would it look like if we asked the difficult yet beneficial questions until the questions were no longer difficult? When you're ready, try it and see.

Life is not about leveling up and competing for the finish line. It is about progressing horizontally, not vertically. We never arrive in this lifetime.

6

COMPARATIVE LIMITING LANGUAGE

"Must be nice," Janice thought in her head as she was scrolling through Facebook one day. Her longtime acquaintance Sarah and her husband were parasailing off the coast of Maui at sunset and were able to capture some beautiful photos, which they posted to remember their magical experience.

A couple days later, Sarah posted some more photos of her and her husband kissing by the beach and a couple videos of them splashing around and playing together in the water. Unfortunately, this, too, surfaced in Janice's newsfeed, sparking additional negative energy.

"Wish I was that lucky," Janice thought. "Sure wish my husband cared enough to take me on a vacation like that." Then Janice dove deeper in thought, which only heightened her frustrations. She thought about how her husband worked all the time, but they never had any time or money to play together.

As questions surfaced, she briefly thought about some choices that she could make but quickly moved her thoughts in another direction because all those choices were too difficult or could lead to disastrous consequences. She was barely aware of all the thoughts rolling around in her head, but she knew it never left her feeling good when she saw Sarah living it up.

Since she felt powerless to the negative energy she was feeling as she watched Sarah enjoying her life, Janice finally settled on another coping mechanism by devaluing the achievements of Sarah and her husband. "After all, they couldn't possibly be that happy," Janice thought. Besides,

Janice had some inside scoop on their life, and she knew firsthand that it wasn't all sunbeams and rainbows as they were portraying on Facebook.

While this didn't feel good to Janice either, for some reason, she felt some sense of relief by undervaluing the genuine happiness of Sarah and her marriage. Thinking Sarah's life wasn't that great seemed to help Janice at least cope with some of the unhappiness in her own life at that time.

Sound familiar? Janice is not the only one to struggle with comparative language, which stems from feelings of jealousy and envy. These are two feelings that are difficult to acknowledge and process because they are also accompanied by guilt and shame as awareness sets in.

Frustratingly enough, the guilt and shame associated with feelings of jealousy and envy often make it almost impossible to talk about. Is Janice a bad person because she has these feelings and struggles with comparative language? Absolutely not! She is human!

Every one of us has struggled with jealousy and envy at some point in life. Many of us developed coping skills to overcome those feelings as children and young adults, and some of us grew into adults who are still battling what can sometimes be all-consuming feelings and thoughts. As children, we sought approval and confirmation that we were enough.

If for some reason those needs were not fully met and our coping skills were delayed as a child or young person in this area, then we may have grown into adults who constantly feel the need to validate and prove ourselves. As children, we did this by listening to the adults in our lives and by looking around and comparing ourselves with others. Hence, some of us grew into adults who are still looking for the parental model to tell us the "right way" and/or by looking around at our peers to assess if we are on the right track and to assess how far off track we think we may be.

AM I JEALOUS OR ENVIOUS OF OTHERS?

How do we know if we are struggling with jealousy or envy? Oh, it's easy; we look for signs. Many signs to watch for are listed in the next section and at the end of this chapter, but here's one example. Phony compliments followed by negative thoughts or talk when away from the person we just complimented is a classic sign of jealousy. Let's say we go to church on Sunday, compliment the pastor's wife on her lovely new dress, walk away feeling some sort of negative energy that's difficult to pinpoint, and then belittle her on the drive home. Now, there could be something else sparking this, but a great go-to when similar scenarios occur is to certainly contemplate whether the comparative mindset is acting up.

Giving insincere compliments of jealousy is when we internally feel negative energy before, after, or while extending the compliment. We do this because we subconsciously know that it is "wrong" to be mad at someone because of their good fortune. When we feel this way, we attempt to be "nice" to save face. The sad thing is, we often don't even realize we are doing this. Jealousy and envy are often toxic and misplaced anger that hide themselves very well. Talk about a blind spot!

These scenarios are not pleasant for anyone involved, and it's extremely obvious what's going on to almost everyone except ourselves when we're exhibiting jealous behaviors. Many of us don't even want to know that we are struggling with these nasty tricksters. Many times, we simply avoid certain people all together for reasons that have very little grounds. We secretly sense something is off, but we won't even go there. When struggling with jealousy and envy, we don't want to see it because then we would be forced to look in the mirror if anything were to change.

A helpful way to identify if we are struggling with comparative language is to monitor our feelings, thoughts, and behaviors by looking for signs. Boy, this is a tough adventure, so get ready! And before we begin identifying jealousy and envy in our lives, let's remember that jealousy and envy are not us! They are symptoms of a comparative mindset that we can modify when we are ready to heal and move beyond its limitations.

IDENTIFYING JEALOUSY AND ENVY

Janice was struggling with envy, which is different than jealousy. Envy is present when we secretly feel or outwardly express resentment because we long for something or someone that someone else has possession of or is engaging with. **Envy** stems from a Latin word meaning to regard maliciously or grudge. The Old French meaning added such meanings as hostility and enmity. When Janice was feeling frustrations while looking at Sarah's social media page, she didn't have ill intent and didn't even understand why she was experiencing hostility and begrudging her, but that is what envy does. It is ugly, makes us feel ugly, and most of the time, we do not know how to cope with these feelings. We certainly do not talk about them because, let's face it, it's ugly, and we don't usually want people to see our ugly side.

Jealousy is different than envy. Instead of begrudging what someone else has or is experiencing, jealousy is when we fear someone is going to take something that we have or are experiencing. Jealousy is usually accompanied by such traits as suspicion, distrust, possessiveness, and insecurities. Jealousy often occurs in situations where we feel anger or resentment because our spouse works with a cute person whom we fear may catch their attention. Or, perhaps, someone else may be excelling at work, and we secretly fear they will get the upcoming promotion instead of us. Maybe we get frustrated and feel left out when one of our best friends is spending time with another friend of theirs. Regardless of the situation, jealousy and envy are uncertainties and insecurities on steroids.

For those who do struggle in this area, don't be hard on yourself. When we're ready to grow, it's easy to recognize some of the symptoms. Keep in mind that we, and possibly those we care about, will likely suffer the consequences of this nasty nature until we decide to squelch the comparative mindset. Accept yourself in the process and be gentle with yourself until you're ready to move a position. Until then, be on the lookout as jealously and envy manifest verbally, in body language, and in actions, and they often affect the choices we make and the people we allow close to us. If you're ready to develop skills to push beyond these limiting thoughts and emotions, here are some things to look for. Check the ones that may apply to your life.

Feelings

☐ Jealousy: fear of losing something or someone
☐ Envy: resentment or longing for what someone else has
☐ Hostility
☐ Begrudging
☐ Enmity or animosity toward someone
☐ Distrust
☐ Suspicious
☐ Unworthiness or not being good enough or as good as someone else
☐ Inferiority or inadequacy
☐ Guilt associated with feeling jealous or envious
☐ Shame associated with feeling insecure or having ill intentions
☐ Inability to wish someone well when feelings of envy and jealousy are surfacing

Thoughts

☐ Internal judgments and insecurities against yourself
☐ External judgments and criticisms against others
☐ Rationalizing or manifesting reasons why someone else's path is different than the one you secretly or verbally envy
☐ Reluctance to engage or be vulnerable with people where envy or jealousy may surface
☐ Malice or hurtful intentions

Behaviors

☐ Undermining
☐ Bad-mouthing or spreading rumors
☐ Violating the trust or confidence of someone
☐ Holding a grudge or being unwilling to work through feelings of anger

- ☐ Coveting
- ☐ Belittling
- ☐ Insincere compliments
- ☐ Controlling
- ☐ Blaming
- ☐ Lashing out
- ☐ Avoiding
- ☐ Terminating relationships
- ☐ Passive-aggressive actions
- ☐ Manipulations
- ☐ Possessiveness
- ☐ Isolating or hiding our ill feelings
- ☐ Gaslighting behaviors or sowing seeds of doubt pertaining to another

ARE OTHERS JEALOUS OR ENVIOUS OF ME?

When others manifest jealous or envious behaviors toward us, it often creates an atmosphere where we question ourselves and whether something is actually wrong with us. We may begin wondering if others see us in a negative light as well. This is a vicious, vicious cycle, so watch for it and stop it immediately! This isn't easy because it goes deeper, even into our developmental years. For many of us during our development, we are told by those who love us that other kids "are just jealous," which is why they are being mean. Well, perhaps, but there are many other potential reasons for unhealthy behavior from children. Relying too heavily on the "just jealous" reasoning can certainly limit our development as children and even into adulthood. Any form of jealousy is from a comparative mindset, and if we think others are jealous of us, we can get sucked into it.

If we feel like people are behaving ill toward us because they are jealous, then we may be temporarily using jealousy to inflate our own ego as a defensive mechanism. Unfortunately, we are not solving any problems or mending any bridges by relying on the "just jealous" statement. Is this statement helpful, then? Oftentimes, we attract things that we internally fear, and we certainly attract things we think of often. So, it is important to not focus on the "jealousy" of others. An alternative to wondering if others are jealous or envious of us is something beneficial. It's called living. Simply living our lives and doing what we do regardless of the view of others is rewarding within itself. When we are living our life, we feel positive and healthy energy and can see signs such as:

- ☐ Self-confidence and healthy self-efficacy
- ☐ Healthy self-esteem (with a touch of humility, of course)
- ☐ Void of comparative thoughts, language, and behaviors
- ☐ Secure with self, not needing the validation or approval of others

- ☐ Having a sustainable and healthy support system with honesty and trust
- ☐ Having a strong sense of gratitude
- ☐ Complimenting or giving sincere accolades with positive emotions
- ☐ Succeeding without measuring successes against others

Chances are, when we check those boxes, we're not allowing our lives to be affected by jealousy or envy. When we do encounter the behaviors of others that create an environment where we feel unsafe, we can do some things to move beyond it, such as self-assess and be open with ourselves to identify if our words or behaviors may possibly be contributing to an awkward environment. If so, we can create a safe space by vulnerably discussing it and modifying our words and behaviors. Once we've identified and taken responsibility for our own participation, we can acknowledge that we are not responsible for the feelings and actions of others. Modify and resolve what we are responsible for and then keep on living. At the end of the day, it is important that we accept, let go, move on, and live our own lives. Sometimes it is possible to mend relationships caught in the snare of a comparative mindset and sometimes it is not; live regardless!

JEALOUSY IN PARTNERSHIPS

My husband called me one day and said, "Man, I have to tell you about this lady I just saw at the gas station." Then he proceeded to tell me a couple details about an attractive woman he saw while he was getting fuel. He said, "You know, one of those people who really have that look that catches your attention and you have a hard time not staring? Well, she was like that, and I had to keep reminding myself not to look. I kept saying, 'Don't look, just don't look.'" And then we started laughing together because I know exactly what that feels like. As a matter of fact, that's happened a few times to me.

One of my best friends and I had planned a few days to explore Chicago a few years ago. We commuted via train, and while walking through the train station upon arrival in downtown Chicago, there he was! Oh my...well, let's just say, my bestie and I had plenty of laughs while trying to control our wandering eyes. Of course, I shared with my husband all our experiences of the day once we got settled in the hotel, including Mr. Wonderful. The worse part was, even a few months later, I dreamed about the train station guy! Oh no, I definitely did not want to be dreaming about another guy! Seriously, I had not been thinking about him, he just popped into my dream. So, I told hubby I saw him again in my dreams, and we laughed that morning, just like we had laughed the night I first saw him.

Some people may think that's too much. Well, maybe so for some, but we are human, and who else do we talk to about our human stic behaviors than if not with one another? We also both realize that we are human with a physical nature that demands we keep it intact to remain healthy. My husband and I have devoted our lives to each other. We do not keep secrets. We do not hide things. Aside from respecting the confidentiality of others, we talk about everything. He's my favorite person in the world to speak with, so why wouldn't I share these crazy human moments with him? We have created a safe space for each other so these, and other trying and strange, conversations are possible.

One other time, my hubby mentioned something about a new friend's wife who was attractive, and we laughed and teased each other for a couple minutes about it. Then he said something to me that was such a compliment. He said, "You know what? I love that we can talk about anything. A lot of people have to hold stuff in and can't really be real with everything because they are afraid of what their partner might think. But we have such a safe relationship that we can be real with one another, and I really appreciate that." I agreed with him completely. No, we are not lusting. No, it doesn't happen frequently. But these scenarios are great examples of the freedom within our relationship that comes from appreciating our humanness and being comfortable enough to talk about it.

One of the reasons we communicate so well now is because we have both worked on our own insecurities. Underlying insecurities feed a lot of negative emotions and defense mechanisms, including jealousy. We are pretty fortunate that we have both worked through much of our individual insecurities, but it was a process, for sure. We did the work, and now our safe relationship is the reward of our efforts. Not every relationship is safe. Imagine what it looks like when our partner is struggling with insecurities. Now imagine what it looks like when we are the one struggling with insecurities. Are we open and honest with our partner during these times? Are they open and honest with us? Does the relationship feel safe enough to be transparent and vulnerable?

What would have happened if I was insecure within myself when my hubby told me about those attractive women he saw? Or what if my hubby was insecure when I told him about the train station guy or my crazy occasional dreams? If we're honest, many of us have not worked through our own insecurities to the point where we create a safe space for some of those difficult conversations. Imagine what it would look like if you could speak with your partner about anything without fearing insecurities? Now, imagine if your partner could do the same. What would it take for your relationship to be safe enough for the tough conversations?

Do insecurities ever surface in the form of jealousy in your partnership? This can be scary because it may indicate one of two things, neither of which are pleasant to acknowledge, and both of which are uncomfortable to address. Either we experience jealousy from outward causes that stem from lacking trust for legitimate reasons, or we feel jealous because we are insecure and our thoughts are being directed by the BS of our past. If my husband feared I may have an interest in someone else, or had cause for distrusting me, his response would likely have been different when I spoke about the guy at the train station. Vice versa, if I had difficulty liking myself or was displeased when I look in the mirror, chances are I would not be so open to him sharing about the woman at the gas station.

Jealousy is not an unhealthy emotion, by the way. My husband and I are in a committed relationship, and if that feels threatened, be assured, I will stand my ground and address the situation. But before I do, I'll look in the mirror and assess whether the jealousy could have been sparked by my own insecurity before communicating it with my husband. One reason is because I do not want to be limited by my insecurities. The other reason is because my husband deserves more respect than being attacked or burdened by my insecurities that I've chosen not to assess and work through. My relationship deserves a healthy me that stems from me loving and trusting myself, which will help prevent insecurities. Regardless, when we are healthy and bitten by the comparative bug, we can easily and quickly process it to assist us in moving away from an unhealthy mindset that can be destructive. We, and our relationships, are worth breaking through the BS of the comparative mindset.

While we have an incredible relationship now, things were not always peaches and cream. Frankly, we still have a hiccup here and there, but we've both developed so much as individuals that we have created a safe space to talk about any challenges we face as individuals or in our relationship. It's not easy; it's work, but we are committed for life. Occasionally, we may jointly agree to table a matter for a brief amount of time to release some personal steam and clear our heads. However, we quickly come back to the drawing board to tackle matters because we will not allow anything to fester through the damaging defense mechanism of avoidance.

Insecurities often lead to avoiding or attacking when we feel jealous or envious. Avoidance in a partnership is the silent disease that erodes the foundation. It's the slow, miserable, silent killer that sucks the breath from a relationship, causing it to slowly die. Projecting and attacking are louder versions of destructive defenses. Avoidance and attacking surface to some degree in most partnerships, but I challenge all of us to watch for these defenses and begin focusing efforts to squelch them. It's work, but my husband and I are committed to having the difficult conversations to keep our foundation strong and healthy. We are also committed to watching our own attitudes when they may reflect an unhealthy mindset that can spark challenges within our relationship. The processing pages at the end of this chapter will assist for those ready to overcome a comparative nature.

PATHOLOGICAL JEALOUSY

For most of us, jealousy can be controlled without causing extreme threats to our lives and relationships. However, varying degrees of jealousy exist, and it is important that we understand exactly where we are on this spectrum so we can monitor and take action to prevent undesired consequences for ourselves and others.

There are a lot of options for those of us who struggle with feelings, thoughts, or behaviors associated with a comparative mindset. Talking to a trusted loved one, doing some research, introspection, personal development exercises, or taking other measures such as life coaching or counseling can often prevent serious consequences.

However, for some, jealousy in certain extremes can by symptomatic of serious underlying problems. In these cases, it is imperative that a proper evaluation be conducted by a licensed professional so that a safe action plan can be created that will promote healing in the lives of the individual and those with whom they engage. While this is not a complete list, some serious symptoms to be aware of are listed below:

- Delusions: whether or not sparked by gaslighting, delusions are still indicative of potential serious challenges
- Obsessions/fixations
- Excessive questioning
- Interrogating someone
- Accusatory communications
- Suffocating partner, friend, or other
- Snooping or invading privacy of other

If you observe some of these behaviors in yourself or a loved one, you are encouraged to speak with your doctor or a professional therapist to rule out potential dangers.

THE MAYHEM OF MORE AND THE ENTANGLEMENT OF "-ER"

A few key points are crucial to really understanding the potential harm of our words. One is that everything that we think and say means something, it stems from somewhere, and it will produce an outcome. Even little words such as *more*, *most*, and add-ons such as *-er* or *-est* can reflect a limiting mindset. In the English language, the comparative degree is expressed using *-er* or the word *more*. The superlative degree is expressed using

-est or the word *most*. Watch carefully for those nasty add-ons in thoughts and verbiage because they are a form of the BS of better. Think about it:

- Good. Better. Best.
- Happy. Happier. Happiest.
- Pretty. Prettier. Prettiest.
- Fine. Finer. Finest.
- High. Higher. Highest.
- Thin. Thinner. Thinnest.
- Calm. Calmer. Calmest.
- Fancy. Fancier. Fanciest.
- Funny. Funnier. Funniest.
- Wise. Wiser. Wisest.
- Prosperous. More prosperous. Most prosperous.
- Handsome. More handsome. Most handsome.

Okay, here's the reality. Wise is more than enough! Even if we become wiser, we'll never be the wisest because someone will always be wiser than us in someone's eyes. So, what's the point of being more wise than wise? Pretty is more than enough! Even if we become prettier, we'll never be the prettiest because someone will always be more pretty than us in someone's eyes. So, what's the point of being more pretty than pretty? These words and add-ons are double-edged swords; comparative words often stem from pride, arrogance, or insecurities. They often lead to resentment and rob us of acceptance and peace. When we do what we can, where we are, with what we have, there's no need for better because there's no need for comparison. I may progress in a horizontal direction tomorrow if I choose, but who and where I am currently is more than enough. No comparative or superlative word phrases will define me because I am indescribable and immeasurable.

HORIZONTAL VERSUS VERTICAL PROGRESSION

Becoming more popular within our culture, which is fixated on self-improvement, is an old gaming phrase: "leveling up" or "level up." In the gaming community, it basically means to increase in power, rank, or skill. Level, of course, has to do with measuring, so the intention is to advance or measurably move up. In life, perhaps it's an upgrade, a promotion, or achieving something greater than previously reached like climbing the corporate ladder or purchasing a more expensive home or other material items. The challenge then becomes, what now?

Within our pressure-induced society, we push ourselves and oftentimes others to **level up**, meaning to upgrade or create some form of positive change. But how long can we do this? What happens when we continue to level up? What do we do then? So, what if we reach the highest rank in the game, kill the final monster, save the princess, and achieve the highest score? Now what? Is the game over? Do we play it all over again? If we do play it again, will it be as fun and interesting? Probably not, because we've already been there and done that. This form of advancement is known as vertical progression in the gaming community.

Our two sons explained the difference between vertical and horizontal progression in gaming like this: **Vertical progression** is about leveling up, acquiring better and stronger gear to battle the next harder opponent, which renders all previous opponents obsolete, as they are now way too easy. Exploring previous realms in vertical progression makes it less fun because we've already been there, so it becomes boring for most, as opposed to the more broad and unlimited possibilities of going horizontal.

Horizontal progression in games is more about having most of the tools at your disposal at the beginning and knowing how to utilize them efficiently and in conjunction with one another to take on more difficult areas or opponents. You can also acquire more tools later that are not inherently better than prior ones but can be utilized more efficiently in certain circumstances. Horizontal progression in gaming is generally more complex than vertical gaming as it requires more thought. Since horizontal progression isn't as linear, many more options are available. Horizontal progression is usually more complex and challenging in using resources, which can add to the fun and excitement.

The point is that within the gaming community, you don't have to level up vertically to be more powerful. Moving horizontally also increases your power. You can climb the vertical ladder and eventually reach the end with less complexity, skills, and resources, or you can move in various positions on a horizontal playing field while gaining knowledge and new skills with never-ending possibilities. It's the same in the game of life. Life is not about leveling up and competing for the finish line. It is about progressing horizontally, not vertically. We never arrive in this lifetime. Life is full of possibility.

It is important that we view life on a horizontal playing field instead of a vertical corporate ladder. Living life in the realm of horizontal progression drastically reduces life's pressures. We can see this by reviewing the upcoming Horizontal vs. Vertical Progression diagram. Within the realm of vertical progression, someone is the best, someone is the worst, and we are usually mediocre—somewhere in between. We're always striving to be better but never actually arrive no matter how high we climb. How does this serve anyone?

The alternative, horizontal progression, is powerful and full of potential. Progressing horizontally is without the comparisons but loaded with possibility. At any given moment, we can move in any direction regardless of what direction others are traveling. There's no need to critique or judge our direction or the direction of others because we can move a position in any direction anytime we choose. There's no race and no finish line. We never arrive, it's never boring, there's always lots of potential, and we aren't competing with anyone.

Horizontal vs. Vertical Progression

Vertical Thinking

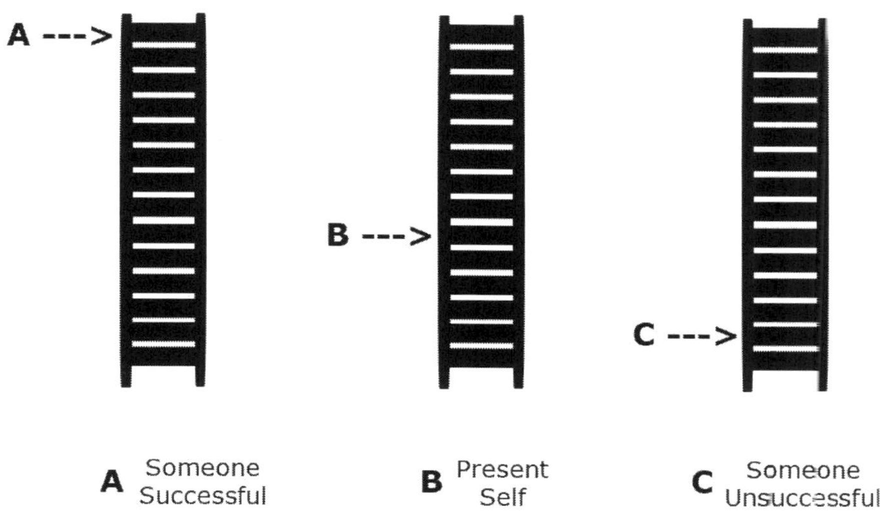

A Someone Successful **B** Present Self **C** Someone Unsuccessful

Horizontal Thinking

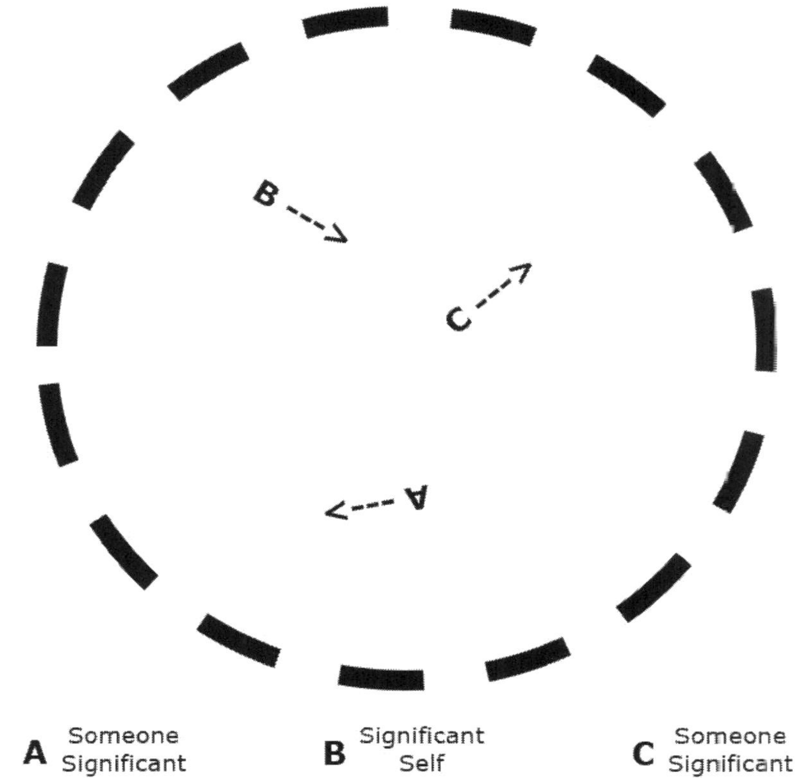

A Someone Significant **B** Significant Self **C** Someone Significant

GRACE IN THE FACE OF COMPARISON

Let's be real for a moment. Sometimes, a comparative nature can be downright ugly. When you're reading this book, it's likely that you may find yourself in one of two positions:

1) I know someone like this: You're nodding your head, thinking, "yep, he or she is just like that." This may give you some sense of justification for the awkward feelings you struggle with during your engagements with that person, who is likely struggling with a comparative mindset.

OR

2) Your inkling tells you this chapter was written for you, but it's difficult to swallow. You may be avoiding guilt and shame or blaming the reasons why you *have to be* this way. Or you may be convincing yourself that you are not jealous or envious at all and that the comparative language you use is nothing more than a necessary response to the ridiculousness around you.

Which one is it? Regardless, both require grace. Yes, grace in the face of comparison is necessary because it is difficult to cope with. Bestow grace upon yourself and bestow grace upon others when you see that comparative nature rear its ugly head. It's the human defensive nature that's ugly, not you or others. Surround yourself with support, be vulnerable, create a safe space where others may feel more comfortable to be vulnerable, and extend loving support to yourself and others to overcome it. We must acknowledge and talk about the beLIEfs and insecurities underlying the comparative nature in order to overcome it.

One way to overcome insecurities is to establish a life of significance. We can have success without feeling significant, but the reverse is not so, as success always accompanies a life of significance. Personal significance is key, and it varies from individual to individual. We often compare our own significance with others, which feeds our insecurities. This is not helpful because every person is walking in unexplored territory daily that cannot be defined or driven by territory already explored by self or others. Every challenge in every season is an opportunity for new exploration. When we explore, we will find infinite solutions and opportunities that have never existed before. This will occur as we replace the limiting language and empty behaviors contained within this book with vulnerable curiosity and fearless exploration. What was that again?

Every day is full of choices between:

Limiting Language and Empty Behaviors	OR	Vulnerable Curiosity and Fearless Exploration

What will you choose today?

We will see you on the other side of that choice tomorrow. And guess what? You'll have another choice tomorrow and another the day after that, so don't forget to give yourself and others a break along the way. In the meantime, ACCEPT! Accept self, others, and trust the Universe has our well-being at heart and is overseeing all our circumstances. We are never lost or forgotten, nor are we ever compared with anyone else.

Every day is a choice between limiting language and empty behaviors or vulnerable curiosity and fearless exploration.

Homework for Overcoming Comparative Language

While it may be difficult to acknowledge, is the comparative mindset holding you captive? Insecurities cause us to notice things we are doubtful or apprehensive about within ourselves and our circumstances. Instead of living a life of fulfillment, the comparative mindset can lead to envy and jealousy, feelings of powerlessness, hopelessness, unfulfillment, or resentfulness.

The comparative mindset relies heavily on assumptions and, my oh my, does it have a lot of assumptions. It is the cousin to the JM and doesn't need to inquire because it already knows what's fair and who has it better than whom because it notices almost everything. Knowing who we are and living out our personal truths assist in not noticing so much what's going on around us. Expressing gratitude is one contributing factor to overcoming the comparative mindset. So is looking at life through the lenses of horizontal thinking versus vertical thinking.

The comparative mindset is so difficult to talk about, which can lead us to isolate. It can be harsh and critical sometimes, which subconsciously leads to feelings of guilt and shame. This can lead to attempts at covering itself up by reminding us how ridiculous or unfair others and their circumstances are. Comparisons are always divisive; that's the point. It acknowledges differences and measures in a manner that someone has the short end of the stick—always. It also likes to justify why it chose a different path than others. However, justification is not necessary; it's just evidence that the comparative mindset is ruling.

If these thoughts, mindset, and attitudes sound familiar, put the measuring stick down and grab ahold of grace and gratitude, which will lead to personal fulfillment. Remember, if expressions of grace and gratitude are not already a part of your daily thoughts, neural pathway development is the way to change this.

TAKE YOUR TIME AND DO THE WORK!

The comparative mindset causes so many challenges for us internally. It begins with uncertainties that run loose in our BS, manifesting as insecurities. Then these insecurities create an unsafe environment where we begin questioning ourselves, our worth, our value, our correctness, you name it. Insecurities can have us questioning anything and everything before we even know what hit us. It doesn't stop there. To convince ourselves we're okay, we compare ourselves to those we see around us. Either we are less than them, more than them, envious of them, jealous of them, angry or resentful of them... The list goes on, and it's miserable for everyone.

Most importantly this week, do not be hard on yourself if you find yourself battling the comparative mindset. At some point in life, comparisons served you to some degree while your self-concept was being developed. Unfortunately, while it was attempting to keep you safe, it taught you how to measure yourself against others, which led to getting frustrated at them, yourself, or both. But now is your time to acknowledge that there is an alternative to the comparative mindset. Through mental exercises, you can build new neural pathways by training your brain to stop measuring yourself and others.

Once again, acceptance is key. Upon catching the comparative mindset in action, remember to stop measuring yourself and your circumstances against others. We are all on a horizontal playing field and can move in any given direction at any time. Our options are innumerable. All our lives are full of potential and possibility, and we can never compare apples to oranges. We are each as unique as our individual fingerprints and even more so because our lives are ever-evolving. There is literally no possible way to compare our lives and circumstances against one another. Through gentle observation, take the time this week to capture comparative limiting language. Then, identify the underlying uncertainties and insecurities and replace them with healthy truths while building neural pathways full of security and gratitude.

OBSERVATIONS OF THE COMPARATIVE MINDSET

Take a few moments to observe the language, feelings, and uncertainty that often accompany the comparative mindset. Then observe how others may experience this mindset and how it may limit you. Check those that apply to your experiences or fill in the blanks with additional observations you have made pertaining to this limiting mindset.

Comparative language:

☐ Must be nice
☐ Wish I had or could...
☐ Wish I was that lucky or fortunate
☐ Devaluing the achievements of others
☐ Defending your position and why it is different than someone else's
☐ Sometimes accusatory or other judgmental words
☐ Other ___________________________

Feelings that often accompany comparative language:

☐ Resentfulness
☐ Bitterness or soreness
☐ Jealousy
☐ Envy
☐ Unimpressed
☐ Other ___________________________

Uncertainty: Are my circumstances enough?

Others may experience me as:

☐ Pungent or hostile
☐ Uptight or suspicious
☐ Phony or as a pretender
☐ Cold-blooded
☐ Uncordial
☐ Arrogant or ungenuine
☐ Sarcastic or rude
☐ Other ___________________________

The comparative mindset may lead to:

☐ Inability to be genuinely happy for the good fortune of others
☐ Inability to congratulate others
☐ Inability to acknowledge others and their achievements
☐ People feeling unappreciated and unacknowledged
☐ People feeling unsafe, disrespected, or invalidated
☐ Few and shallow relationships
☐ Counterfeit joy—appearing happy over feeling happy
☐ Other ___________________________

Daily Journal Practice

Following are journal topics and exercises for the next seven days, but feel free to continue such exercises until you feel yourself being able to automatically capture and replace the comparative limiting language within your mind. It will take some time, but the neural pathways will develop as you do these exercises daily, and eventually, you will no longer find it necessary to write things down. The brain will learn to process automatically as you train it through such exercises as those contained within this program.

Day 1: Journal Your Battle with Comparative Language

- Take a few moments to journal about your struggle with comparisons.
- Write about the insecurities that form the comparative mindset.
- Where might these insecurities have come from?
- What does life look like if you are free of these insecurities?

Day 2: Journal the Uncertainties of Insecurities

- What uncertainties surface amid these insecurities?
- What can you accept amid these insecurities?
- Where are you attempting to level up? What does it feel like?
- Where might you be attempting to progress vertically? Horizontally?

Day 3: Thought Capturing

Write down any comparative thoughts you have today, also including jealousy and envy. Pay special attention and log *all* the insecurities relating to a comparative mindset. When did you find yourself comparing yourself with others?

Day 4: Thought Replacement

Now replace the comparative thoughts from Day 3 with words of security and gratitude by observing, gathering data and information, listening to and trusting that small, still voice inside. What is possible with this mindset?

Day 5: Thought Capturing and Replacement

Write down all comparative, jealous, or envious thoughts you have today and immediately replace them with secure and grateful thoughts through gentle observations.

Day 6: Thought Capturing and Replacement

Again, write down all comparative, jealous, or envious thoughts you have today and immediately replace them with secure and grateful thoughts through gentle observations.

Day 7: Transition from a Comparative Mindset to a Grateful Mindset

Categorize and list all your concerns of the day into the comparative mindset column or the secure and grateful mindset column. Once listed, use grace and gratitude to lead you to calm contemplation by reframing all the items in the comparative column to make secure and grateful statements.

Continue thought capturing and replacement exercises to build neural pathways that support a secure and grateful mindset.

PRACTICE AND BUILD THE NEURAL PATHWAYS OF A SECURE AND GRATEFUL MINDSET

Thoughts of the Comparative Mindset:	**Thoughts of the Secure and Grateful Mindset:**

Reframe comparative thoughts with thoughts of security and gratitude:

JOURNAL TOPICS TO CONTEMPLATE FOR OVERCOMING THE LIES OF THE COMPARATIVE MINDSET

Grab your notebook or *The BS of Better Journal* to contemplate and process overcoming the comparative mindset. Below are cues and questions to begin assessing the costs and the payoffs of allowing the comparative mindset, but don't stop here. Remember, journal those prompts that stand out to you and ask yourself other difficult questions and concerns that may not be listed but are hiding deep within yourself. You already know these concerns; this is your time to listen! Identify and observe the comparative mindset so that you can stop what's causing those sore feelings of bitterness and resentfulness when you are ready.

Inquisitive Alternatives:

- ☐ What other thoughts, words, body language, or behaviors surface during the comparative mindset?
- ☐ Who and what am I grateful for in my life?
- ☐ Who do I care about that I can genuinely compliment?
- ☐ Who do I care about that I can genuinely congratulate on a recent accomplishment?
- ☐ In this moment, to whom can I extend grace?
- ☐ I accept myself by...
- ☐ I accept others by...
- ☐ I accept my circumstances by...
- ☐ I will extend grace and respect to myself by...
- ☐ I will extend grace and respect to others by...
- ☐ The gift I can give to myself now that will make a significant impact on how I will feel about myself is...
- ☐ Other ______________________

Neural Pathway Development Support

It cannot be reiterated enough that neural pathway development is crucial for sustainable healthy change in thoughts and behaviors. Heightening self-awareness, committing to personal reflection time, and completing acceptance and action plans daily and weekly will develop the neural pathways that serve you. For additional daily processing support, please see **Appendix A – Neural Pathway Development Support**. What would it look like if we asked the difficult yet beneficial questions until the questions were no longer difficult? When you're ready, try it and see.

> **"What you WANT is irrelevant; what you've CHOSEN is at hand."**
> **~Spock**

7

EMPTY-COMMITMENT LIMITING LANGUAGE

"Seriously, how difficult can this possibly be? Why does this have to be so hard? It didn't used to be. Why do I make commitments to myself and break them? Why do I not work toward the things I say I want? Why do I not prioritize my time for the things that interest me? I'm *trying*, but I never succeed in this area. I *want* this so bad but can't make it happen. I *wish* I had the fortitude to do this. I *hope* this comes through for me, but I always let myself down. I *want* and *hope* for this but often don't put forth the effort to chase it. I've *tried* for this multiple times over the years but don't follow through. This is important to me, so why don't I allow myself to do it?"

Kelly was beating herself up because she let herself down yet again on her weight loss journey: year after year, yoyo diet after yoyo diet, joining yet another gym and canceling the membership six months later having only worked out a handful of days. She bounces back and forth in her mind with reasons and questions. "If my thyroid wasn't messed up, I'd have more energy, wouldn't pile on as much weight, and could lose weight faster and keep it off." Then she toggles the other way. "Yes, that's true, but it's still your thyroid and your body. You're still responsible for it no matter how easy or difficult. You know what to do, Kelly! Just do what you know you're supposed to do!"

The battle in her mind rages on every day throughout the day, like an ongoing and irritating toothache. "I've *tried*, and I can't stick with it. I *wish* I had so-and-so's body style, then it wouldn't be so difficult. I *hope* these new diet pills work; the last ones sure didn't. I would sure *like to* join the gym again, but I don't know if Joan will go with me this time. I hate going by myself..." On and on, her mind goes. Empty thoughts. Empty words. Empty commitments. They all leave her void of what she's longing for, yet the cycle in her mind doesn't stop. Kelly isn't the only one who struggles with this mindset.

Why do you think Kelly is struggling with doing something she says she's so passionate about? Self-sabotage and other self-defeating behaviors could be manifesting, but most of the time, it goes back to the mind being on cruise control. I say this all the time and I will keep saying it: We don't do what's healthy; we do what's familiar. If Kelly for the past few weeks has not been eating healthy and exercising, simply put, those neural pathways are not programmed in her brain. Usually, we don't even think about these options because they're not there in our brains. This is why weight loss groups, accountability groups, daily or weekly check-ins, life coaching, daily cues or prompts, and other such support methods are so helpful. These methods remind us and bring information to our brains that assist in developing neural pathways that focus on the objective.

Yes, we may think about weight loss every day, but it's the *way* we think about it that makes a huge difference. If we are shaming ourselves for the weight we gained, for not eating healthy nor exercising yesterday, or for other reasons not even pertaining to weight loss, chances are, we are not supporting healthy neural pathway development. Instead, we are reinforcing negative pathways that already exist and are a big reason why we are stuck in the first place. Condemnation doesn't lead to healthy neural pathway development for sustainable change. Our minds are on cruise control, and whatever we've been doing the past few weeks is likely what we'll keep doing until something drastic takes place.

CRUISE CONTROL KEEPS US FROM WHAT WE WANT

"This is so stupid!" I said to my husband on the phone while driving alone to Colorado to visit one of our sons. I had rented an SUV for the journey to save miles on my car, and it was acting strange. The cruise control would not work properly; it seemed like it was not getting fuel at certain times because it kept slowing down and then it would pick back up. This went on for a few hours. I am known for being a patient person unless someone is hurting or disrespecting someone else, but this really stretched my patience. It was a 14-hour drive, and at this rate, it was probably going to take me 18 hours. **All I wanted** was for the car to drive normally! I mean, really, is that too much to ask? Nice mindset, huh?

I kept **trying** to figure it out, but it was so aggravating, making a normally enjoyable trip extremely frustrating. My husband is mechanically inclined and a whiz at troubleshooting problems, even over the phone. Man, I sure **hoped** my husband could shine some light on this situation. When he asked me what the problem was, I was so frustrated that I did more complaining about the problem than explaining the details. My husband calmly kept asking me questions. After he gathered enough information, he said that it sounded like it may be some type of radar or sonar detection within the vehicle.

While he was speaking, the car started doing it again. I felt validated in my complaints and reiterated to my husband, "See," although he couldn't see anything, "there it goes again!" He inquired what was different: "What's around you?" I noticed I was approaching an 18-wheeler, which I shared. Huffing and puffing more, I said to Scott, "**I sure would like to** have rented a normal car that wouldn't be sucking all my energy right now! This is so stupid!" Scott patiently listened to me ramble and then told me to go around the tractor trailer as my vehicle continued to slow down. So, after checking the mirrors to see if it was safe to merge, I put on my blinker and changed lanes. As soon as I was most of the way in the passing lane, to my amazement, the vehicle automatically sped up. I couldn't believe it. I thought for sure there was something wrong with that stupid car!

My husband then explained to me what was going on. The automatic emergency braking (AEB) system is part of the driver-assist technology in certain vehicles. It can pick up on surrounding vehicles, pedestrians, and other obstacles while driving. Radar mounted on the front of the vehicle detects how close you are to objects in front of you, and when it detects you're too close, it engages the AEB system to slow the car down.

I love the open highway with my foot easily accessible to the speed of a supercharged engine. I can drive for hours, listening to my favorite jazz CD while enjoying the freedom of the open road. With that being the case, I rely heavily on a vehicle's cruise control to keep my tendency to speed in check. On rare occasions, I've found myself driving three digits without even realizing it. Therefore, cruise control is a great tool to keep myself and others safe while I enjoy my drive.

However, this vehicle had programming that was too cautious for my tastes. It was slowing down to protect me from things that were not a real threat. So, after understanding my husband's explanation, I spent the next 30 minutes paying close attention to the vehicle. I learned more about the vehicle's programming as I studied when the automated braking system engaged. I paid close attention to the distance between my car and other vehicles and quickly started predicting when the AEB system would engage. With this knowledge and predictions, I could maneuver the car around situations to keep the radar from sensing a supposed problem.

When the radar seemed overly sensitive, I would manually override the system, make my own reasonable judgments and act accordingly, and then reengage it when I felt it would no longer be unnecessarily triggered. I learned how to work around the radar's sensitivities. Once I did that, I developed an appreciation for the programming. I worked with the vehicle instead of being frustrated with it and fighting against it. I learned how to work within its parameters, disengaging it when it wasn't serving me, and this made the rest of the trip more enjoyable and probably safer. Once I learned to appreciate the vehicle's programming, it opened the door for me to explore where I wanted to allow this automatic programming to work for me and where I wanted to manually override it. Hmmm, there might be something to this.

Initially, I had allowed my frustration to build up for hours before taking any action. By the time I decided to take action, I was so convinced that the *stupid* car was messed up, I was not open to possible solutions to the problem. It was easier for me to keep believing the car was the problem instead of solving the problem. I wasted time on cruise control with empty-commitment words like **want**, **try**, **hope**, and **would like to** instead of stopping the vehicle, doing a little research, developing an action plan to alter my frustrating circumstances, and then solving the problem. When I finally opened my mindset to the idea that perhaps there was a solution, it changed everything. Cruise control often keeps us spinning our wheels. When we listen intently to ourselves, we can hear it, but most of the time, we push those faint internal cries off to the side. We keep on cruising because that's what we've been doing so that's what we keep doing.

UTILIZING AND OVERRIDING CRUISE CONTROL

I thought I had **tried** everything. I **wanted** a peaceful drive to visit our son. I **would like to** have rented a simple vehicle that worked. I **hoped** Scott could help me. All the **wanting**, **trying**, **hoping**, and **would-like-tos** got me nowhere as I drove for hours frustrated. This whole scenario got me thinking, as it is similar to our lives. We cruise right along in our vehicles, which is like our lives. Our mind is in the driver's seat. The radar is like our emotions, the programming that sets the criteria for the radar to signal us is our belief systems, and our defense mechanisms are like the AEB system.

You may want to read that again, but let me explain it this way: Cruise control is like the regulatory measure that our brains attempt to consistently coast along within. It's the familiar neural pathways in our brain that house our habitual thoughts and behaviors. Our brains prefer the path of least resistance, the one that requires the least amount of thought and energy to implement. Another book in this series will talk more about the brain, but basically, our brains will choose what is familiar over what is healthy any day unless intentional action is implemented to change course. Again, we don't do what's healthy but rather what is familiar. Familiar isn't always the healthiest course, but it certainly breeds a sense of safety because we've already determined that we can cope with and survive whatever is deemed familiar.

It is important to recognize that every day we wake up with our familiar cruise control engaged. That cruise control will keep us functioning with the least amount of effort as possible and will keep us pointed in the direction where we feel the safest. We have automated responses or defense mechanisms toward most situations based on our varying internal and external life requirements and expectations, which we have each learned and established. These internal and external requirements and expectations are directed not by what we want or by what is healthiest, but rather by what the mind deems familiar because only then is it predictable, safe, and acceptable.

Over time, this became the programming we live by and formed our beLIEf system (BS). This BS programming houses the criteria for the rules and expectations of our radar, and our radar is our emotions. When our emotional radar detects a potential threat, it will engage the AEB system to change some aspect of the current course to protect us, engaging our defense mechanisms. This radar senses and alerts us of a potential problem so that we can proceed with caution in a safe and predictable direction. When that radar detects a problem, it triggers us, and one of two things will occur. Either our automated emergency braking system, which is our defense mechanisms, will engage, or we can disengage those automated responses and make calculated decisions by doing a manual override.

While these defense mechanisms are beneficial and have protected and served us well in many instances, they have also been a grave disservice in many areas of life. Therefore, the key here is to know ourselves so well that when these automated responses attempt to kick in, we manually take the control away. Becoming a master at manual overrides is not an easy feat, but it's crucial for a healthy and joyful life of peace and significance. It's also crucial for taking action to obtain the things we say we want.

The manual override is dependent on our individual values and preferences in lieu of the programmed BS. The manual override allows us to see beyond the emotional state of the moment to make calculated choices based on objectivity and an openness to various forms of information. How much easier would our life be if we could set the programming of our vehicle's cruise control? Imagine writing your own radar programming based on your personal values and preferences instead of a distorted BS. Even more powerful, imagine having the ability to disengage all programming when the parameters seem too sensitive or rigid in certain circumstances. How would that change some things in life? Can you see the value in learning about the BS of your own programming and altering it to suit who and where you are now? With a little intention and a heightened sense of awareness, you can do just that! We are going to do some exercises to increase your personal awareness so that you can begin reprogramming your own cruise control or overriding it when it is not serving you. But before we do, let's explore the language we often use when we are not getting what we say we want but are not quite ready to do the work to get there.

WANT – WHAT DOES THAT WORD MEAN ANYWAY?

Unfortunately, most of our lives, we are in cruise control and not really pursuing what we think and say that we want. Oh sure, I hear the mind chatter now and totally get it! We have enormous reasons why we are not pursuing our wants; after all, we have enormous responsibilities and people to tend to, which consumes most of our time. And of course, external circumstances play a huge part in our availability for the things we desire. However, if we frequently find ourselves lacking in our desires, then we must look deeper in the mirror because our needs are not being met in one way or another.

Wanting means we are lacking or void of something we desire. **Trying** means we are lacking efficient efforts that lead to the results we desire. Trying means we are ineffectively attempting but not achieving. **Hope** means we are trusting and anticipating for something we lack. **Would like to** means we are expressing our preference for something we lack. All these words are expressions of lacking. If we want something, do we have it? No! If we are trying for something, are we doing it? No! If we are hoping for something, do we have it? No! If we would like to do or have something, is it present in our life? No!

Lack! And do you know what that means? **Lack** is the state of being without or not having enough of something, being deficient, short, inadequate, insufficient. The word lack stems partially from the Middle Dutch word *laken*, meaning lack and blame. You know where we're headed with this, right? When we are lacking, we blame. We do most of the time, don't we? We blame ourselves, someone else, or circumstances for our lack.

If we are lacking something as an adult, who is responsible for filling that lack? Obvious, right? But it's not so easy to take responsibility for filling that lack. This is where blaming and complaints come in. Oh yes, every time we complain about something or blame (which often looks like excuses, or reasons, if we're working it to lessen the blow of the reality), it is an indicator that we are not pursuing what we want.

When we use empty-commitment language, we are telling our brains that we lack something, sparking thoughts and feelings of deficiency, scarceness, inadequacy, privation, emptiness, and insufficiency. How will we ever find fulfillment with our minds programmed with such void neural pathways? We won't! We don't! It is important to identify areas we may feel we are lacking in; we individually decide what those areas may be, by the way, not someone else, and not out of obligation. We decide, independent from anyone else, if we are ready for movement to fill the lack in our own lives.

READY OR NOT

Once we recognize an area we feel void in, we have the option of making one of two choices: 1) accept ourselves until we are ready to create movement, or 2) prepare for movement when we are ready. What is ready, anyway? **Ready** defined means to prepare mentally and physically. We sometimes get this nudging feeling when we are getting close to being ready for movement. We feel ourselves sort of wanting to participate, and when we start preparing mentally and physically, we know it's almost time. There's a silent whisper of hope and possibility fluttering around. Many times, it happens after a scare or challenging time.

Ever play hide-and-seek? Remember that freeing and sneaky feeling of taking off when the seeker begins counting? It's exciting, and our brains create a storm contemplating the most elusive spaces possible. Anyone ever get in trouble for hiding somewhere you weren't supposed to? Yeah, me too, but wasn't it great? Man, we could come up with some ingenious places, couldn't we? Funny enough, most of the time we thought for sure we were the only ones to think of that place.

Remember picking the perfect spot and crouching down, trying to calm your breath and snickering as not to be heard in this all-original location? Remember the feeling of trying not to laugh as you hunkered down, shoulders closely hugging your neck, because that sneaky feeling was so much fun? Those were the great moments!

But hey, what about those times the seeker was almost to the magic number and we still hadn't found a place? Our fellow playmates were loudly whispering, "over there" or "over here" or "get down, here they come." Remember that feeling of fumbling around trying to find a place, confused and lost as the anxiety steadily increased with every number the seeker yelled? Oh my goodness, I'm scared and laughing right now just thinking about that feeling; 92…93…94…come on, come on, do something, make a choice, get somewhere fast! The seeker continues and hopelessness starts to set in; 98, 99, 100…READY OR NOT, HERE I COME!

Then BAM, it hits us. We lost. The seeker turns around, and we are the first one they see. "Found you! You're out!" the seeker says as they merrily skip along to find the next poor goober. But our minds start racing. "Wait, they're still playing. Am I the only one to not have found a spot? Forget it, I quit. May as well give up; everyone else already has the best spots anyway. I'm tired of playing this stupid game."

Remember those times? Those were the not-so-great moments. The brain protected us by reminding us of all the reasons we weren't ready because it felt like it was supposed to be ready like everyone else. The same thing happens in our lives as adults. We feel like we are supposed to be ready. After all, we see so many other people doing it, there must be something wrong with us, right? No! One important aspect to keep in mind is that we are not always ready, and that's okay. Sometimes we are not mentally prepared, or maybe we're not ready to invest much effort in certain things for a number of reasons. If we allow internal and external pressures to push us when we are not ready, it can have ill effects. We may feel frazzled, experience physical anxiety, and make choices that will not serve us or others out of haste if we push into areas we are not mentally and physically prepared for. Let's face it: sometimes, we're just not ready, and that's that.

Empty-commitment words indicate we are lacking in an area but are not ready to do what it takes to fill the void. We are not ready to take the responsibility necessary for change, so we pretend to put forth some effort, although minimal, yielding little if any rewards. Of course, we are not ready because the neural pathways in our brains that have been strengthened are void of optimistic opportunity in this area we say we want, hope for, would like to, and are trying for. So, let's pause for a moment and be gentle with ourselves.

These pathways were at one time beneficial to us, even though they may not be serving us now. I will repeat this over and over. The point of this is to heighten awareness, not to pressure ourselves into complaining, blaming ourselves, and feeling guilty for lack of effort. We put forth plenty of effort every day somewhere doing something, but maybe not in an area we say we want because we aren't ready to work toward it right now. So, a simple acknowledgment of what is going on under the surface can be helpful without all that pressure. In certain areas, we may want to sit the bench for a bit. If so, accept the bench while there instead of being frustrated with yourself or others for being there. Acceptance keeps us at peace until we are ready.

You know, we are all abundant in something, and it costs us. For some of us, perhaps it's long working hours and financial rewards. For others, maybe it's plenty of time spent with our children, yielding the rewards of many "I love you"s. For some, maybe it's hours spent watching TV, safe away from the fear and frustration of the outside world, or maybe it's staying surrounded by drama so that we don't have time to see our own limitations. Yes, we are all abundant in something.

Inquiring into our own areas of abundance can be enlightening. One mental note to hang onto is that while we are investing in one area and growing in abundance, we will be lacking in another area. This is why balance is so important. Is it healthy to spend *all* our time working, or taking care of our children, or watching TV, or engaging in drama? Probably not. So, keep an eye out for balanced abundance and measure it only by what is important to us as individuals, not by anyone else. Keep in mind that abundance is not abundant unless it is balanced. We all invest somewhere, and it costs us something.

The reality here is that the opposite of lack is abundance, and we decide what we will be abundant in by the neural pathways we choose to strengthen in our brains. Sometimes that's career, sometimes it's health, sometimes it's relationships, sometimes it is busyness or quietness, etc. As we mature in areas over time, we often find more balance in more areas.

However, sometimes circumstances occur that create temporary seasons where we frankly feel fortunate to simply survive. "Screw balance today, my goal is to keep my head above water!" Ever feel like that? Yes, we all do. That's another reason acceptance is crucial. The point here: Identify and observe where we are and then accept it until we are ready for movement. Sometimes we want to be on cruise control, even though it may not be the most comfortable and we may get triggered. Sometimes it's easier that way until we're ready to tackle something new. When we are ready, we can use the empty-commitment language as an indicator that something in our lives may want more attention than we've been giving it. We can simply acknowledge this and accept the bench until we're ready to get our hands dirty and do the work. We'll know when that is when we begin to prepare mentally and physically. Until then, accept!

WHEN WE'RE NOT READY

This book is being written during the COVID crisis in the United States. Our lives, along with those of many others in our area, have drastically changed. Most of the places where we used to go, we don't go anymore. Most of the things we used to do, we don't do anymore. So many things have changed! Right now, my husband and I are living in our fifth wheel on our small plot of ground while building a small cabin for our retirement plans while scaling and managing our six-figure part-time business. We made a lot of sacrifices to make most of our dreams come true. Sometimes those sacrifices can be demanding. It's easy to lose sight of some of our priorities during such times.

The circumstances took a toll on me personally. I allowed certain things to change that I wish I wouldn't have. But I did, so now what? Well, the big thing that changed for me was gaining the majority of the 60 pounds back that I had lost a year before. I did not gain the weight back because I couldn't eat healthy or exercise. I gained the weight because I allowed myself to eat unhealthy and I chose not to exercise when my circumstances made it more difficult to do so.

Oh yes, there are many reasons why, but it doesn't change the end result and the consequences of my action, or inaction. At night now, I'm back to throwing the sheet over myself real quick, hoping that my husband will not notice the extra roll around my waistline that I'm bringing to bed once again. Yes, we have raised five children, but we still make it a priority to have fun in the bedroom. And man, right about now, that's a lot more difficult mentally and physically. Stairs are more challenging, and my joints are a lot sorer again. It's more difficult to keep up with our precious little grandbabies, and I don't have near the energy I did after losing all that weight the year before. Can anyone else identify with this? It's uncomfortable. I don't like it. For quite a while, I wasn't ready to do anything about it.

Am I down on myself? No! Do I battle thoughts, feelings, and behaviors because of it? Yes! But I refuse to be entrapped by the disappointment and embarrassment of my weight gain. Instead, I gently observe my thoughts and behaviors, make choices, and extend acceptance and grace at the end of each day. I remind myself almost daily, sometimes multiple times a day, of certain personal truths that assist me in making choices that will yield the results I desire. Do I make desirable choices every day? No! I also am not fooling myself by pretending that I'm trying something that I'm not actually taking action on. I'm not acting like I want something that I'm not willing to invest energy in at this time and am fully aware that when I'm ready, I'll take the action. But for now, some days I choose to eat healthy and move more, and some days I don't. Through it all, I've made it a point to extend to, and receive grace from, the mirror.

I do this by talking gently with myself and setting reminders on my phone, hanging them on my fridge or purse, journaling, and putting notes in my car and on my desk. Just little uplifting and supportive notes remind me what's important because, in the midst of busy life, I can easily forget and lose track of what I desire while on cruise control. Some reminders sound like this: 1) Exercise is not an obligation. It is a choice that when made yields the results of a healthy body that I enjoy and feel comfortable in. 2) A healthy food regimen is not a restrictive prison keeping me from my favorite tasty treats. Tasty treats are not rewards; they are scrumptious choices that come with a heavy price when indulged upon. 3) I am indescribable and invaluable regardless of my weight, but that rock'n bod sure feels good when you're ready for it.

Do you see the acceptance and grace I extend to myself with a touch of humor? This acceptance and grace while appreciating the humorous side of humanity is exactly what keeps me in a state of joy regardless of my weight or circumstances. This is why my husband and I have so much fun in our marriage, with our children, and with our grandbabies. It's why our friendships are fun, lighthearted, and safe. Am I always happy? No! But happiness is not joy. Happiness is enjoying a temporary moment or circumstance. Joy is the sustainable foundation in my soul that reminds me daily that I am invaluable and that life is on my side regardless of choices or circumstances. Happiness is a fleeting feeling; joy is a healthy mindset. We can have a happy moment, but if our attitude is not healthy, we will never experience or sustain joy.

For this reason, my sole professional objective is to assist in ***Reducing Life's Pressures***. Our joy is greatly affected by the pressures we allow and place upon ourselves. The limiting language we use often reflects our mindsets. If we are using better, inadequate, guilt-ridden, judgmental, worry-infested, comparative, empty-commitment, victimization, or other forms of limiting language, there is a high probability that our joy is being diminished. Think about it. It's tough to maintain a joyful mindset when we're pressuring ourselves with these forms of BS. At the end of the day, joy is what most of us secretly long for but have trouble hanging on to. That is because it is crowded out by all the BS we allow and engage in, which is exactly why I took on ***The BS of Better*** program. The homework in this chapter gives us an opportunity to reflect on areas that we can decide to take action on or accept in order to experience a joyful mindset.

Intentionally disengaging the cruise control of our minds is not easy, but through daily processing, it is absolutely possible and probable. It will be a battle because the mind will try to keep us on cruise control where it is familiar, predictable, and safe. But the more we practice intentionally making calculated choices daily, the easier it will become. Remember, one key factor is self-awareness—knowing, respecting, and accepting ourselves so well that we can disengage the cruise control and make a calculated choice based on the results we want to experience. Empty-commitment words leave us lacking, which often diverts our attention to blaming ourselves, others, or our circumstances for being void of our desires. Blaming is never helpful, so nip those thoughts and behaviors in the bud as soon as you recognize them. Instead, capture and replace such thoughts with acceptance and action plans that will promote a sustainable mindset of joy and fulfillment. Okay, let's get to work by spending the next week processing homework that will build healthy neural pathways that promote us yielding our desires.

Cruise control will not manifest our desires; intention backed by action and acceptance will.

Homework for Overcoming Empty-Commitment Language

Do you find yourself longing for something but not obtaining it? Ever feel void or empty? Ever make commitments to yourself or others and break them? Empty-commitment language represents something we are lacking in but not ready to tackle. Our internal cruise control keeps us in a pretend state that says we are making attempts at fulfillment by trying, wanting, hoping, wishing, and so forth, yet we remain void.

Assessing our level of readiness to take action is important in order to avoid feelings of disappointment and emptiness. If we are ready to take action, we can develop action plans and simply take small steps daily that will eventually lead us where we desire to be. No attempts are even necessary, just consistent and steady movement with one foot in front of the other daily. However, if we are not ready, the alternative is to create acceptance plans so that our peace and joy can remain intact until we are ready for movement.

TAKE YOUR TIME AND DO THE WORK!

Remember, most of the time, we do what is familiar instead of what is healthy. Therefore, it is important that we monitor our thoughts and behaviors to ensure we yield the results we would like to see in our lives. Our brains love cruise control but are programmed with sensitive information, like radars waiting to detect something odd in order to protect ourselves. This information will easily trigger us and throw us right into our defense mechanisms if we are not observant. It will also keep us stuck in familiar, yet unproductive, habitual thoughts and behaviors that make it difficult to put forth energy that will yield the rewards we desire.

This happens a lot when we are experiencing a mindset that is not committed to investing in the things we desire. Cruise control will not manifest our desires; only intention backed by action and acceptance will. There is a fine line here because if we place too much emphasis on the action itself, we can become overwhelmed and exhausted. Yes, we want to take action, but not at the expense of accepting ourselves where we are right now. When healthy, assessing our personal priorities and creating an action plan to achieve our desires will reduce the pressures and triggers in our lives. This will assist in promoting a mindset of joy, but only when packaged in acceptance and grace.

This week, remember to extend grace and acceptance to yourself regardless of the choices you make. Gently observe the empty-commitment language and how it may be affecting your life and the lives of those you care about. Notice the things you want, wish for, hope for, and try to do and then notice how those experiences make you feel, whether or not achieved. Hold your journal close this week and process all your actions and your inactions. Record how you extended grace to yourself amid both action and inaction. It is important to note that the objective of this chapter is not to reduce you to a human doing. You've had enough of that. The goal is to liberate you into a human being that gently observes your desires, aligns your thoughts and behaviors with them, and extends acceptance and grace regardless of choice and outcome.

OBSERVATIONS OF THE EMPTY-COMMITMENT MINDSET

Take a few moments to observe the language, feelings, and uncertainty that often accompany the empty-commitment mindset. Then observe how others may experience this mindset and how it may limit you. Check those that apply to your experiences or fill in the blanks with additional observations you have made pertaining to this limiting mindset.

Empty-commitment language:

- ☐ Trying
- ☐ Want to
- ☐ Would like to
- ☐ Hope to
- ☐ Wish
- ☐ Other ________________________

Feelings that often accompany empty-commitment language:

- ☐ Continual longing
- ☐ Void
- ☐ Uncommitted
- ☐ Unfulfilled
- ☐ Unsatisfied
- ☐ Disappointed
- ☐ Unhappy
- ☐ Hollow or without substance
- ☐ Other ________________________

Uncertainty: How can I minimize feelings of failure, disappointment, or hopelessness surrounding my present decisions or lack thereof?

Others may experience me as:

- ☐ Unreliable or flighty
- ☐ Untrustworthy or unstable
- ☐ Insatiable or discontented
- ☐ Undisciplined or wavering
- ☐ Other ________________________

The empty-commitment mindset may lead to:

- ☐ Voidance of heartwarming desires
- ☐ Wavering thoughts and behaviors
- ☐ Repeatedly shifting directions due to lack of commitment
- ☐ Procrastinating or poor time management
- ☐ Poor follow-through
- ☐ Wanting more than achieving
- ☐ Other ________________________

Daily Journal Practice

Following are journal topics and exercises for the next seven days, but feel free to continue such exercises until you feel yourself being able to automatically capture and replace the empty-commitment limiting language within your mind. It will take some time, but the neural pathways will develop as you do these exercises daily, and eventually, you will no longer find it necessary to write things down. The brain will learn to process automatically as you train it through such exercises as those contained within this program.

Day 1: Journal Your Battle with Empty-Commitment Language

- What did you wish today?
- What did you hope for today?
- What did you long for today?
- Where did you feel void, empty, or disappointed today?

Day 2: Journal Your Battle with Trying

- What did you try but not achieve today?
- How did you feel about your level of commitment in this area?
- How did you extend acceptance and grace to yourself in this area?

Day 3: Gently Observe Others, Explore, and Learn

- Without comparison, spend the entire day and evening gently observing the commitments others are keeping with themselves.
- What rewards are they receiving due to their commitment to themselves?
- Through gentle observation and without comparison, what can you learn about yourself from watching their behaviors and seeing their rewards?

Day 4: Thought Capturing

- Write down any empty-commitment words or actions you notice within yourself today; try, wish, hope, want, would like to, secret longings, broken commitments, etc.
- Define the word **action** and describe what it looks like in your life.
- Define the word **acceptance** and describe what it looks like in your life when you are not ready to take action.

Day 5: Thought Replacement

Take the empty-commitment thoughts, words, and actions from Day 4 and replace them with thoughts, words, and actions of fruitful and fulfilling thoughts and actions mingled with acceptance and grace in lieu of expectation and pressure.

Day 6: What Am I Ready For? What May Stop Me?

- What commitment(s) are you ready to explore at this time?
- What might prevent you from keeping these commitment(s) to yourself?

Day 7: Acceptance Plan

- In the areas you are not ready to explore or alter at this time, journal words of acceptance and grace that will support you with no expectations or pressure as you work to develop neural pathways that are fruitful and fulfilling.
- How will you extend grace to yourself and others regardless of your readiness to change at this time? Who can support you?

Continue thought capturing and replacement exercises to build neural pathways that support a fruitful and fulfilled mindset.

PRACTICE AND BUILD THE NEURAL PATHWAYS OF A FRUITFUL AND FULFILLED MINDSET

Thoughts of the Empty-Commitment Mindset:	Thoughts of the Fruitful and Fulfilled Mindset:

Reframe empty-commitment thoughts with those of a fruitful and fulfilled mindset:

JOURNAL TOPICS TO CONTEMPLATE FOR OVERCOMING THE LIES OF THE EMPTY-COMMITMENT MINDSET

Grab your notebook or *The BS of Better Journal* to contemplate and process overcoming the empty-commitment mindset. Below are cues and questions to begin assessing the costs and the payoffs of allowing the empty-commitment mindset, but don't stop here. Remember, journal those prompts that stand out to you and ask yourself other difficult questions and concerns that may not be listed but are hiding deep within yourself. You already know these concerns; this is your time to listen! Identify and observe the empty-commitment mindset so that you can stop what's causing those hollow feelings of being unpleased or unfulfilled when you are ready.

Inquisitive Alternatives:

- ☐ What habits are on cruise control that are serving me?
- ☐ What habits are on cruise control that are not serving me?
- ☐ What would I like to increase abundance in?
- ☐ What reward(s) am I ready to invest energy in?
- ☐ How will I accept what I am not ready to invest in?
- ☐ What reward is worth the price of commitment at this time?
- ☐ What fulfillment may materialize by choosing to override habitual thoughts and behaviors at this time?
- ☐ Other ________________________

Neural Pathway Development Support

It cannot be reiterated enough that neural pathway development is crucial for sustainable healthy change in thoughts and behaviors. Heightening self-awareness, committing to personal reflection time, and completing acceptance and action plans daily and weekly will develop the neural pathways that serve you. For additional daily processing support, please see **Appendix A – Neural Pathway Development Support**. What would it look like if we asked the difficult yet beneficial questions until the questions were no longer difficult? When you're ready, try it and see.

It's not the size of the difficulty; it's the mindset with which we approach the difficulty that makes it more or less difficult.

8

VICTIMIZATION LIMITING LANGUAGE

"You just don't understand, that's not possible," Jenny snapped at her best friend Beth a few years ago.

"Look, Jenny, I'm not trying to add pressure to your life or make things more difficult for you, but this is not the first time you've fallen into situations like this. There's a pattern that is not serving you, and it's going to continue repeating unless *you* change it."

"I KNOW THAT, BETH! But this time is different!" Jenny proceeded to give reasons why she was stuck in yet another mess. She capped it at ten, which were all valid reasons, but she could've listed more. Of course, hardly any of them were her fault, and she was powerless to change most of them.

At that time, Jenny found herself hopeless and helpless yet again in a season, looking for any ray of sunshine while transitioning between seasons. Unfortunately, these rays of sunshine were usually little more than fleeting circumstantial changes that brought her temporary relief before falling into yet another pit that left her feeling the exact same way.

This circle of crazy was exhausting not only for Jenny, but for everyone in her life. The pattern of drama that surrounded her lack of responsibility to create stability not only wore her out but strained her relationships. Most people, jobs, friendships, partnerships, etc., in her life were fleeting, and those who remained were guarded because they didn't know what to expect from season to season. It was too difficult for most people to hold on even though they really cared about her, and she slowly slipped through the fingers of most. While Jenny recognized these patterns to some degree, and sometimes felt like a burden to others, she simply didn't see a way out.

These patterns in Jenny's life were frustrating for her and all those who loved her. While these words may be painting her as difficult, she was anything but! She worked and loved hard, supported so many, and was an incredible and amazing woman. That's why she made friends so easily, was able to engage in new relationships so quickly, and impressed business owners to hire her on the spot over and over; I'm telling you, this woman was a rock star! She was extremely intelligent and contributed a lot within the roles she assumed.

The challenge: she didn't realize how amazing she was, which created insecurities and uncertainties that led to one drama after the next. The dramas, not Jenny, were exhausting to people, and there is a huge difference! Jenny, like the rest of us, was an incredible person who simply had her own form of limiting language and behaviors to overcome. That's it! Like Jenny, we are all fighting some form of battle. It can be from failure to failure, victory to victory, or somewhere in between; our mindset decides. A fixed mindset leads to powerlessness and failures, but a growth mindset leads to learning and victories.

Jenny had hopped from failure to failure so much over the years that her confidence was basically nonexistent at one point. However, as the seasons rolled on, within each transition, Jenny began finding a little piece of herself that she didn't know existed. She started transitioning from a fixed mindset to a growth mindset. The more she failed and survived, the more aware she became of her internal strength, which continued to grow with every setback. Yes, her initial reactions were usually still finding reasons outside of herself for her troubles. But, with each battle, she fought a little harder and a little smarter, working on her self-awareness and focusing on where she could accept responsibility and personally create powerful change for herself and those she cared about.

At this time, however, the biggest challenge Jenny faced was the cloud of failure that she knew everyone saw when they looked at her. It was *terrible* and felt inescapable, like she had "loser" tattooed across her forehead, which certainly added to the daily challenges she faced. So, what's wrong with Jenny?

Are you ready for this? NOTHING! Nothing is wrong with Jenny. Her environment, mindsets, and behaviors during adolescent and adult development look different from some of us, yes, but isn't that the case for all of us? Yes, it is. Nothing is "wrong" with Jenny. She was diagnosed with a couple of mild mental health concerns that are requiring her to work harder in certain aspects of her journey, but the biggest challenge she has now is the fact that she and a few others think something is wrong with her.

Now, she has labeled herself—and assumes everyone else has too (some have, some haven't)—as difficult. We all do this to ourselves and others to some degree, and it is crucial that we at least become aware of it because the biases we form and react from can be devastating to ourselves, others, and our society. What is it going to take to get over the human nature of labeling people? I understand our nature is to mark things and people as safe or unsafe to keep ourselves safe, but there must be a graceful and compassionate way to do so.

The damage we cause to ourselves and others is simply not worth staying in this fixed mindset of self-preservation. The brave souls are those who venture beyond their own fears and frustrations into the realm of someone else's reality without criticism. We do that when we no longer feel the need to validate ourselves and our own positions. Acceptance of others follows acceptance of self. We know we have accepted ourselves when we no longer feel the need to validate our positions because we are relieved of the internal pressure to be more.

Why is this important when it pertains to a victimization mindset? Because **victimization** is *powerlessness*. We are only powerless when we feel like we are not enough and need to be better. This often comes from the societal pressures we feel to be normal. What is **normal,** anyway? Is there such a thing? Do you know anyone whose photo could be placed in the dictionary next to that word? No! Then why are we so insistent on making sure *we* are normal? What exactly does that mean? Does it mean healthy? Does it mean functioning? Does it mean successful or significant? It's all subjective and irrelevant. We've all been dealt a hand, and some are much uglier than others, but all of us have concerns. We all win when we all make it.

IDENTIFYING AND OBSERVING THE VICTIM MINDSET

One way to look at a victim mindset is this: A victim mindset is a response to internal and external pressures that leads to thoughts that say, "my challenges are too difficult," "I am powerless," "this is too hard," "I can't do this," etc. Sometimes, circumstances do seem too difficult for all of us. Fortunately, most of us have taken enough risks and succeeded enough times among the failures that some level of internal assurance tells us we can overcome whatever challenges surface in the future. However, that assurance has not been established in everyone's mind, and it's not set in stone. Almost all of us question our own competency, capabilities, and resilience at some point. Some of us have matured in our coping skills to be able to handle it with little effect, and some of us are good at masking how hard we've been hit. But we all face these types of uncertainties.

Just like we all have uncertainties, we also all have opportunities. Sometimes the victim mindset tries to get us to take advantage of someone else's opportunities, and sometimes we allow our own opportunities to be given away to someone who refuses to find their own. When we notice a loved one who struggles with a victim mindset, it is not helpful to project our opinions and solutions on them, nor is it helpful to give them our opportunities. Their struggles are their opportunities for learning and growth. The opportunities for learning and growth may look different for each person, but let's be real, we *all* have uncertainties as well as the opportunities to overcome them!

Ever think or say things like the following?

☐ Things never work out for me.
☐ It's always one thing or another...no matter how hard I try.
☐ I can't because...
☐ I already tried that...
☐ I would, but...
☐ If this or that would not have happened...
☐ If someone else would do or would have done...
☐ It's not possible for me because...
☐ Did that, but it didn't work...
☐ It's not my fault, I've tried everything I could.
☐ I'm doing the best I can.
☐ I didn't mean for this to happen.
☐ Why does this always happen to me?

What about statements like these?

☐ Many of my problems lead to behaviors that imply there are no solutions.
☐ My closest friends and family always give me wonderful advice, but none of it will work for me.
☐ I've had a lot of relationships over the years, but most of them tend to end or I move on for some reason.
☐ I did everything I could in that relationship, and it ended because they...
☐ I was the best employee they could ask for, and I'm no longer there because they...
☐ My closest friends and family just don't understand.
☐ I'm entering into a new personal or professional relationship, and this time it will work out because they are not like all the ones in the past.

The list goes on, but the underlying mindset is the same; it's the powerlessness and irresponsibility of the victim mindset (VM). Hold on, hold on, keep reading. If you can identify with this mindset, you're not a bad person. You're not a bad person! Got it? You're like the rest of us, but your beLIEfs, BS, and defense mechanisms look a little different from some. If you do not identify with this mindset, chances are when reading this, you were visualizing someone in your mind whom you personally know that does struggle with it. The VM can often wreak havoc everywhere, and it's easy to pinpoint. But it sure can be difficult to cope with and to love through.

While reading this chapter, please remember to keep grace at the forefront of your mind whether you are struggling with a VM or someone you love is. If you struggle with the VM, extend grace to yourself and those who love you as you patiently work together. If you love someone who struggles with the VM, extend grace to them as they work through their challenges and to yourself as you cling tightly to them. There is a healthy way to engage with each other, even amid the VM. The VM often demands action as it is helpless, but it is possible to love and support each other. It requires grace, intention, healthy boundaries, mutual agreements, and working together to maintain a safe environment to communicate through the awkward and powerless moments when the VM is active. Be patient; calming the VM is a long learning process, but it is doable!

ENGAGEMENTS OF THE VICTIM MINDSET

Let's start by increasing awareness of ways to identify this little booger so we can catch it in action. Along with the statements already mentioned, the victim mindset often engages in behaviors that create an unsafe and uncomfortable environment for its host and others. Much of the time, in place of self-love, self-care, and accepting responsibility, victimization often uses self-pity, blaming, attention-seeking behaviors, and other such tactics to fulfill the void and helplessness inside. Sometimes it looks like the following:

- **Loves attention:** The victim mindset usually attracts loads of attention; unfortunately, it's usually negative attention. Seeking the pity of others for its many misfortunes and undeserved calamities, the VM frequently amplifies the pain and distress while seeking more and more attention, preventing itself from investing any time in responsibility and action-oriented thoughts and solutions.
- **Empress of drama:** "Woe is me," the victim mindset says yet again, while outsiders, especially those closest to the individual struggling with the VM, silently think, "Here we go again…another train wreck," or "Another day, another drama."
- **Restless endurance:** Because the victim mindset doesn't solve its own problems, it stays in a state of restlessness. But it doesn't give up, oh no, it is full of endurance, which is why it will tell its stories

of woe to anyone who will listen. It will typically keep feeding the same fire and invite as many as possible to join in on the fun until another fire is started elsewhere and it has a new story to tell. This restless endurance spreads like a wildfire and is never-ending.

- **Denying responsibility:** It's never the victim mindset's fault, and even when it is does acknowledge some level of responsibility, it certainly isn't powerful enough to overcome the challenges to solve the problem. It can't, and that's the verbiage that doesn't change. The VM changes the reasons it can't with most new challenges, but rarely ever changes to the position of being able. Why? Because it can't!
- **Master of self-pity:** The VM loves phrases like, "I've done everything I can, but..."; "No one cares"; "I'm all alone, and no one understands my troubles"; "My problems can't be solved like that because..."; "It's more comfortable for me to wallow in the familiar place of self-pity." It's so frustrating for those struggling with this mindset because it leaves the individual feeling powerless, hopeless, and lacking in confidence for any real change.
- **Self-centered:** There's not much time to inquire of the challenges of others or how others are doing because the VM keeps the individual housing it so self-absorbed that it has a hard time genuinely thinking about the possibility that others may be having a difficult time. The VM keeps us so focused on the unhappy circumstances in our own lives that we don't have time left to contribute to anyone else's life. Therefore, this mindset robs us of reciprocal bonding with others, which is why few long-lasting relationships stay in our lives when we allow the VM to rule for long.
- **Blaming:** Since the victim mindset is incapable of finding its own solutions, it must blame someone or something else. To look in the mirror would require accepting responsibility for initiating change, which it is incapable of. So, the VM blames the present boss, forgetting that it blamed the boss before that and the boss before that. It blames the new partner, not realizing it blamed the partner before that and the partner before that. If there is no person to blame, it will grab ahold of any circumstances to push the blame on. The VM will never find opportunities amid challenges, but rather will blame outside sources for robbing itself of all opportunities.
- **Rejecting opportunity:** Speaking of opportunity, there is no change, no solution, nor will there ever be with the VM. This mindset is so familiar with failure that there is rarely ever any need to even try, because, after all, it can't. The VM has already been there, done that, and nothing will work. It's special, not like anyone else. Its

problems are too big for opportunities that work for other people. There's no point to trying anything. It can't succeed, remember?

WHEN DOES CHANGE OCCUR?

I'd like to say that one day we wake up and decide that the people and things we've been telling ourselves are important actually *are* important enough to become a priority. That, bizarrely, we wake up one day and decide it's time, and then we become responsible and take action. On rare occasions, this does happen for some when the pain of staying the same becomes greater than the pain of investing in change. However, most of the time, change occurs through a lot of painstaking and intentional trial and error.

That's the reality for most; even when it doesn't look promising, we do it anyway. We choose to get our hands dirty, take the risks of potentially making mistakes and falling on our faces, and then get up and keep going anyway. Why? Because it's important—important enough to work for, important enough to invest energy in, important enough to change to yield the results we've told ourselves we really want in our lives. Not because we *should* or are *supposed to*—no! We eventually pursue what is important as we recognize that *we* are important enough to invest energy in. It starts by identifying our importance in the mirror and then daily choosing to fight for it. While it's not easy, it is possible! It's not only possible, it's probable when we are ready. One big difference between those who do and those who do not create healthy change is that while both recognize it's difficult, one does it despite that fact.

"Marriage is hard. Divorce is hard. Choose your hard.
Obesity is hard. Being fit is hard. Choose your hard.
Being in debt is hard. Being financially disciplined is hard. Choose your hard.
Communication is hard. Not communicating is hard. Choose your hard.
Life will never be easy. It will always be hard.
But we can choose our hard. Pick wisely."
~Devon Brough, in *The Mind Journal*

Yes, life is difficult. No, we never really know how things are going to progress or wind up. However, to experience peace and joy, movement through personal responsibility is necessary. One of my favorite leaders of all time said it so well:

"You don't have to see the whole staircase, just take the first step." ~Martin Luther King Jr.

Peace and joy in life are byproducts of prioritizing what we individually deem important and then taking the first step toward it. Where we invest our time signifies what we deem important in that moment. This can be extremely difficult for the victim mindset. There are no judgments here, so relax and simply observe thoughts and behaviors to see where energy is being invested, and that will reveal what's really important at that moment. For the VM, it is often survival commingled with powerlessness, which is why it often looks like one chaotic episode after another. It avoids responsibility to changing course because it has convinced itself that it is powerless to do so.

The powerlessness of the VM invests more energy into finding reasons why it can't do what it says it wants to do rather than investing thought and action in what could yield important outcomes. Because the VM is not producing what the host deems important, it must then validate reasons, which ultimately become repetitive excuses for irresponsibility, inactivity, and powerlessness. Over time, this wears on others, which is why those battling with the VM usually have more shallow and temporary relationships. People can only walk on eggshells for so long before they become exhausted. The difficulty in the relationships is not only the VM running wild, though; it is also attributed to those around us not understanding what is going on. Sometimes people who love us when we're struggling with the VM give up because they are exhausted. However, if we all explore together and choose to patiently grow together, it is possible to establish healthy long-term relationships. Avoidance and termination are not the only options when the VM is present.

No, it's not easy, but it is possible. Unfortunately, the victim mindset's powerlessness makes the lives of those around us uncomfortable. And oftentimes when others attempt to share the uncomfortableness they feel with us, the VM overreacts, becoming extremely emotional, shutting down completely, or exercising unhealthy defense mechanisms. When the VM is running wild and avoiding responsibility, it will likely say and do things that make others feel unimportant or unsafe. This will likely cause those who care about us to put up guards of protection and fear getting too close. So many of you know someone whom you feel guarded around because of an active VM. Everyone must set their own healthy boundaries, but other options besides giving up and moving on exist.

Although healing is tough, acknowledging some of the behaviors is the first step to overcoming the VM, regardless of who is hosting it. It's hard because the VM is often comfortable riding the free train to nowhere/anywhere and later asking for help cleaning up the mess once it derails. Why? Because it didn't have the money or resources to purchase the train ticket to the place it really wanted to go to in the first place. The VM always has a great excuse for never arriving at its destination.

Therefore, instead of planning and working to chart its own healthy course, it hops on another train to nowhere/anywhere, usually at the expense of someone else, and the cycle continues.

This vicious cycle often exhausts the host and those close to that person. The exhaustion felt by the person allowing the victim mindset amplifies powerlessness, which makes the exhaustion itself become one more reason why it can't. The exhaustion experienced by those in proximity often leads to alienation or terminating the relationship. This becomes one more excuse of why the VM can't because now it doesn't even have support; it's all alone, no one understands, no one else has these types of troubles, and the beLIEfs continue leading to hopelessness and devastation as more people give up on the relationship.

If you recognize this cycle, don't be hard on yourself or others. We all practice the VM at some time. Awareness is a beautiful place to start when attempting to modify any limiting mindset. This means observing thoughts and behaviors and gently communicating and working through the victim mindset by exercising commitment, accountability, and responsibility for making subtle and repetitive changes to develop new neural pathways in the brain. Creating an atmosphere for small and repetitive successes is huge for overcoming the VM.

The difficulty for the victim mindset is that it has already convinced itself that it is powerless, that it has already tried everything, and that nothing will work. The VM does not want to hear that it is capable, that there are plenty of options, nor that things can change. The VM is so used to failure that it cannot comprehend anything that resembles victory. The victim mindset can get creative when it realizes that others are onto it, even so much as making pretend attempts at responsibility for appearance's sake so that it does not lose the support of others altogether. Be careful when you see the VM doing this because people catch on really quick and can feel deceived, which is likely to make the connection feel unsafe and unhealthy for others.

THE VICTIM MINDSET WILL DISSIPATE AS IT EXPERIENCES VICTORIES

If things are going to change, the host of the victim mindset must begin to experience individual moments of victory by accepting responsibility. Even the smallest of feats is crucial in overcoming the victim mindset. One powerful tool that can assist here is making checklists: daily, weekly, monthly, and annually. Every little victory empowers! Making lists, committing to and completing any healthy tasks, and checking them off the list will empower the host, which is the first weapon in defeating the victim mindset. Seriously, add anything that feels healthy to your checklist. Here's a sample list:

☐ Get up with my first alarm instead of hitting snooze.
☐ Make my bed.
☐ Brush my teeth.
☐ Take my shower.
☐ Dress for my day.
☐ Make one commitment to myself and keep it today.
☐ Finish one task that is really important to me.
☐ Research one topic that interests me for 30 minutes today.
☐ Write two pages in my book today.
☐ Cook my supper instead of eating out.
☐ Do my dishes.
☐ Go to bed in time for me to get at least 7 hours of sleep.

Create your own list and make it personal. Notice how there is ownership in the list: my alarm, my bed, my teeth, my shower, my day, my commitment, important to me. The victim mindset does not like ownership because it requires accountability and responsibility, so start by creating a list that claims ownership.

Some may have read the sample list and thought, "Man, that's a breeze. I do more than that in a day standing on my head." Others may have read the list and thought, "Geez, that's a little overwhelming. I'm lucky to get my teeth brushed daily." Listen, there is NO comparison here! This is a judgment-free list for you to observe actions and work toward accomplishing things, any things that will strengthen the neural pathways that say, "I can!" By the way, the sample list was my list at one time when I was battling depression during a national health and economic crisis. Many days I didn't check off every box, but the days I did were empowering and kept me going. Even the smallest of successes defeats failure. The VM is not used to succeeding, so assist it by providing any opportunities for victories, large or small.

GETTING REAL ABOUT SUPPORT

The objective of overcoming the victim mindset is establishing and living independence by loving and believing in self. When we find ourselves in need of continual support, we may be lacking independence, self-love, and confidence. Help is not a bad thing; we all occasionally need assistance. However, when we find ourselves in the support line frequently, it is important to explore the circumstances around our dependence in certain areas. Let's not be hard on ourselves for seeking help sometimes. Frankly, some of us could benefit from a little dependence here and there. Many of us are terrified of asking for any help, which can be unhealthy as well. It's about balance—give and take within the confounds of our world and reciprocal relationships.

Our gut, and those around us, if we listen carefully, will tell us if our level of dependence or independence may be imbalanced and causing or intensifying challenges. Think about this: **independence** is liberation, individuality, and the ultimate expression of freedom. We know when we feel liberated and free, responding to the world as an independent individual. There are, however, times when outside help promotes our independence and freedom. Isn't that beautiful? When balanced, we feel healthy. When imbalanced, we feel unhealthy, which is often manifested in our personal and professional relationships.

We can explore this balance by asking ourselves questions when we feel off. Explore the following questions but also listen to your gut here. What other questions may assist in finding balance?

1) What support am I seeking because I feel lonely or rejected?
2) What support am I seeking because I feel incapable?
3) How am I neglecting myself or others by avoiding my responsibilities? Remember, it's not any easier for someone else.
4) What support am I extending when I really don't want to?
5) What support am I avoiding that may add value to my life and others?
6) What support am I asking for that is a replacement for the actual support that will bring about healthy and sustainable change?
7) How will I avoid needing this type of support in the future?
8) Who am I taking advantage of?
9) Who is taking advantage of me?
10) What am I pretending not to know?

Boundary Time

When it comes to providing tangible support for adults, there is a fine line to explore. The idea is to help, not enable. Tricky, isn't it? You know you've been there, and it's tough to see exactly where that line is. This may help:

> **Helping is an isolated opportunity to provide an assisted solution, packaged within a life lesson, for an adult who may be lacking in capability or responsibility.**

Helping is healthy; tangible support can be enabling. Tangible support is when someone else is bearing the weight, sometimes repeatedly, for an adult who refuses to learn capability or accept responsibility. This is a form of learned dependence, which is not healthy for anyone. It is dangerous. Helping is giving assistance, where the person helping and the person asking for aid are both shouldering the weight of the solution. Help is extended temporarily as someone is learning how to do it themselves. If aid is given without being packaged in the form of a life lesson that promotes capability and responsibility in the future, it is not helpful.

As parents, most of us provide our children with tangible and intangible support over the course of about two decades as we daily help them learn life lessons that promote self-sufficiency. At some point, the support transitions from less tangible to more intangible so the child will gain confidence and independence. Failure to do so can lead to an unhealthy dependency or codependency. Gauging age-appropriate assistance as a child develops and transitions into adulthood is a crucial component of child-rearing. But it doesn't stop there. As adults, we also have the responsibility of exploring that fine line with any adult between tangible support and healthy help.

> **Enabling is allowing someone to shuck, in lieu of shoulder, their own responsibilities.**

One truth that few will dispute is that no one gets something for nothing. Some put it as, "you reap what you sow." Others say, "what goes around comes around." You get the idea; we don't get something without first investing in it, and if we do, someone else did the investing. Franklin P. Jones worded it so well: "When you get something for nothing, you just haven't been billed for it yet." When we are reaping something we have not invested in, someone is footing the bill. That can be emotionally, mentally, physically, or financially.

This concept is the reason every guardian or parent's responsibility is to teach their child how to fish instead of always providing the fish as the child develops. Responsibility builds independent and self-sufficient characteristics, which are crucial components of adulthood. Be forewarned: some children pick up on this concept quickly; some learn later into childhood or in their teenaged years. And some well into adulthood never quite master these truths. Adults who have not mastered this concept have fallen victim to the victim mindset. The longer these dependent behaviors have surfaced, the more difficult they will be to get rid of.

As adults, if we are not providing for ourselves and are refusing responsibility for self-sufficiency, we are suffering from the victim mindset and forcing others to suffer as well. Although difficult to acknowledge and even more difficult to alter, these mindsets are created to protect us during certain seasons, and at some point, they actually served us. The difference between someone with a victim mindset and someone without is that the person without it already grew out of their victim mindset. Oh, you mean they matured in this area? Yes!

These are some tough words, but remember, let's not be hard on ourselves if we look in the mirror and see the VM. It's certainly not helpful to look at others with a critical nature, pointing out the unhealthy behaviors that accompany the VM. The purpose of ***The BS of Better*** program is to identify and observe. That's it. Should we or others decide to modify behaviors, then let's go for it, but with zero expectations, no shaming, blaming, guilting, nor finger-pointing! Simply identify and observe. We and others will modify behaviors when we are ready; it will begin through observations but will not occur until we feel safe. Boundaries are crucial, but they can be set in place with grace instead of frustrating finger-pointing. So...

> **Let's keep a solid foundation of acceptance for self and others because growth does not occur in an atmosphere of condemnation.**

Here's the point: Responsibilities are burdens that reap some type of reward once they are met. Unless there is a serious cognitive delay, every adult and most children beginning in early childhood assume responsibilities so that we may reap rewards. Whether it's children deciding to brush their teeth so they don't rot so they can look cute and eat their favorite foods or adults deciding to go to work to have money to pay bills, buy food, and do things they enjoy, everyone (except infants) has responsibilities. Even infants mature.

The victim mindset's number one responsibility is to shuck responsibility, and it looks daily for ways to do that. The VM attempts to take us back to infancy, a place where someone else carries all the burdens, does all the work, and allows us to reap the rewards. For a six-month-old, this is wonderful and healthy. For a 16-, 26-, or 36-year-old, it is not cute or healthy; it's uncomfortable. Here's why...

Someone must shoulder the burdens to reap; that's what **responsibility** does. When we accept responsibility, we are agreeing to shoulder the burden to reap a reward. We love shouldering the burden for infants because they are innocent and not developed. However, as we cover in this book, development is crucial; we must mature to be happy and healthy and to allow those around us to also live happily and healthily. Think about this: when the victim mindset says, "I can't," it is saying, "I won't agree to shouldering this responsibility." Well, if the reward is going to be reaped, someone must say, "I agree to shoulder this responsibility," or "I will."

Rewards transpire when we are healthy because we say, "I can and I will accept the responsibility for creating this reward." The victim mindset thinks it can't, so it says "I won't." These phrases go together:

I will = I can, and I agree to shoulder the responsibility
I can't = I won't, and I refuse responsibility

See the challenge the victim mindset creates? If we can't or won't, who will? Every time we say I can't, we are also saying who will. The victim mindset has its hands out begging for someone else to shoulder its responsibility. It reminds us that life is too hard, it's too much, no one else has it this bad, my difficulties are extraordinary...lie, lie, lie, beLIEfs! There is *zero* truth in this mindset. No one is without difficulties! It's not the size of the difficulty; it's the mindset with which we approach the difficulty that makes it more or less difficult.

Let's take a deep breath and begin identifying and observing so we can calmly consider alternatives when we are ready. A great place to start while identifying and observing is to ask this question every time we hear the lies of victimization. Let's start practicing now:

I can't because...	Who will and how?
I would, but...	Who will and how?
It's too hard for me!	Who will and how?
It's not my fault!	Who will and how?
If this or that would not have happened...	Who will and how?
If they would not have done this or that...	Who will and how?

Get it? Regardless of the reason (the victim mindset's nice word for *excuse*), the responsibilities must still be met to survive or reap rewards. So, who will meet those responsibilities, and how will they do it if the VM keeps the host from doing their part? At the end of every reason or excuse, the question still exists: Who will and how? The reason (excuse) does not make the responsibility go away. It simply prolongs it or shoves it onto someone else's plate who is already juggling their own plates full of responsibilities.

The victim mindset is lacking in or void of self-sufficiency. When we do not shoulder our part, then we are pushing our responsibilities onto someone else's shoulders. This is why most hosts of victim mindsets have primarily shallow and temporary relationships, personally and professionally. It's exhausting to watch and participate in for the host and others close by, causing these relationships to struggle. The struggle resembles the following chart showing the **Healthy vs. Victim Mindsets**.

Healthy vs. Victim Mindsets

Independency & Responsibility of the Healthy Mindset

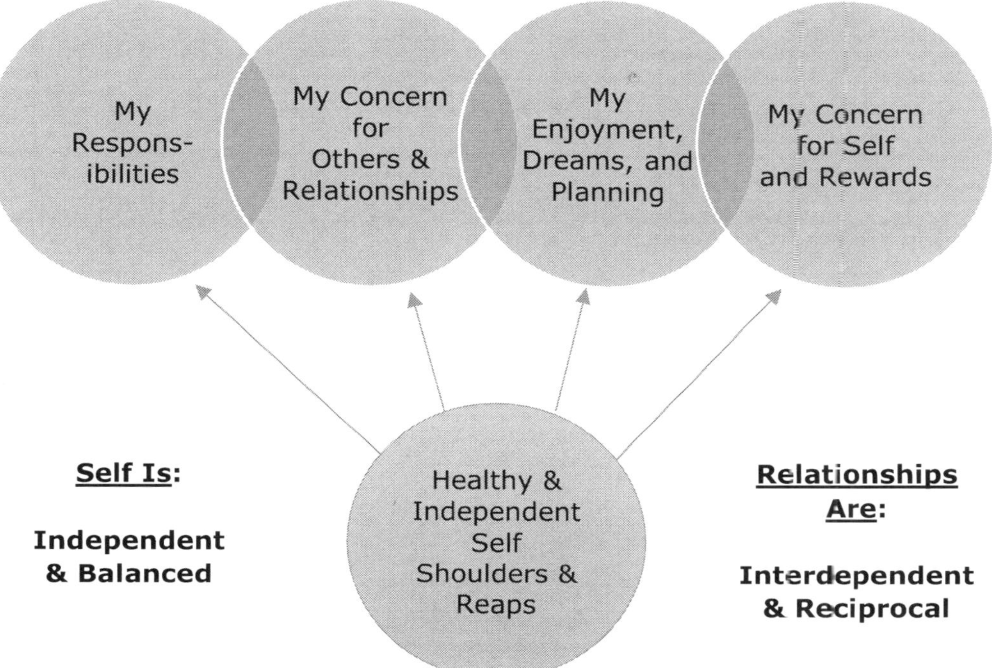

Dependency & Codependency of the Victim Mindset

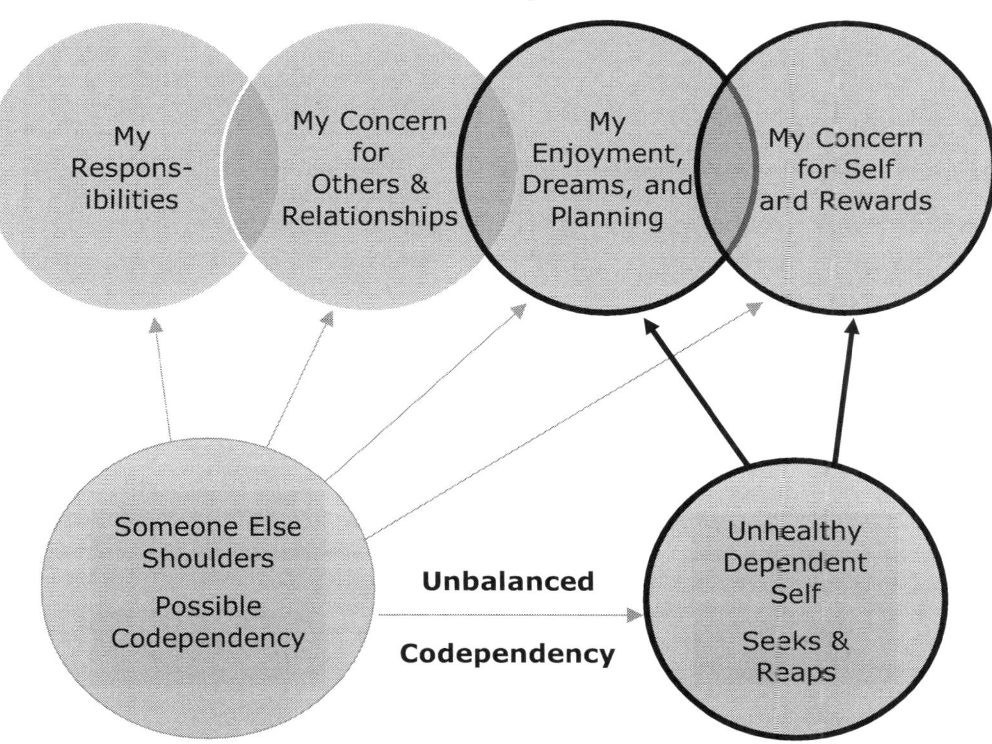

A healthy mindset yields rewards through accepting responsibility and confronting anything that attempts to steal our independence. A healthy mindset allows us to shoulder our own responsibilities; our concern for others and relationships; and our enjoyment, dreams, and plans while expressing a balanced concern for ourselves. Being mature in the areas of shouldering our own responsibilities reaps rewards and leads to a balanced lifestyle that is rich in healthy, reciprocal, and interdependent relationships.

An unhealthy victim mindset frequently yields fewer rewards independently by avoiding responsibility when possible. Many of the rewards reached are often temporary; primarily because someone close by is shouldering the victim mindset's responsibilities. Compounded with irresponsibility, the VM also often lacks genuine concern for others, which drastically affects relationships. The VM focuses on its own enjoyment, dreams, and plans, while expressing concern primarily for itself, which is often experienced as selfish and narcissistic by those attempting to relate to the host.

The immaturity of the victim mindset allows for it to stay in a seek-and-reap mode at the cost of almost anything or anyone, forcing responsibility onto others and forming an unbalanced codependency. This VM creates an environment that is often engulfed in exhaustive drama and problems, which eventually terminates most personal and professional relationships. But as stated, the VM has extreme difficulty accepting responsibility, so upon termination, it blames the other parties and extraordinary circumstances to avoid responsibility. Instead of being rich in rewards and healthy relationships, the VM keeps the host rich in repetitive failures and temporary relationships.

Many beautiful and invaluable individuals struggle with the VM, and so many wonderful rewards and relationships await those individuals on the other side of responsibility. It's never too late to begin focusing, developing, and maturing beyond victimization. Let's *not* be hard on ourselves when we relate to this mindset; assuredly, at some point, it served us well as a survival tactic, which is why it gained such power in our minds. Don't focus on the why and how; simply start by focusing on the "who will" for now as we lovingly accept ourselves and commit to identifying and observing thoughts and behaviors that are not serving us and others.

CONVERTING INTENTION INTO FRUITION

There are varying reasons why an intention never comes to fruition. The foundation of all those reasons are uncertainties based on fear. If we feel a strong urge to do something with an intention, it is common for fear to surface. Anytime we do something that is unfamiliar or difficult, of course we are going to feel fear. Our brains innately fear unfamiliarity. It can be something simple and minor, or it can be something drastic and life-changing, but if it's unfamiliar, we will fear it. The VM, unfortunately, often exaggerates these fears and will drag us straight into "I-don't-know-how" mode.

Sometimes it's a simple conversation that we will avoid at all cost because it may feel uncomfortable, and we fear that feeling or the outcome of the conversation. Of course, some scary times call for drastic measures, but we often continue living with an unhealthy and unsafe mindset for several reasons. One could be that we don't want to lose someone or something. Another could be that we don't see a way out; this means we can't figure out the "how to."

It is so uncomfortable being stuck in the don't-know-how mindset because we refuse to explore or learn how. We all do this to some degree at certain times in life, so if you notice being stuck in this mindset, don't be hard on yourself. Simply identify and start observing. You will create movement when you are ready to know how. Until then, when victim language surfaces, suggesting that you can't or there isn't a way, replace that BS with a healthy personal truth that will empower you and encourage you right where you are. Maybe it sounds something like this:

☐ I'm not quite sure at this moment, but I am open to figuring it out.
☐ This is a temporary season; I have survived and even thrived amid other challenges, and I will certainly do the same here.
☐ These circumstances are confusing and difficult; I acknowledge the uncertainty and will work through the fear to make the situation healthy and safe.

Or maybe it sounds differently for you, but creating a path for an intention to come to fruition requires a mindset that is the opposite of a victim mindset. It requires a readiness for responsibility that is tough to see for the VM. Victimization is a special kind of mindset that always carries with it a pair of glasses that filters out everything it does not want to see. The challenge with these glasses is that everyone else can see what's not working, while we remain blind to it. How do we know when this is happening? That is even easier—those around us will tell us. And when they get tired of telling us, they will likely avoid us or walk away altogether. This is a painful price to pay because we refuse to remove the glasses that accompany the VM.

When we see this going on, we can identify and observe the cost of this behavior and the cost of altering it. Sometimes it requires a lot of effort, and frankly, sometimes we're not ready. However, in most scenarios, the time comes when the cost of staying the same is too great. We get tired of paying the price for something that yields pain and consequences instead of joy and reward. When that realization hits home, we remove the blinding glasses of victimization and ask ourselves these two crucial questions:

What is not working?
What am I ready to do about it?

When that realization hits home, we are usually exhausted, those around us are exhausted, and we and/or those close to us have paid a heavy price. We conclude that the VM is not worth it anymore. That is when we know we are ready to sow and reap despite how difficult the efforts of change may be. A lot of avenues are available for overcoming the VM, none of which will be much fun or easy but will certainly be worth the efforts.

We can start by journaling every day the things we are identifying and observing. That's it for now. We will devise plans and take action when we are ready, but the VM is stubborn and prefers to put us and others through a lot of pain first before it raises the white flag of surrender to change. For now, identifying and observing are crucial, requiring us to remove the blinders. If we don't, one day, possibly many days, we are likely to wake up and realize our blinding VM cost us much more than we ever anticipated paying.

Therapy can be a helpful option for those struggling with a VM. Man, does the VM hate that thought. The VM relies heavily on inability and irresponsibility and doesn't like the idea that change is even an option. Therefore, those of us really ready will be faced with a battle, but working with a therapist to identify the rewards of our efforts will be helpful. Oftentimes, the VM stems from trauma, developmental delays, or other underlying challenges. Specific types of therapy can be helpful depending on individual needs. For instance, cognitive behavioral therapy (CBT), eye movement desensitization and reprocessing (EMDR) therapy, exposure therapy, and other forms are specifically designed to break through the challenges of the VM and possible underlying causes.

The BS of Better program is not designed to diagnose or recommend specific therapy as treatments vary depending on individual needs, which must be assessed by physicians or licensed therapists. However, this information is being included because it is important that we consider the great value in seeking professional assistance when the pressures of any mindset keep us entangled for a period of time. It's not only the VM that is a symptom of potentially damaging concerns that keep us stuck in situations that are unhealthy.

So, it is important that we listen to ourselves and care for ourselves enough to break through the uncomfortableness of seeking professional assistance. Seeking therapy does not mean we are broken or messed up. It means that we are strong enough and love ourselves enough to consider many options in making self-care a priority. We dream of a day when things will "be better," but our intentions rarely come to fruition when the VM is active. Counseling can often assist with creating a plan based on our individual needs and objectives that is more likely to come to fruition. This is especially important when we feel down on ourselves or are struggling in relationships or in our careers. Therapy is nothing to be feared. However, the pain we live with daily because we refuse healthy support through therapy is frightening.

THE PIT TO THE PEDESTAL?

Don't you feel bad for the victim mindset? That's the point. The victim mindset's mission has been accomplished! If you are one of the amazing people who have identified some of these limiting thoughts, language, and behaviors described in this chapter, thank you for reading this far. Life lessons and learning opportunities are not easy, and it takes a lot of courage to look in the mirror and truly consider putting in the work necessary to modify our mindsets and our circumstances. It is hard, and while many of us look around at how "well" we see others functioning, just know it is hard for everyone else too. Maybe in a different way, but it's hard for us all no matter how we package and present ourselves to the world.

I cannot tell you the hundreds of times people have acted surprised that I have and have had some pretty big challenges. Why? Simply because of the way I package myself and my challenges. Let me be vulnerable with you, okay? Having survived childhood and adult trauma, I have a good poker face and have utilized many tools to keep things moving in a healthy direction most of my life.

I absolutely love my life and wouldn't change anything about it. However, I do not always have everything together, but from the outside, it usually looks like I do. I hate this, but people jokingly say stuff to me like, "I think to myself, what would Brigitte do or say here?" And when I am vulnerable, people always act surprised, saying things like, "I would have never guessed," or "You always seem to have everything together."

Stop it! Stop placing anyone in your mind on that level because it is a fallacy. Yes, I have a lot of education and experience working with the mind and emotions. Yes, I have overcome a lot and accomplished a lot; so have you! But that is not where my life transformation took place. The transformation occurred and continues to occur through my individual commitment to increasing self-awareness, personal growth, and learning new tools to overcome my ever-evolving limitations and challenges. This will be the case until I leave this life. Am I a rock star? Well, I humbly say, Yes! But I'm not on some stage or pedestal because I have my life together. No! If there is a pedestal, then we're all on it together. We're all equal and wonderful, and we're all fighting battles.

My triumphs and confidence did not come from my degree in psychology or any other degrees or training certifications. It came from the desire to explore a growth mindset and the commitment to personal awareness and behavioral modification when I'm ready to change something that is not presently serving me, while accepting what I am not ready to change. Yes, I wrote this book for YOU, but I also wrote it for ME, because I do not always have my ducks in a row no matter how it looks from the outside. ***The BS of Better*** program you are working through right now is but one of the outcomes of my personal development. Is everything in here correct? I don't know, but so far, it's the revelations and tools that have supported me to the place I am now. Who knows what program will evolve in 10 years, 5 years, 2 years...hey, even in 1 year? I don't know, and I'm okay with that. This is the maturation my heart longs for others to experience when ready.

I do not always *feel* like I am enough, but that does not change the fact that I *am* more than enough. So, I accept and love myself despite those feelings and thoughts right where I am. One large contributing factor to my being okay with this is that I fought to reach, and continue to fight to sustain, a place of self-love and acceptance in the moment. That will never change! It's a long hard battle, and it's what transformed my life and what will transform anyone ready to look in the mirror and embrace it. I have built and strengthened the neural pathways of self-love and acceptance in my brain. This is what naturally attracts people in my life. This is what makes people feel safe; because I love and accept myself, I am able to love and accept others without condition. I truly do. But trust me, that took a lot of self-reflection and personal development.

While writing this, I'm fighting with myself trying to figure out why this part of my journey is unfolding within the victimization chapter, and here's what I've discovered. The victimization mindset stems from lack of self-love and acceptance, which leads to a comparative nature that feeds the victim. The victim mindset kept me looking around at others and feeling like my circumstances were special, too difficult, or different, feeding the idea that I **couldn't** do certain things because of external reasons holding me back. I am easily triggered by the victim mindset because at one time in my life, I felt and lived with the victim mindset driving.

This mindset insisted that neither I nor my circumstances were normal, not like everyone else, which is why I had such a hard time until I broke free of the beLIEfs. I lived by selfish lies—it wasn't me, but the victim mindset I allowed. I felt powerless because of the beLIEfs I allowed my mind to ponder. In reality, I overcame the victim mindset by living powerful while I was feeling powerless. It was a daily, moment-to-moment choice. "Is this thought powerful or powerless?" "Is this act on powerful or powerless?" Over and over, I asked myself these questions and fought to align my thoughts and behaviors with the powerful woman I knew myself to be despite the distorted, preprogrammed beLIEfs of powerlessness. It took a lot of work, but you know what? I'm worth it!

So, first, stop looking around at others to assess your normalness! So many strive to move from their perceived pit to a perceived pedestal that we forget to simply look in the mirror. This is serious! Stop searching for normal! Have you ever defined that word? Well, here it is: regular, typical, conforming, lack of deviation from what is considered to be usual or expected. Oh, puh-lease! You can keep *normal* because, that right there, I'm never going to be and have no desire to be! Is this bad? No!

However, some of us strive for normal, which is only some idea of what is expected, and we feel safe within this realm. Is that bad? No! However, what we have here is polar-opposite tendencies and positions, and when those positions collide, none of us naturally feel safe. The comparative nature that has us comparing ourselves and our circumstances has us looking at people who are wired differently; it's like comparing apples to oranges.

So, the objective is not to be concerned with whether we prefer being normal or being different, the objective is to ensure a safe space for everyone involved. Someone who prefers stability and relies heavily on clear expectations may not feel safe with someone who dreams big and takes huge risks without counting the costs. The point is, we'll never find our answers by striving to be normal or by rejecting it. Normal doesn't really exist except within the confines of limited perceptions.

These limiting perceptions give us some distorted idea that those who are normal are on some middle ground; those who are in the pit are not normal, and those on the pedestal are above normal. Can we agree to stop this madness? Stop striving to go from the pit to the pedestal. When feeling like you're in a pit, simply ask someone to throw you a mirror. Attempting to define our own normalcy by looking around at others will get us nowhere fast. Mere acceptance acknowledges the humanness of us all and reminds us that normalcy is unnecessary and futile. We all have needs and are doing our best to meet those needs. In the process, we sometimes bump into one another. Our mindsets make this process more pleasant or less pleasant.

MEETING MY OWN NEEDS

Many decades ago, humanistic psychology proposed that we are driven by higher needs, especially the need for self-actualization, which is basically the need to fulfill our own individual potential. It is important to not confuse self-acceptance with self-actualization; these are two different things. It is possible to reach self-acceptance without becoming self-actualized. We may never fully reach our own potential, but it is much more likely that we will do so after first reaching a place of self-acceptance.

The victim mindset likes to remind us that we cannot meet our potential because...well, you name it. When this happens, remember to not begin with self-actualization if that feels overwhelming. Begin with accepting self in the moment and taking some form of action to experience success; even within what we may deem as the smallest of endeavors exists an opportunity to experience a victory. When we think or say, "I can't," we are referring to our inability to meet specific personal need(s). It is important to identify what those needs are and start working through the possibilities of meeting needs by exercising personal responsibility.

Abraham Maslow's hierarchy of needs is a helpful place to start if the VM has the reigns. This is important because the VM attempts to keep us in a mindset of failure or fear of failure. The only way to disrupt the victim mindset's fixation on failure is to experience victories. Acknowledging victories, of all shapes and sizes, is crucial, and so is putting ourselves in scenarios that will create opportunities to experience these victories. For the exercise on the next page, take some time to reflect and journal about what and how your individual needs are being met at this time.

Meeting My Hierarchy of Needs

Some have interpreted Maslow's hierarchy of needs as requiring one set of needs to be met before the next level can be pursued. This theory has been debunked through many studies, so do not look at this chart with an expected order of achievement. You choose where to focus energy and personal responsibility based on what you individually deem important at this time. Acceptance while accepting responsibility is key!

Ability to meet personal needs	The needs I am not meeting are:	The needs I am meeting are:
Physiological Needs: Personally creating a way to provide basic necessities of survival such as food, water, shelter, warmth, sleep		
Safety Needs: Personally creating an environment that feels secure, stable, and unafraid		
Love and Belonging Needs: Personally creating a sustainable support system of friends and family by forming healthy relationships built on reciprocity and respect		
Esteem Needs: Personally creating an environment that contributes to my achievements, self-esteem, and the respect and acknowledgment of others		
Self-Actualization Needs: Personally creating an environment that pursues and fulfills my unique potential		

Choice is the opportunity for positive or negative energy moving forward.

Homework for Overcoming Victimization Language

While attempting to meet our needs in this ever-changing world, we face hardships. Here's a story about one of them. Once upon a time, there were two women driving side-by-side on a split four-lane highway; they were in separate sedans approaching a red stoplight with no cars ahead of them in either of their lanes. They were both wearing their seat belts, driving the speed limit, and gently putting on their brakes with the anticipation of stopping at the red light, which they were both carefully watching. Both ladies were safe drivers, had never had accidents, were not in a rush, and the traffic was light.

Within three seconds of approaching the red stoplight, it turned green. Lady A took her foot off the brake and proceeded ahead, obeying the green light she now had. Lady B kept her foot on the brake, took her eyes off the green light for one second to look to her right, then to her left, and then slightly to the left in front of her in the two lanes proceeding in the opposite direction. Lady B then kept her foot on the brake because she noticed an oncoming car approaching the light rather quickly with their blinker on to turn in front of her. As Lady B came to a stop, Lady A had not noticed the turning vehicle, which plowed into her, totaling her car. Unfortunately, the driver of the turning vehicle did not have insurance.

Whose fault was the accident? Does it really matter? Fault in this instance is irrelevant because it is after-the-fact and cannot be changed. However, the victim mindset loves finding fault and shifting the blame to avoid responsibility for cleaning up the mess. It uses the no-fault excuse to get assistance. Of course, the driver of the turning vehicle is at fault, but without insurance, Lady A is still responsible for cleaning up the mess because she participated in the accident. Lady B avoided the accident by observing and taking precautions. The host of the victim mindset will always benefit from observation and taking responsibility amid hardships.

Here is the cold hard truth about hardships: they happen to us all, no matter how strong or weak we may appear. I'm over here doing my thing and—boom—hardship. You're over there doing your thing and—boom—hardship. In between every amazing time is a hardship or two, maybe more. While you're doing your thing and facing your hardship, what happens when I knock on your door to assist me with my hardship? Does your hardship go away? Do you put it on hold? Does someone else take care of your hardships and responsibilities while you help me with mine? Tough questions, right?

Well, that's sort of what happens when the victim mindset has the reigns. During someone's else's victories or hardships, we're knocking on their door, interrupting their time, with our hardships. Their life is still going on, but they're pausing to help us with our hardship. Now, this is a wonderful thing unless it's abused. Helping builds bonds, and we all benefit from giving and receiving, so keep on helping, world! However, the VM takes it to a different level...an uncomfortable level. The VM indulges in taking advantage of others through their commitment to us.

That hurts, doesn't it? Yes, it does. So, help. Be helped. But don't take advantage of it. And when we see the VM kicking in, look for ways to accept responsibility despite the difficulty level. Remember, it's not the size of the difficulty, it's the mindset with which we approach the difficulty that makes it more or less difficult. The following pages will assist in identifying and overcoming the victim mindset. So, take the next week or two to explore and process the effects the VM may be causing in your life. Oh, yeah, don't forget to keep grace in your quiver: grace for self and grace for others. Now, let's get started.

TAKE YOUR TIME AND DO THE WORK!

The VM questions its own capabilities, so these exercises will likely feel uncomfortable and difficult to follow through on. Do the exercises and follow through anyway. When you realize the rewards are worth the effort, you'll make a way because no reason, challenge, excuse, or level of familiarity will suffice.

Initially, start by identifying, observing, and journaling about your mindset, language, and behaviors during *every* challenge. Don't worry about changing anything right now (unless it is unsafe, of course). Simply catch and journal about things where you feel weak, powerless, frazzled, out of control, inept, incapable, not meeting responsibilities, etc. No need to take action, simply journal these things. Start and stay here for a week or two until you master the crucial first step of identifying the victim mindset.

Next, when you are ready, and only when you are ready for movement, start looking closer at your journal and consider the things that could be done when challenged—explore all options. When you are ready for movement, create a movement plan by listing everything you could personally do. On occasion, you may ask for help; caution here, as you should only delegate when you are able to compensate. Then, take consistent action. No matter how small, move in the direction you desire by accepting responsibility to create as many opportunities for success as possible. This will begin defeating the lies of the victim mindset that keep you comfortable with failure because it does not believe it can. It (the VM) can't, but YOU can!

If you realize that you are battling the VM, repeatedly processing the topics and questions on the next few pages will assist you in winning the war. Don't be afraid to ask yourself the difficult questions. The VM will tell us every time that we can't, there's nothing we can do, no matter how much we "process," it won't work—beLIEfs, all beLIEfs! Doing such exercises will rewire those beLIEfs, and that's why the VM doesn't want us to even go there. Well, go there anyway; every day, go there because the more you process, the less power the VM has over you. It will take weeks, maybe even months, but you can overcome the VM by developing healthy neural pathways in your brain through daily exercises. You deserve the freedom and power that comes with conquering the VM and so do those who love you. When you're ready, you'll enter the final battle to end this nasty war in your mind and in your relationships. Remember to keep grace and acceptance in your quiver every day.

If you are being affected by the VM that has its grips on someone you care about, make sure to complete the exercises included in the **Daily Journal Practice When Loving Someone Entrapped by the Victim Mindset**.

OBSERVATIONS OF THE VICTIM MINDSET

Take a few moments to observe the language, feelings, and uncertainty that often accompany the victim mindset. Then observe how others may experience this mindset and how it may limit you. Check those that apply to your experiences or fill in the blanks with additional observations you have made pertaining to this limiting mindset.

Victimization language:

- ☐ I can't because...
- ☐ I would, but...
- ☐ If this or that would not have happened...
- ☐ If someone else would do or would have done...
- ☐ It's not possible for me.
- ☐ It's always one thing or another, or this always happens to me.
- ☐ Did that, it won't work.
- ☐ I tried but...
- ☐ It's not my fault.
- ☐ No matter how hard I try...
- ☐ Other ________________________

Feelings that often accompany victimization language:

- ☐ Hopelessness
- ☐ Powerlessness
- ☐ Deprivation
- ☐ Null or insignificant
- ☐ Unsuccessful
- ☐ Other ________________________

Uncertainty: Am I capable?

Others may experience me as:

- ☐ Needy
- ☐ Exhaustive
- ☐ Unreliable or unstable
- ☐ Irresponsible
- ☐ Idle; wheels spinning
- ☐ A casualty; weak
- ☐ Surrounded by drama
- ☐ Other ________________________

The victim mindset may lead to:

- ☐ Recurrent failures
- ☐ Needing continual support
- ☐ Codependent relationships
- ☐ Short-term or shallow relationships

☐ Burned bridges
☐ Isolation from people avoiding the drama or high maintenance
☐ Other ________________________

Expose and Overcome the Victim Mindset

When you are ready to defeat the VM, take charge by daring to ask yourself questions like those below. But don't stop here. Instead of questioning yourself or others, question the uncertainties and beLIEfs that have held you captive far too long. This is just a starting point. Get creative in your explorations. There's so much in store for you and those you care about. The VM is terrified of your awakening, but the world awaits you!

1) Who is responsible for moving forward from right here and now?
2) List all options and possible solutions. List *all*, no matter how difficult.
3) What solutions can I carry out on my own?
   - Even if difficult, what *can* I do?
   - Since I can, I will by...

4) What solutions *require* some form of support? **Require** means absolutely necessary; it does not mean making things easier.
5) When support is needed:
   - How will I keep from needing such support in the future?
   - How will I support the supporter? How will I ensure reciprocity in the relationships?
   - Am I hopping from hand to hand, giver to giver, or am I seeking support from those who genuinely love and care about me?
   - Am I open to hearing what my emotional supporters are saying to me?

6) Have I experienced similar challenges before?
   - If so, what did I not learn then?
   - Where may I consider maturing now?

7) What do I love about myself? What do others love about me?
8) What gifts do I possess? Yes, gifts—you have plenty! List them *all*.
9) What significance and successes have I achieved up to this point?
10) Am I creating situations that will lead to significance and success? If not, what steps will allow me to do so?

Daily Journal Practice for Overcoming the Victim Mindset

Following are journal topics and exercises for the next seven days, but feel free to continue such exercises until you feel yourself being able to automatically capture and replace the victimization limiting language within your mind. It will take some time, but the neural pathways will develop as you do these exercises daily, and eventually, you will no longer find it necessary to write things down. The brain will learn to process automatically as you train it through such exercises as those contained within this program.

Day 1: Journal Your Battle with Victimization Language

- Take a few moments to journal about your struggle with the victim mindset.
- How has your life and the lives of those you care about been affected by the VM?
- Journal about your fears of overcoming the VM.

Day 2: Gently Observe Responsibility

- Define the word responsibility in your journal and describe what it looks like when you live it.
- Who is responsible for moving forward from right here and now?
- What are your ongoing responsibilities?
- Which ones are you meeting at this time? Not meeting at this time?

Day 3: What Am I Ready For? What May Stop Me?

- Journal anything that might keep you from accepting responsibility and taking action to meet these responsibilities.
- List what you are ready to explore and the action you are ready to take in overcoming the limitations of the VM.
- What value comes when you accept responsibility and take action?

Day 4: Identify the VM

- Write down any words you thought or said, or actions you exhibited, that portray that of a VM this past week.
- How did you feel, and what actions did you take?
- Someone is always shouldering your responsibilities. Which ones did you shoulder? Which ones did someone else shoulder for you?
- What did you learn this past week? What worked? What didn't work?

Day 5: Shouldering Responsibility and Taking Action

- What solutions can I carry out on my own right now?
- What solutions may require some form of support?
- How will I keep from needing such support in the future?

Day 6: Thought Capturing and Replacement
Take the VM thoughts, words, and actions from this past week and replace them with thoughts, words, and actions of powerful responsibility, acceptance, and grace in lieu of expectation, blame, and pressure.

Day 7: Acceptance Plan

- In the areas you are not ready to explore or alter at this time, journal words of acceptance and grace that will support you with no expectations or pressure as you work to develop neural pathways that are powerful and responsible.
- How will you extend grace to yourself and others regardless of your readiness to change?

Continue thought capturing and replacement exercises to build neural pathways that support a responsible and powerful mindset.

PRACTICE AND BUILD THE NEURAL PATHWAYS OF A RESPONSIBLE AND POWERFUL MINDSET

Thoughts of the Victim Mindset:	Thoughts of the Responsible and Powerful Mindset:

Reframe victim thoughts with those of a responsible and powerful mindset:

JOURNAL TOPICS TO CONTEMPLATE FOR OVERCOMING THE LIES OF THE VICTIM MINDSET

Grab your notebook or *The BS of Better Journal* to contemplate and process overcoming the victimization mindset. Below are cues and questions to begin assessing the costs and the payoffs of allowing the victim mindset, but don't stop here. Remember, journal those prompts that stand out to you and ask yourself other difficult questions and concerns that may not be listed but are hiding deep within yourself. You already know these concerns; this is your time to listen! Identify and observe the victim mindset so that you can stop what's causing those feelings of hopelessness and powerlessness when you are ready.

Inquisitive Alternatives:

- ☐ Since I am responsible for moving forward, some things I *can* do now are…
- ☐ One action I will take *now* is…
- ☐ When new challenges arise, I will stay on my course anyway by…
- ☐ I commit to and allow myself to succeed at __________ regardless of __________ by…
- ☐ I will maintain ownership of my responsibilities by…
- ☐ I will create and protect reciprocal relationships in my life as I support my supporters by…
- ☐ Daily, I will succeed at…
- ☐ I am capable of…
- ☐ Other ________________________

Neural Pathway Development Support

It cannot be reiterated enough that neural pathway development is crucial for sustainable healthy change in thoughts and behaviors. Heightening self-awareness, committing to personal reflection time, and completing acceptance and action plans daily and weekly will develop the neural pathways that serve you. For additional daily processing support, please see **Appendix A – Neural Pathway Development Support**. What would it look like if we asked the difficult yet beneficial questions until the questions were no longer difficult? When you're ready, try it and see.

Daily Journal Practice When Loving Someone Entrapped by the Victim Mindset

Following are journal topics and exercises for the next seven days, but feel free to continue such exercises until you feel yourself being able to automatically capture and replace enabling tendencies within your thoughts and behaviors. It will take some time, but the neural pathways will develop as you do these exercises daily, and eventually, you will no longer find it necessary to write things down. The brain will learn to process automatically as you train it through such exercises as those contained within this program.

Day 1: Journal Your Battle with Setting Healthy Boundaries

- Take a few moments to journal about your struggle with enabling.
- How has your life and the lives of those you care about been affected by lack of healthy boundaries?
- Journal about your fears of overcoming enabling.

Day 2: Gently Observe Enabling

- Define the word enable in your journal and describe what it looks like when you live it.
- Who is responsible for setting healthy boundaries here and now?
- What are your ongoing challenges with enabling?
- Which healthy boundaries are you setting and keeping at this time? Not setting and keeping at this time?

Day 3: What Am I Ready For? What May Stop Me?

- Journal anything that might keep you from setting healthy boundaries and taking action to experience a peaceful mindset.
- List what you are ready to explore and the action you are ready to take in overcoming the limitations of enabling.
- What value comes when you establish and keep healthy boundaries?

Day 4: Identify Enabling Tendencies

- Write down any words you thought or said, or actions you exhibited, that portrayed enabling this past week.
- How did you feel, and what actions did you take or not take?
- What responsibilities are you shouldering that do not belong to you?
- What did you learn this past week? What worked? What didn't work?

Day 5: Establishing Boundaries and Taking Action

- What boundaries may I consider right now?
- What is the difference between healthy support and enabling?
- What support am I extending that is healthy? What support am I extending that is enabling?

- How will my words and action assist in preventing the need for tangible support in the future?

Day 6: Thought Capturing and Replacement
Take the enabling thoughts, words, and actions from this past week and replace them with thoughts, words, and actions of healthy boundaries. Disrupt the expectations, blame, and pressure of others that attempt to force action that is uncomfortable for you. Do this by extending acceptance, grace, and self-care for yourself so you will have the energy to offer healthy support for others who are exercising responsibility.

Day 7: Acceptance Plan

- In the areas you are not ready to explore or alter at this time, journal words of acceptance and grace that will support you with no expectations or pressure as you work to develop neural pathways of healthy boundaries and peace.
- How will you extend grace to yourself and others regardless of your readiness to change?

Continue thought capturing and replacement exercises to build neural pathways that support healthy boundaries and a peaceful mindset.

PRACTICE AND BUILD THE NEURAL PATHWAYS OF HEALTHY BOUNDARIES AND A PEACEFUL MINDSET

Thoughts of the Enabling Mindset:	Thoughts of Healthy Boundaries and a Peaceful Mindset:

Reframe enabling thoughts and behaviors with those of healthy boundaries and a peaceful mindset:

There's no joy when we're not moving unless we've accepted where we are.

9

THE LIMITING LANGUAGE OF UNCERTAINTY

"I don't know what to do. I know I'm sick and tired of feeling sick and tired. Continually scratching my head and taking actions that always lead to the same place. It's exhausting. I'm happy but don't experience joy in my soul where I am right now. I don't want to work in corporate America anymore, I want to do my own thing!" she told her husband as they lay in bed while she contemplated yet another job change. "I know there's more to life, but I can't pursue it because..."

She continued by listing all their bills and responsibilities and expressing her desire not to make her husband's load heavier. She was well aware that if she pursued her interests, someone would have to pick up the slack, and it would be her husband, who already had more than a full plate. Besides, he had his own dreams, and she didn't want hers to take precedence over his. That wouldn't be fair. He supported her by saying things like, "Babe, I want you to do what you want to do. We'll figure it out." She would say similar things to him, but neither would take the leap. He knew it wasn't possible; the numbers didn't add up, and secretly, she was terrified too. They both had a lot of obligations and individual big dreams, but the uncertainties were enormous—too big for either of them to bite the bullet.

This "she" is me! The "he" is my hubby. This occurred at the beginning of our adventures to self-sufficiency via self-employment. Man was it tough! About 15 years prior to this conversation, our relationship began with a blended family, we were upside down nearly a half million dollars, and we'd fought a long, hard battle for one another and our five children, whom we both had full legal custody of. We had gone through so many emotional and financial struggles that, just thinking about it, makes me want to take a 24-hour nap to recover. Between court battles, legal expenses, building a new home for our children, getting acclimated to blending a family and all the responsibilities, and still reaping some of the nasty seeds we previously sowed amid terrible pain...man, tough doesn't cover it! We had no physical support from anyone, little emotional support, and quite a few people breathing down our necks. We pretty much isolated socially from most people because it seemed that they either avoided us like the plague or wanted to cast stones at us. Uncertainties were everywhere!

Grace, resilience, determination, and our undying love for each other and our children got us through. And now, we're in this new place so many years later. Children are all grown, healthy, and thriving, so we sold the home we raised them in, bought a fifth wheel to live in, and set out on an adventure. To where, you may ask. No clue! We had many ideas yet still so many obligations. We were on our feet financially, but the nest egg wasn't very big because we had to break almost every egg open to feed our children and give them everything we could up to that point. Between buying them five cars, sports, private schooling, braces, helping with some college, and paying for weddings, funds went fast. Retirement was still pretty far away for us, so paying the bills by trading our time for a paycheck was the necessary means. So, we devised a plan! One thing my hubby and I are good at is planning, which is why we get it done. It may take a while, but we do it. People do not typically complete or achieve what they don't plan, and we mastered that early on, which is one reason we made it through less scathed and scarred than we did.

THE BS ROAD TO SUCCESS

Part of our plan along this new adventure was making my schedule more flexible. Being a life coach and professional speaker brought in some funds but not a lot. I had more time than I knew what to do with and less money than I wanted to support our joint endeavors but no real plan. So, we decided to take a trip and explore other options. My husband had started a side hustle a few years prior that had potential, but he didn't have time to do much with it. Can anyone relate? Many of my entrepreneurial clients find themselves in similar predicaments when starting out. The uncertainties of starting or scaling a business are insane, which is why most of those who do it stop at some point. But we were determined. Off we went. We hopped in our vehicle, drove to the other side of our state for a convention, questioning everything in the process, including the high ticket price we'd paid to get into this convention to explore our crazy possibilities.

At this convention, we thought of every reason why it may have worked for these other people but why it probably wouldn't work for us. We did enjoy talking with many people because we were determined to learn as much as we could. But really, the most empowering part of that four-day weekend was the time we spent dreaming with each other and hashing out details. It was fun chasing each other naked around the hotel room like kids again, turning off our phones, and looking into each other's eyes. This was a retreat for us that revived not only our marriage, but it literally exploded our business. We were still skeptical but also full of possibility when something happened on the drive home. It still brings tears to my eyes.

My husband said, "Write this stuff down." So, I took out my notebook, and we strategized all the way home. We settled on a business model to promote our business in the service industry. When we got home, we committed to the uncertainties we were ready to face. We've earned nothing less than six figures in that part-time service business ever since that trip! We continue to thrive while investing in top-of-the-line equipment to offer the highest quality service in our industry and area. To date, we have a five-star rating, 100 percent satisfaction rating, and get referrals almost every single day. Has everything been peaches and cream? No! Have we made mistakes? Yes, but we take responsibility and learn from them! But, most important, we're doing it!

My husband puts it like this: "You gotta decide which uncertainties you're going to commit to conquering and then start somewhere." The uncertainty doesn't go away because we've made a commitment and started moving. No, oftentimes movement amplifies the uncertainties at first. But then one day, you wake up, look back, and go, "Holy cow! How did we get here?"

Be forewarned though, we're not always ready, and my hubby and I certainly were not for quite some time. We tried to fool ourselves and *say* we were ready but couldn't because...[insert excuse here]. But now we see the reality of that BS. When we were ready, we started moving. But even if there is a road to success, it's a never-ending and ever-changing one. Most of my life, I was searching for some BS road to success, but thankfully, I finally woke up and chose a different route! The "road to success" was more like the never-ending road to disappointment anyway.

SUPPORT WHEN MOVING

Be cautioned: movement can be a lonely place. Even those closest to us are likely to not understand where we're going, and they probably will not know how to support us when we start moving. Any type of change brings about more uncertainties for us and those who love us. When people saw our company growing and us building our dreams, most people quietly observed at first. Then, when the fruits of our labor and our potential were more visible, they started being more verbally supportive, and many people started referring others to us. These referrals eventually became blessings that we didn't expect, and we were so grateful for the support when it came. We were blown out of the water because, while we were in the trenches alone at first, there was only one guy getting his hands dirty and supporting our efforts. He went out of his way to invest in us mentally, emotionally, and physically. While Johnny was our first supporter, he certainly would not be our last. Now there's so many that sometimes we are brought to tears by the love and support.

If they'd known where we were heading, more people would have supported us sooner, but honestly, we didn't even know our potential. It's important that we don't get our feelings hurt in the middle of such transitioning. We're all trying to figure it out, so it is important to accept and appreciate the support that is being given anytime and keep going, regardless of what phase we're in. Don't expect support, but appreciate it if it comes. Uncertainties can be divisive; don't allow it!

Even when people are supporting us, it can be a lonely journey because we have to figure out with whom it's safe to speak about the endeavor. Growth comes with huge challenges and uncertainty, and human nature makes it difficult sometimes. Do we talk to our friends and family? Probably not, because they don't understand our struggles unless they've been through them, and some may even think we're bragging when we start talking about our successes. It's a strange thing. For example, when they ask occasionally how it's going, when we do share, it feels awkward or we're met with silence. It can hurt. Sometimes it hurts really badly, but there's no reason to take offense.

The observations of our friends and family come from their own expectations that we've assisted them in building when it pertains to our lives. They only know where we've previously been. When we start breaking out of those molds, it's confusing for us, so you know it's confusing for them. Things start changing, and as much as our friends and family want to support us, they battle their own challenges and uncertainties. Depending on people's mindsets when we share, they could pat us on the back and congratulate us or they could silently walk away, telling others that all we do is flaunt and brag about our successes.

Yep, both have happened to us. No, we're not mad because, frankly, we've acted out our fair share of hurtful human tendencies as well. This is yet another time to extend grace to ourselves and to others. And when grace is not being reciprocated, keep extending it anyway. *Dis-grace* is just uncertainty with a loud voice. Put in your earplugs and keep on moving or doing what you're doing! We are all moving in and out of various mindsets throughout each season, so let's remember to extend grace regardless of which side of the table we're on, with or without support.

Don't be afraid to share your successes if you feel it. It's even tough for me to write this portion of the book and share some of our struggles and successes. Some people are private and never share anything and can seem stuck up to people. Others tell all and get accused of flaunting or boasting. We never win in those goofy battles, so squelch them as soon as they surface and move on. If you're private and don't want to share your secrets and successes, don't! There's no rule that says we must.

I personally made the decision to share our struggles and some of our triumphs because I am grateful for those who did that for us over the years, and it made a huge difference in our lives. Our expansion in large part was due to the support we later received, much of which were from strangers who had become our clients. It's like we had to build the foundation by ourselves and then support started rolling in. The Universe rolled out the red carpet when it saw we weren't giving up because we kept moving forward once we were ready.

Most of the support we did receive was from fellow business owners and entrepreneurs we met who knew exactly what we were going through while scaling our business. They not only shared their struggles and sympathized with us because they get it, but they highly encouraged us to keep going because they saw potential in us. They gave us tips and tricks along the way. I'm not afraid now to tell people that pursuing your dreams is scary but possible by busting through uncertainties. It's not only possible, but highly probable when we're ready for movement, accept where we are, and align with our authentic selves. We are also aware that the mindset that is not ready for movement is often envious of the people who are moving. But when we bump into that mindset out there in the world, we keep on moving past it!

WHEN WE'RE NOT READY FOR MOVEMENT

For those not ready for movement, accept where you are, otherwise it'll drive you crazy while living what feels like unhappily ever after. There's no joy when we're not moving unless we've accepted where we are. Acceptance of the present is the starting point, regardless of decisions for movement. And movement is not necessary to experience joy. On the contrary, many people put the brakes on after years of successful movement to search out and experience the joy of quiet again. Some of us long to move, some of us long to slow down, but both require acceptance to experience and walk in joy.

When we are ready for movement, we start conquering uncertainties while being prepared to face failures and more uncertainties. When we are not ready for movement, we do the same as we must still conquer uncertainties while being prepared to face failures and more uncertainties. While we are avoiding one choice that may accompany challenges, we're considering another that will also be accompanied by challenges. If we are not moving, the challenge is acceptance of where we are. If we are moving, the challenge is acceptance of where we are going and acceptance along that path.

It's a hopeless feeling when we are not moving but feel like we want to. When we are moving, we don't know what challenges we may face, but there's a sense of hope because we are subconsciously anticipating that our movement will take us where we want to go. Again, movement is not necessary for joy, but when we feel like we want to move, it's important to listen to ourselves and explore it.

THE VICIOUS CYCLE OF MOVEMENT

So, let's say we've made the decision to move. But alas, we arrive at our destination after much persistence and hard work. Then, soon after, it's *been there, done that,* and the cycle begins again. Are we ever really satisfied? The adaptation level phenomenon suggests probably not. This is an exhaustive human tendency that tells us we've gotta keep rolling. We strive and strive and climb and climb the stairway to success, thinking if we could just get to stair 3000 on a 5000-stair case that we'll be happy, right? So, we pick a reasonable goal—I mean, we're not smart enough or strong enough to reach 5000, but hey, we can definitely hit 3000.

So, we huff and puff and hope and struggle and...YES! Finally, we reach stair 3000! We hit our goal! We are content and happy for a while and then...discontentment sets in because we're almost always striving for something or someplace else. Once we reach our goals, the brain adapts quickly and then asks, "Now what?" What used to be our ultimate goal now becomes our new norm, and we find ourselves searching for something else.

A mental challenge always exists no matter how many times we experience successes; that's why success within itself is never enough. It's not about satisfaction; it's about acceptance in every single season of life. Acceptance while aligning with our authentic self is the ultimate goal for the human mind. Uncertainties stop this process, cause us to doubt, and use divisive tactics that separate us from ourselves and others. We can accept and align with our authentic self as we get more comfortable with neural pathway development exercises that let us adapt a new belief system that supports instead of limits us.

ACCEPTING AND ALIGNING WITH OUR AUTHENTIC SELF

Why do we do what we do? Three primary foundational mindsets lead to most of our thoughts and behaviors. These mindsets are obligatory, egocentric, and authentic. The obligatory mindset is when we do things because we think we *should* or are *supposed to*. A pressure-induced reason throws us into looking outside of ourselves, comparing, and searching. Imagine what it looks like when we make a mistake from that mindset. We're really hard on ourselves—maybe also on others—and we blame.

Egocentric is the next mindset. Sometimes, we do things for selfish or narcissistic reasons. We do something to get something in return. When we look at it with this mindset, we're expecting other people to do their part, we get disappointed, and we focus on equality and fairness, making sure that we are not taken advantage of. When in this mindset, we might experience a lot of temporary things. Because our intention is to get what's coming to us, there is usually an end. We continue until we conclude that we're not going to get what's coming to us, then we move on. During one of the coaching certifications I took, my trainer, Gary Kuzmich, gave me an eye-opening reminder. We all manipulate to get what we think we deserve sometimes. This is when the egocentric mindset is active.

The last reason we do what we do is because it aligns with who we are. This is the authentic state of mind when we know who we are and our thoughts and behaviors reflect such. We know ourselves, our vision and mission, and the values and personal priorities that align with the responsibilities within the roles we have chosen for ourselves. When the authentic mindset is active, it is freeing to not do things because we think we're supposed to or for selfish reasons.

I've had people ask me, but what does this look like? How do we live in a state of mind that is authentic instead of egocentric or obligatory? The answer is to stay in a heightened place of self-awareness. When we train our brains to think about what we are thinking about, this is possible. We will always teeter back-and-forth between these mindsets, but look for certain identifiers.

Here's a simple one. Do you know those times when you feel torn between doing what you're supposed to do and then secretly arguing with yourself that what's expected is unfair or unjust to you? This is a perfect example of the obligatory and egocentric mindsets at odds. That torn feeling we are experiencing is actually the authentic mindset attempting to push its way through the chaos. The challenge is that most of us developed exercising the obligatory or egocentric mindsets more so than the authentic mindset.

Think about it: How many people can you think of during your development that modeled a lifestyle that was dominated by authenticity? Probably not many, if any at all. As a matter of fact, those who do live authentically do not fit within the molds of those who are exercising from a place of obligation or self-centeredness, which makes it difficult to understand or appreciate those who are walking in authenticity. The obligatory and egocentric mindsets are intimidated by the authentic mindset, and they clash sometimes. Someone walking in an authentic mindset can't be manipulated, and that's tough for the other two mindsets to accept.

Most people expect everyone else to do what they are supposed to or that everyone else is selfish. Whoever is dominated by the obligatory mindset will expect that everyone else should do what they are supposed to be doing, just like they are doing. That fosters distrust and uncertainty when someone dominated by an obligatory mindset experiences someone who is dominated by an egocentric or authentic mindset.

If someone is dominated by an egocentric mindset, they anticipate that everyone else is selfish like they are. This breeds distrust because they ultimately know that even if someone does do something nice for them, they're only doing it for selfish reasons and to ultimately gain something from them. When they experience someone who is manifesting authenticity, they have a hard time believing that someone would do something nice for nothing. The egocentric mindset reminds us that those authentic nice people must be up to something.

See the challenges and why we bump heads with one another often? These different mindsets make it difficult to understand our own and one another's intentions and motivations. The obligatory and egocentric mindsets distrust everything and everyone, which forms uncertainty. These mindsets question self, others, Creator, circumstances, you name it! The authentic mindset is based on trust. It knows itself and stays self-aware. It accepts its own humanity and realizes it will never arrive but is doing what it can today with the knowledge it currently possesses, knowing full well that could change tomorrow. Trust is the foundation that overpowers every uncertainty in the authentic mindset. Trust is the only cure for uncertainty.

MOVING BEYOND THE LIMITATIONS OF UNCERTAINTY

Here's the cold, hard truth: If my husband and I had not broken through the lies and divisiveness of continual uncertainties, we would have never achieved anything. And I'm not talking about finances because money and assets are minimal in our eyes, and they do not define us or our value. It's the beautiful relationships and freedoms we have that make our lives so rich. But uncertainties tried to rob us of everything! It didn't work. It will never work because we see uncertainties for what they are. Uncertainties are the doors of opportunity. We are not too afraid to open those doors. Were we afraid? Yes! Often! Are we now? Yes! Sometimes! Will it stop us? No! We're afraid sometimes, but fear is not big enough to keep our hands off the doorknobs of opportunity. We fight fear with trust—trust in ourselves, trust in one another and others, and trust in our Maker.

Since uncertainty is a reflection of distrust, to some degree, we must identify where that distrust is in order to process uncertainty and use it to propel us forward instead of letting it hold us back. Standing on our personal truths amid distrust will increase our power to take action in a manner that promotes us in lieu of limiting us. Having the courage to move beyond our uncertainties will enhance our abilities to trust in the future, but it does require action in the face of distrust within the present moment.

Uncertainty is of great help to us as it assists us in avoiding things that may disappoint us. But keep in mind that there will always be those times when we are disappointed because disappointment comes from unmet expectations. However, uncertainty and inaction will always lead to disappointment. When we take action that is in line with the truth of who we are, we can, at minimum, experience inner harmony and learn from those instances where we may be disappointed when our actions did not yield our desired outcomes.

The exercises on the following pages will assist in identifying uncertainty, in using it to guide us, and in calming it when it may be an overreaction based on our limiting BS. This is a two-part exercise; Part 1 promotes a heightened awareness and processing of doubt versus trust, and Part 2 teaches us to move beyond uncertainty using our personal truths instead of relying on the lies of our distorted BS. The questions in Part 2 will assist in identifying those personal truths to create a foundation upon which we can establish action plans. This requires replacing the BS lies with truth. When in doubt of yourself, others, or Creator/Universe, reflect on the following exercises.

Part 1: Raising Awareness and Processing Distrust

1) The level of trust I feel with **myself** in this instance is:

Doubt		**Uncertainty**		**Trust**
1	**2**	**3**	**4**	**5**

The underlying factors that are feeding trust or distrust in myself are:

2) The level of trust I feel with **others** in this instance is:

Doubt		**Uncertainty**		**Trust**
1	**2**	**3**	**4**	**5**

The underlying factors that are feeding trust or distrust in others is:

3) The level of trust I feel with **Creator/Universe** in this instance is:

Doubt		**Uncertainty**		**Trust**
1	**2**	**3**	**4**	**5**

The underlying factors that are feeding doubt or trust in Creator are:

Part 2: Replacing the BS with Personal Truths

When Doubting Self

Lie: I am not enough, I am unworthy, I am undeserving, etc.

Truth: I am invaluable, covered by grace, and:

Lie: I can't.

Truth: What I can do is:

When Doubting Others

Lie: The beliefs, values, words, or actions of others are limiting me.

Truth: The value I find in the beliefs, values, words, or actions of others is:

Lie: I don't have enough support.

Truth: The support I do have is:

When Doubting Creator or Circumstances

Lie: My past is preventing my future.

Truth: The lessons learned from my past that promote my future are:

Lie: I don't have enough time, money, or resources.

Truth: The time, money, and resources I do have are:

These are action-oriented statements. If we are not ready to take action, we will hit a wall in exploring such questions. However, when we are ready, we do not run from action-oriented questions; we seek them. Ready or not? Ready or not is only relative to your readiness to yield your desired outcome; it has no bearing on your value. Remember, you will never be any better than you already are! You are invaluable right where you are, always have been, always will be. The goal will always be horizontal progression only when you are ready to move to another position, never vertical progression sparked by some fallacy of increased worth or power as you climb some BS ladder!

All peace and opportunities for progress come first from acceptance, which is the foundation for trust. Trust is the foundation for being vulnerable. If we do not accept ourselves, others, and our world, then we will not trust ourselves, others, and our world. If we do not trust ourselves, others, and our world, then we will not be vulnerable with ourselves, others, and our world. Acceptance, trust, and vulnerability are prerequisites of movement and growth as all peace and progress rely fully on this trio. So does genuine connection. Any connections and communications not based on this trio are lagging and disabled to some degree.

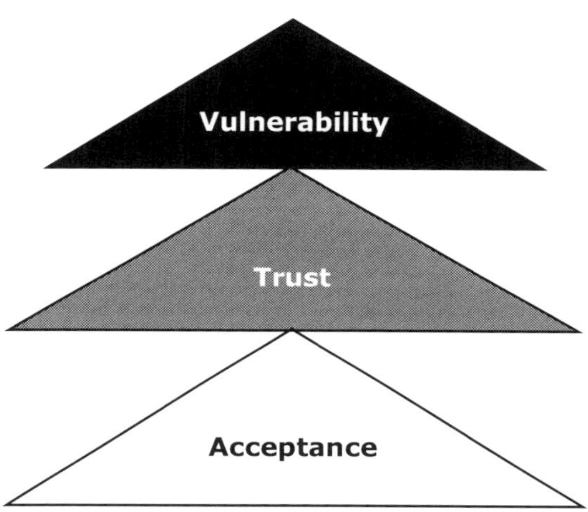

THWART TRICKY THOUGHTS

Uncertainty always makes us uncomfortable. We mentally defeat uncertainty when we choose acceptance, which leads to trust, which leads to vulnerability. This mindset ultimately leads to open and healthy dialogue with ourselves and others. When we face any form of uncertainty, our mind starts rolling in a direction to address or escape these uncertainties. Unless redirected, the mind will always travel along the neural pathways that are the most familiar and search for the easiest and quickest way to resolve the uncomfortableness of uncertainty.

While on the edge of contemplating or worrying about the choice of action while facing uncertainty, our mind plays tricks on us. To thwart those tricks, we must understand what they are. Now, these tricks are different for everyone, depending on many things such as cognitive and emotional abilities, past experiences, personality styles, aspirations, or expectations. These tricky thoughts may even vary for individuals depending on what season of life they are in at the time the uncertainty surfaces.

This is certainly not an all-inclusive list, but note some of the tricky places our minds go during uncertainties. Check any of the following cognitive distortions that sound familiar to you.

- ☐ **All-or-none thinking or overgeneralizing:** It's either black or white, with no gray area. Polarizing thoughts tell us it's all good or all bad.
- ☐ **Catastrophizing:** When we feel like the sky is falling, we run around in our minds like a chicken with our heads cut off, inflating the difficulties.
- ☐ **Projecting:** Like verbal projectile vomiting, we basically spew our emotions and traits onto others. Just because *we* do doesn't mean *they* do.
- ☐ **Filtering:** Negative filtering is seeing things through lenses that take in all the negatives but filter out the positives. Positive filtering is the opposite.
- ☐ **Predicting:** Jumping to conclusions, mind reading, and fortune telling, we think we know exactly what is going to happen so we can cope with it.
- ☐ **Unsubstantiated rules:** We enforce rules on ourselves and others without really understanding where these rules came from or their importance.
- ☐ **Justification:** Self-preservation at its finest, we make excuses for ourselves to minimize potential damage.
- ☐ **Delusions:** We have a false sense or belief not based on reality. In high stress or anxious times, we all may experience this to some degree.
- ☐ **Conforming:** We see things the way others see them or adapt areas of our lives based on others. This includes chameleon-like thoughts and behaviors.
- ☐ **Exaggeration:** We make the positives bigger to get more attention or exaggerate the negatives by making mountains out of molehills.
- ☐ **Personalizing:** We make things about us that aren't really about us. It's important to allow others to exist by not making everything about us.
- ☐ **Need for control:** We've already covered this one, but when we feel out of control, we attempt to control.
- ☐ **Need for fairness:** Certain personality styles demand fairness, which is a fallacy. The fair train leads to nowhere and cannot be calculated.
- ☐ **Blaming:** We blame ourselves or others.
- ☐ **Emotional reasoning:** Reasoning with our emotions instead of facts or reality, it often accompanies anxiety and depression.
- ☐ **Expecting others to change:** This stems from our desire to control others.

- ☐ **Mislabeling:** Sort of like overgeneralizing, but we project negative labels on self or others because of an unfavorable characteristic.
- ☐ **Mr. or Ms. Right:** Some of us struggle with feeling the need to always be right. None of us want to be considered a know-it-all, but some of us only feel safe if we are.
- ☐ **Reap-and-sow fallacy:** We don't always reap what we sow. It rains on the just and the unjust alike. This is a fact we must accept to live in joy.

MOVING BEYOND COGNITIVE DISTORTIONS

Those are some cognitive distortions that our minds like to use to play tricks on us when it is uncertain or confused. At the core, they are all used to avoid uncertainty. It is important to identify these distortions and shift our minds in a healthy direction. Below are some processing exercises that may assist you to do this. So, grab your journal and reflect.

1) When triggered, write down the distorted thoughts and limiting language that are coming to mind.
2) Write down who you are: your values, vision, mission, power statement, or whatever your personal truth is. With my coaching clients, we co-create a Personal Compass for each client that consists of this information. If you have not yet identified these personal truths for yourself, I highly encourage you to connect with a life coach or possibly a therapist who specializes in providing these services. If we do not know who we are, how will we ever live authentically? Again, list your personal truths and explore how that person responds amid uncertainty instead of resorting to cognitive distortions.
3) Now, standing firm on your personal truths and from a place of mindfulness, find the value in the moment or circumstance. Then, genuinely respond by aligning thoughts and behaviors with your personal truths in a manner that benefits everyone involved, including yourself. Take an action you are ready to take and accept.

Many people ask how long it will take to build neural pathways in doing these exercises, and I am hesitant to respond. Why? Because there is no value in my giving you a measurement by which to critique yourself. So, I will pose a question and give a response, but ultimately the answer lies within you and me as individuals.

How long will it take to develop those neural pathways? It's like building muscle in your body, although it does not take as long to build mental muscles in our brains as it does in our bodies. However, one frightening part of mental muscles is that they weaken much quicker than our physical muscles when not exercised. Therefore, if there is a mental practice that you have found that is serving you, keep at it! Or, within a few short days, they will begin dwindling and disappear before your eyes and be hard to build back up.

One reason it is so difficult the second, third, fourth, etc., go-round is the shame we carry for the failure that we experienced during our former attempts. Let it go! Just keep in mind that this is going on, accept yourself where you are, create a plan for moving forward horizontally, and lovingly extend grace to yourself right where you are regardless of action or inaction. As we practice, we will begin recognizing the different types of limiting language, be able to reframe our thoughts, and process healthy choices in a few short seconds.

ALTERING OUR BELIEF CYCLE USING A GROWTH MINDSET

The roots of our beLIEf cycle look like this:

1) Our **uncertainties** are the root of our beLIEfs.
2) Our **beLIEfs** are the root of our belief systems (BS).
3) Our **BS** is the root of our perceived truths that we act upon daily.
4) When our **perceived truths** face discrepancies, insecurities surface.
5) **Insecurities** force us to reevaluate our uncertainties.
6) This forces us to **reject** the discrepancy (opponent) or **modify** our beLIEfs.
7) Modifying our beLIEfs is an extremely difficult thing to do because if we modify them, it **changes**, at least in part, **our entire BS**, which forces us to accept new perceived truths and alter the neural pathways hardwired in our brains. This is a process. It takes intentional calculated choices frequently throughout each day until our hardwiring has been reprogrammed.

Uncertainties are at the foundation of our beLIEfs as our beLIEfs were formed to protect us from our uncertainties. We're so used to it, we don't usually question them. They seem normal because they are familiar and because we've rationalized why we've accepted them as a necessary part of our lives. The uncertainties are so obvious if we look for them in our thoughts, words, and actions and we justify them. Let's look at some variations in the language we use when uncertain versus the language we use when we feel safe:

"I'm sick of it! I'm quitting! My boss doesn't appreciate anything I do!"
vs.
"I wish my boss well and will respectfully transition to a more suitable position if our issues do not resolve through healthy communications."

~

"I've had it! My husband is never going to change. I want a divorce."

vs.

"I am going to live the healthiest version of me and model the love and respect I desire so that we can come to a resolution, together or apart."

~

"Things are never going to change in this organization; I'm done!"

vs.

"As I grow personally, perhaps we can respectfully engage in the difficult and uncomfortable conversations necessary to create healthy change together."

~

Do you see the difference? Uncertain minds want to hide or fight; inquiring minds remain calm and want to explore. We can easily tel which mindset is active, the **uncertain** or the **inquiring** mindset, by assessing our feelings. If we are feeling exhausted and debilitated, the uncertain mind is likely in control. If we are feeling empowered and productive, the inquiring mindset is likely in charge.

We can see more signs of a healthy mindset by looking at the following Growth vs. Fixed Mindsets chart. Take a few moments and check which side of the chart your thoughts and feelings are on today or this week. Are you observing or measuring? Then go to the next step: Are you observing whether your thoughts and actions are healthy and aligned with your genuine self, or are you measuring whether your thoughts and actions are good/worthy or bad/unworthy? See the difference? Check the boxes that align with your mindset today and then come back and review it again in a few days.

Experiment with this chart when you feel triggered and again when you feel calm and in your element. Journal your thoughts every time you explore the growth versus fixed mindset exercise. This will assist your brain in being mindful of what state it is settling in.

GROWTH VS. FIXED MINDSETS

Check the areas that display an active growth or fixed mindset below.

√	Growth Mindset Inquires	Fixed Mindset Stays Uncertain	√
☐	Observes	Measures	☐
	whether		
☐	Healthy & Aligned	Good/Worthy or Bad/Unworthy	☐
	which reflects		
☐	Trust in Self & Openness	Wavering Trust or Distrust	☐
	which focuses on		
☐	Ability & Authenticity, Personal Passions & Prioritites	Being Right & Correct, One-Sided Prioritites	☐
	which sparks		
☐	Unconditional Acceptance, Authentic Connection, Forgiveness, Tolerance	Conditional Acceptance, Phony Connection, Judgments, Criticisms	☐
	which leads to		
☐	Horizontal Progression, Endless Options & Opportunities	Vertical Progression, Restrictive Options & Opportunties	☐
	feelings are usually:		
☐	Peace, Joy, Fulfillment, Curiosity, Acceptance & Love without Condition, Grateful, Hopeful, Interested, Free, Focused, Relaxed, Patient	Fear, Anger, Disappointment, Regret, Hopelessness, Ungrateful, Doubt, Despair, Scattered, Worried, Stressed, Impatient	☐
	behaviors are likely to be:		
☐	Flexible, Inquiring, Open, Sincere, Explorative, Healthy Boundaries, Unbiased, Accessible, Safe, Mindful, Forgiving, Empowered, Tolerant, Approachable, Acting Healthy	Rigid, Controlling, Demanding, Conditional, Manipulative, Biased, Closed, Unsafe, Opinionated, Violating Boundaries, Intense, Unforgiving, Acting In, Acting Out	☐

Our feelings and behaviors are easy indicators of which mindset we are presently choosing to engage. For this reason, it is important to pay close attention to them. Taking a couple minutes to journal our thougths and behaviors a few times daily helps tremendously so that we can catch and reprogram a limiting mindset or strengthen the empowering mindset. Remember, these mindsets are running off of the neural pathways we've previously strengthened, and changing them will not be easy. Transitioning to a healthy growth mindset by overpowering our beLIEfs requires consistent identification and observation. Once we practice and get familiar with monitoring our feelings and thoughts throughout the day, choosing a healthy mindset and options becomes quicker and easier.

I have developed a journal for ***The BS of Better*** program that is specifically designed to facilitate consistent identification and observations daily within ten weeks. The layout of this journal greatly enhances the probability of neural pathway development for sustainable growth and change. However, it is also possible to develop neural pathways without this specific journal. The program journal can be found at www.brigitteranae.com, but let me pass the basic strategy along now for those who may wish to use a blank journal or notebook.

Writing and monitoring are crucial components of neural pathway development, so please get some form of journal or notebook that will allow you to write daily and weekly reflections for at least ten weeks. *The BS of Better Journal* is broken down into daily reflections that take a total of approximately 10 minutes per day and about 10 minutes additional each week for 10 weeks, which is only about one percent of the week focused on ourselves and personal growth. That's a pretty easy and doable task for those who are ready to develop new neural pathways that lead to the change we desire to see in our lives, wouldn't you say? The point is, it doesn't take much. This small investment of time consistently focused on developing the mind will change the dynamics of the brain to serve us now and in the future.

The basic journal format covers these five areas:

1) Identify limiting language used that represents limiting mindsets daily:

    ☐ Language of Better

    ☐ Inadequacy Language

    ☐ Guilt-Ridden Language

    ☐ Judgmental Language

    ☐ Worry-Infested Language

    ☐ Comparative Language

    ☐ Empty-Commitment Language

    ☐ Victimization Language

☐ Language of Uncertainty

2) Uncertainties are expressed as FEAR. Identify and utilize each:

Feelings and Triggers Acknowledged

Explore with Optomistic Observations

Align Thoughts with Healthy Self

Reframe with Healthy Opportunities

3) Daily reflections and a question of the day
4) Weekly reflections geared toward what is working and not working
5) Weekly preparation focusing on looking back at the previous week and looking ahead to the upcoming week

At first, doing these types of mental exercises takes more time and may seem a little redundant with not much movement. It's sort of like that first few weeks at the gym or when you're on a new exercise regimen at home. Our mental muscles are not used to this form of thinking, so it may feel tiring and maybe a little hopeless in the beginning. Without obvious and immediate results, it is common to question the validity of our efforts and wonder if there's a point to the exercises.

You may feel like giving up because of this. However, the more we practice identifying and reframing our thoughts, the easier it becomes. Eventually, it will not even be necessary to look at the processing pages as the questions and concepts themselves will become the new neural pathways in our brains. After a few consistent weeks, when challenged and facing uncertainty, we will automatically recall such processing questions that will redirect our thoughts and actions within milliseconds.

What may take two or five minutes at first will eventually take seconds or less. The more we exercise and build healthy neural pathways, the stronger and more familiar they will be.

The neural pathways that are strengthened in our brain become our options for choice.

That's important, so you may want to reread it. If we do not strengthen healthy neural pathways in our brains, healthy concepts will not be options when choice is available. However, the opposite is also true.

As these new neural pathways gain strength, they will become our new familiar, which we will eventually migrate to with little thought or effort. Our attention all of a sudden will shift. Once we've experienced something repeatedly, it becomes familiar. Healthy habits are familiar habits; unhealthy habits are familiar habits. Familiar is what we are strengthening when we cognitively make the choice to practice these new thoughts and behaviors consistently.

As we practice, we will begin recognizing the different types of limiting language, be able to reframe our thoughts, and process healthy choices in a few short seconds. The chapter summary includes various types of homework to assist in processing uncertainties. Choose the one(s) that resonate with you and work them repeatedly until the exercises develop neural pathways in your brain that allow healthy automated responses.

MOVING BEYOND UNCERTAINTIES

This entire book has basically been about uncertainty. Every chapter represents a form of limiting language that surfaces because a limiting mindset is uncertain about something. At the heart of most of these are three major uncertainties that keep us in a whirlwind: (1) Am I enough?; (2) Are others enough?; and (3) Are my circumstances enough? Our circumstances are usually related to our connection with the Universe or Creator. Ultimately, when we are questioning our circumstances, we are likely questioning if we've found enough favor from Creator or in the Universe to warrant the circumstances we want.

Feeling the need to be *better* is an uncertainty that says we are *not* better. Questioning whether we are enough is an uncertainty of whether we actually are enough. Without question, uncertainty is the biggest challenge of acknowledging our individual value and self-worth, an obstacle that prevents us from pursuing the things we truly long for.

For many of us, uncertainties surface because we feel our world is not enough, that somehow we cannot trust the Universe to work in our favor. Subconscious thoughts secretly fester beneath the surface, leading us to question if the world is for us or against us. Oftentimes, this specific uncertainty is fueled by the fear that we somehow must not be valuable enough for the world to protect us. Maybe we have not done enough, perhaps we deserve to be punished for some private or public wrongs we have committed, and the list goes on. Ultimately, this may lead to a subconscious feeling that Creator or the Universe has an enormous gavel ready to bop us on the head at any given moment. We feel that the world somehow is not capable of watching our backs and keeping us from the unbearable things we fear, especially if we make mistakes.

I'm not sure about anyone else's reality, and I'll never have an opinion on how others give care to their spiritual lives. It's a personal journey, and my nose has no place in anyone's spiritual journey except my own. But speaking for myself, I have an assurance with every uncertainty that only comes from my Maker. It's like the icing on the cake and the strawberry on top of my malt. That's what the God I serve personally gives to my soul. He cradles me because I believe in Him, and there's no consolation like that of which God can give to those who are open to Him.

Many of us not only question daily if we will be true to ourselves, but we also question whether we will find favor and support from those we engage with and from Creator. Perhaps if we are good enough or do enough right, then we will somehow earn this favor that will make us worthy of yielding whatever it is we are hoping for. When the door of pain and challenge opens, and we begin experiencing some of the difficulties that come with being human, then that becomes all the more validation that we must not be enough.

We touched on this some in Chapter 5: Worry-Infested Limiting Language. Along with learning how to contemplate in lieu of worry, it is important that we also work to restore trust and receive grace. Grace is free. It is always free, and so is trust. Ultimately, uncertainty finds its roots in distrust. We may distrust ourselves, others, or the Universe, but if we are experiencing negative energy and having difficulty pushing ahead, there is distrust somewhere. And if we are coming down on ourselves or someone else, grace is lacking.

Distrust is a helpful emotion that guides us, so in no way am I suggesting that we get rid of distrust. On the contrary, it is important that we feel distrust, listen to it, and contemplate what this helpful emotion may be signaling to us. Within this chapter are exercises that will assist us in recognizing distrust, using self-reflective tools to guide us through it, and calming distrust when it may be overreacting.

We need this gauge because life, people, and circumstances do not always make sense. As a matter of fact, they usually do not. Unfortunately, when it doesn't make sense but is in our favor, we frequently and quickly can forget to recall how safe, supported, and able we really are. We will talk more about this in another book in this series, but a strong component of recollection is the emotion associated with the information going on as we are experiencing life events.

When events occur with strong emotion, whether positive or negative, they are driven more powerfully into our memory. This is why we remember so vividly the beautiful moments like our wedding days, birth of our children, vacations, and those devastating moments like divorce, death of our parents, or when we've been violated in some form. The memory of these hard and unpleasant times is not so much the difficulty as ruminating on them is. Rumination is often a strong side effect of negative experiences and leads to uncertainties in moving forward with confidence.

DON'T RUMINATE – MEDITATE!

When we find ourselves ruminating on the negative events or emotions, one thing that can be helpful is to meditate on pleasant experiences. This can be in many forms, from expressing gratitude to mentally taking your thoughts to places you've only seen in photographs or recalling a pleasant memory. Many types of meditation exist: reflection, affirmations, mindfulness, movement, exercises to anchor our attention, expressing gratitude, visualizations, body awareness, spiritual meditations, relaxation techniques.

The idea is to transition the mind from ruminating on negative energy to meditating on positive energy. The more familiar your mind becomes with meditating instead of ruminating, the stronger those neural pathways with positive and healthy response options will become.

One exercise I often use with my clients is Thought Capturing and Replacement, which you've been doing in each chapter's Daily Journal Practice. When we find ourselves dwelling in negative energy or unhealthy thoughts, we have the option of replacing that energy with positive and healthy thoughts. Below is an example of an exercise that can be helpful. Warning: if you do this once or twice, you will not see the benefits of it. The objective here is to teach our minds that there is an alternative to ruminating by showing it *repeatedly* how to meditate. Repetition is the key! Repetition is the key! Repetition is the key! Okay, okay, you've got the message.

Follow these three steps for this exercise: (1) Identify the negative energy when it intrudes our thoughts. (2) If this energy is not prompting us to take necessary and immediate action, take a moment to capture the thoughts that are feeding that energy. (3) Replace those thoughts with thoughts that bring us positive energy and meditate on those.

The idea is to stop our minds from running down those familiar neural pathways filled with negative energy and to begin establishing new neural pathways filled with positive energy. Practice, practice, practice is the only way this is going to happen. Did I mention practice? If we have identified that our thought life is not serving us as often as we would like, we must build healthy thought pathways through creating them and forcing our mind to practice dwelling there instead of the old pathways that are not serving us. The goal is not to meditate for a long period. It could literally be one minute. Instead of focusing on *longevity*, the benefits will come from *frequency*. The more frequently we transition our minds in a healthy direction, the more frequently it will naturally gravitate there. This is done only through intentional reminders and taking action.

I have alarms set on my phone that remind me to do a mind check every four hours during my workday. When the alarm goes off, I do a quick self-assessment of how I am feeling and what my mind is dwelling on at that moment. If it's healthy, helpful, and bringing me positive energy, I express gratitude and continue with my day until the next self-check in four hours. If it is not healthy, helpful, or bringing me positive energy, I do the quick thought capturing exercise below. When I first started this, I would write it down, but now that I've done it so often, my mind goes through this exercise and quickly gets me moving with that positive energy most of the time. Uncertainties are lying thieves, and it's time to question them to death!

Thought Capturing and Replacement

For those serious about starting this practice, feel free to copy this page and utilize it as often as possible throughout the day until your mind naturally takes you there automatically. Studies vary, but it could take four to eight weeks of daily practice to develop a new habit, so keep that in mind and be patient with yourself. We've spent years developing our present thought patterns, and they will not be altered quickly. Make sure to extend grace to yourself as you explore this transition.

What negative energy am I experiencing?

What am I ruminating on?

What positive energy can I meditate on?

Acceptance while aligning with our authentic self is the ultimate goal for the human mind.

Homework for Overcoming the Language of Uncertainty

The purpose of this exercise is not to point out everything you are doing "wrong," as measuring in such a limiting fashion is unhelpful. Tendencies are most frequently behaviors developed over the course of time in response to our self-image and surroundings. The purpose of this exercise is to build neural pathways in the brain that help us remember to simply pay attention to these tendencies so that we can decide if they are serving us. When you notice any tendencies present in your life that are not serving you or others, do not be hard on yourself. Simply observe their existence, recognize they were created at some point for a reason, and that they can be modified. Identify existing tendencies by checking below any life aspects where tendencies may surface that are not beneficial for yourself or others. Then, assess and focus on when they surface by asking yourself questions pertaining to each tendency present like the following:

- What are the circumstances surrounding the existence of this tendency?
- Who, what, when, where, how, and why does this tendency surface?
- What responsibility can I take for altering or eliminating the existence of this tendency in my life?
- How would my life and the lives of others be enhanced by replacing this tendency with healthy responses?
- What resources might I consider to assist in minimizing this tendency if it is difficult to modify on my own?

Listen, life doesn't have to be so difficult and pressure induced. Everyone can do something to reduce life's pressures. We can all transcend the limitations of human nature through neural pathway development and connection with self, others, and Creator. It starts by inquiring internally, asking those action-oriented questions like, where would I like to thrive or mature at this time? We are all continually learning and will develop until we pass from this life. Adult maturation is growth in an area that brings us feelings of wholeness, health, and authenticity. No one else can design your development plan but you. This book is loaded with thought-provoking concepts and questions, but it will only scratch the surface. There's so much more out there for you to explore. Remember, uncertainty is the door to every opportunity. Don't be afraid to knock or barge on through when it makes sense for you. Let's process one more time over this next week.

OBSERVATIONS OF THE UNCERTAIN MINDSET

Take a few moments to observe the language and feelings that often accompany the uncertain mindset that is doubtful and divisive. Then observe how others may experience this mindset and how it may limit you. Check those that apply to your experiences or fill in the blanks with additional observations you have made pertaining to this limiting mindset.

Uncertain, doubting, and divisive thoughts and language:

☐ Doubting or debilitating questioning of self
☐ Doubting or debilitating questioning of others
☐ Doubting or debilitating questioning of Creator
☐ Doubting or debilitating questioning of circumstances
☐ Distrusting the intentions or motives of self
☐ Distrusting the intentions or motives of others
☐ Distrusting the intentions or motives of Creator
☐ Other ________________________

Feelings that often accompany uncertainty, doubt, and divisiveness:

☐ Confusion
☐ Uncertainty or doubt
☐ Unsettled
☐ Skeptical
☐ The need to control
☐ Fear or anxiety
☐ Loneliness
☐ Other ________________________

Uncertainty: Can I trust myself, others, Creator? Am I safe?

Others may experience me as:

☐ Cynical
☐ Controlling
☐ Distrustful
☐ Unpleasant
☐ Closed or guarded
☐ Dominating
☐ Oppressive
☐ Divisive
☐ Other ________________________

The uncertain mindset may lead to:

☐ Isolation
☐ Abandonment or rejection
☐ Loneliness, separation, or alienation

- ☐ Inability to take reasonable risks
- ☐ Being stagnant or stuck
- ☐ Feeling like an angry loner
- ☐ Other ________________________

Daily Journal Practice

Following are journal topics and exercises for the next seven days, but feel free to continue such exercises until you feel yourself being able to automatically capture and replace the limiting language of uncertainty within your mind. It will take some time, but the neural pathways will develop as you do these exercises daily, and eventually, you will no longer find it necessary to write things down. The brain will learn to process automatically as you train it through such exercises as those contained within this program.

Day 1: Journal Your Battle with Uncertainty

- When do you mostly find yourself uncertain?
- Who or what is involved? Self, others, Creator, circumstance?
- How are you manifesting acceptance, trust, and vulnerability?
- What may be keeping you from acceptance, trust, and vulnerability?
- What cognitive distortions have you recently experienced?

Day 2: Journal About Movement Amid Uncertainties

- Who supports you?
- Are you ready to move now or create a plan to accept?
- How are you and others affected by the adaptation level phenomenon?

Day 3: Identifying Your Authentic Self

- Who are you?
- What is your personal and professional vision and mission?
- What are your values?
- What are your personal priorities within this season?

Day 4: Thought and Mindset Capturing

- How is the obligatory mindset manifesting in your life during this season?
- How is the egocentric mindset manifesting in your life during this season?
- How is the authentic mindset manifesting in your life during this season?
- Where are you manipulating to get what you think you deserve?
- Where are you uncertain? Where are you inquiring?

Day 5: Observing and Aligning with Authenticity

- Who do you know that you experience them as aligning with their authentic self?
- What stands out about them?
- What battles have they conquered to walk in this place?
- What would it take for you to walk in an authentic mindset?

Day 6: What Am I Ready For? What May Stop Me?

- Are you experiencing indicators of a growth mindset or a fixed mindset right now?
- What commitment(s) are you ready to explore at this time?
- What might prevent you from keeping these commitment(s) to yourself?

Day 7: Acceptance Plan

- In the areas you are not ready to explore or alter at this time, journal words of acceptance and grace that will support you with no expectations or pressure as you work to develop neural pathways of a healthy and trusting mindset.
- How will you extend grace to yourself and others regardless of your readiness to change at this time? Who can support you?

Continue thought capturing and replacement exercises to build neural pathways that support a healthy and trusting mindset.

PRACTICE AND BUILD THE NEURAL PATHWAYS OF A HEALTHY AND TRUSTING MINDSET

Thoughts of the Familiar and Uncertain Mindset:	Thoughts of the Healthy and Trusting Mindset:

Reframe familiar and uncertain thoughts with those of a healthy and trusting mindset:

JOURNAL TOPICS TO CONTEMPLATE FOR OVERCOMING THE LIES OF THE UNCERTAIN MINDSET

Grab your notebook or *The BS of Better Journal* to contemplate and process overcoming the uncertain mindset. Below are cues and questions to begin assessing the costs and the payoffs of allowing these uncertainties, but don't stop here. Remember, journal those prompts that stand out to you and ask yourself other difficult questions and concerns that may not be listed but are hiding deep within yourself. You already know these concerns; this is your time to listen! Identify and observe the uncertainties so that you can stop what's causing those doubts and divisive tactics, which lead to loneliness and feeling the need to control, when you are ready.

Inquisitive Alternatives:

- ☐ What I trust about myself is...
- ☐ What I trust about the other person is...
- ☐ What I trust about Creator is...
- ☐ What I trust about my circumstances is...
- ☐ Distrust and attempting to control add pressure to myself and others by...
- ☐ I accept by...
- ☐ I extend grace by...
- ☐ I trust and release control by...
- ☐ Trusting is worth the risk because the rewards and value I see in trusting myself, others, and Creator are...
- ☐ The value I see in reducing life's pressures is...
- ☐ I trust and release control of...
- ☐ To reap reward in lieu of consequence, I commit to...
- ☐ Other ________________________

Neural Pathway Development Support

It cannot be reiterated enough that neural pathway development is crucial for sustainable healthy change in thoughts and behaviors. Heightening self-awareness, committing to personal reflection time, and completing acceptance and action plans daily and weekly will develop the neural pathways that serve you. For additional daily processing support, please see **Appendix A – Neural Pathway Development Support**. What would it look like if we asked the difficult yet beneficial questions until the questions were no longer difficult? When you're ready, try it and see.

Keep processing! After you finish reading this book, look back through the chapters and see what areas you may desire to spend additional time processing. Where would you like to mature? What rewards do you desire?

Daily and consistent processing will transform your life and reduce life's pressures within mere weeks.

Final Thoughts

Yes, there are uncertainties and questions to be asked, not of ourselves, others, Creator, or circumstances, but rather of the uncertainties themselves. Uncertainties are lying and divisive thieves! Question them to death! **Intentionally take your time and do the work!**

Can We Make the World Better?

> "Whatever you did, your life is still meaningful. Each of us is more than the worse thing that we've ever done.
>
> "If we can look at ourselves closely, we can change this world for the better. We all need grace. We all need mercy."
>
> ~*Just Mercy* (2019 film)

What Now?

Every day is our chance...
to change the world...
not by being better...
but by defining better...
and living immeasurably.

Within each day, within each moment, lurks an opportunity. There's always an opportunity to extend acceptance and love while walking in grace and gratitude. Taking advantage of those opportunities will reduce life's pressures for us and our world by stopping the debilitating and destructive BS of Better.

Cheers to Reducing Life's Pressures,

Brigitte Ranae

When we love ourselves,
we create a life we love!
Love never fails!

A

APPENDIX A – NEURAL PATHWAY DEVELOPMENT SUPPORT

It cannot be reiterated enough that neural pathway development is crucial for sustainable healthy change in thoughts and behaviors. Heightening self-awareness through such questions as follows while committing to personal reflection time and completing acceptance and action plans daily and weekly will develop the neural pathways that serve you. You, and only you, will figure out what those healthy pathways are. Practice will strengthen them. Through gentle observation in the mirror, doing the self-reflection work repeatedly and consistently, you will create the paths that serve your uniqueness.

Referring to these pages as a journal guide will assist in reprograming your brain to look beyond the challenges and limitations in the moment. The more frequently such exercises are completed, the quicker and stronger the neural pathways will develop. It does not take years. When consistent, we can modify our thought life and behaviors in weeks and experience ***Reducing Life's Pressures***. Assuredly, this will yield a high return when you are ready, but remember, practice self-acceptance until you are ready! Explore what you're ready for with grace.

HEIGHTEN SELF-AWARENESS – POWER QUESTIONS

What am I pretending not to know?

What am I avoiding?

What am I afraid to acknowledge?

PERSONAL REFLECTION

One area I often feel like I am letting myself or someone down is:

When I think about this area of life, I feel:

Appendix A

What I would like to change is:

When I think of making changes in this area, it is hard because:

Feeling I should be better in this area adds pressure to my life by:

The value I see in creating change in this area is:

Making a change in this area would benefit myself by:

Making a change in this area would benefit others by:

ACCEPTANCE AND ACTION PLAN OPTIONS

Which action or acceptance plan resonates with me at this time?

☐ Because I want to reap the value and benefits this change would bring in my life, this week I commit to:

☐ I'm not quite ready to commit to making changes in this area yet, so this week I will work on accepting myself right where I am by:

☐ Someone that I can safely discuss my goals and challenges with in this area and ask for support from this week is:

☐ Even though I am struggling in this area right now, and not quite ready to invest energy in modifying it, I am invaluable and so are the other people who may be involved or influenced by my words and actions. Therefore, I will:

A) Lovingly acknowledge the challenge when it surfaces by:

B) Extend grace and respect to myself and others when this challenge surfaces by:

C) Remind myself of the following truths that reflect self-acceptance and acceptance of others when this challenge surfaces:

ABOUT THE AUTHOR

Brigitte Ranae is well known for success in her life coaching practice where she works with those looking to modify limiting thoughts and behaviors to reduce life's pressures. She facilitates personal development and wellness in the lives of individuals, families, and organizations. Brigitte is an author and course creator and obtained her psychology degree from Central Methodist University in Fuller, Missouri. She also studied industrial/organizational psychology, child development, and office systems and technologies; has multiple coaching certifications; and has been a life coach for over 15 years and a business consultant for most of the last 25 years. She and her husband Scott built a six-figure income by successfully scaling a part-time business that opened a lot of doors and freedom for their family. Brigitte is passionate about supporting other business owners as they pursue their goals as well.

While this summarizes her career, that is not who she is. Brigitte is a woman who is free-spirited and full of life. She enjoys expressing without reservation and likes to play and explore. By embracing her own freedom, she creates a safe space for others to do the same. She strives to be a blessing to herself and others through healthy interactions and does this by giving and receiving unconditional love and acceptance freely and by daily living her primary values, which are honesty, respect, and compassion. Scott and Brigitte have raised five loving, hardworking, free-thinking individuals with beautiful hearts who grew from their children into their friends. They are also the proud grandparents of precious grandchildren with the anticipation of many more to come. Brigitte's truest joys come from spending time in reciprocal relationships with family, friends, colleagues, clients, and Creator.

Brigitte specializes in emotional regulation, behavioral modification, communications mastery, relationship coaching, leadership training, habit formation, and spiritual healing. For additional information on booking Brigitte for speaking engagements, group training sessions, or to inquire about life coaching services, please email info@brigitteranae.com. Brigitte has multiple upcoming publications, including online courses and additional support resources in her ***Reducing Life's Pressures*** series, so feel free to visit her website www.brigitteranae.com for future updates.

Made in the USA
Columbia, SC
09 June 2021